Letts

Study Guide

GCSE
Success

German

GCSE
Success

Rod Hares and Helen Pollard

Contents

This book and

Stay on course! Use these pages to get to know your course.

No matter which exam board you are using, you have to do...
- a listening and a reading exam
- two controlled writing assessments
- two controlled speaking assessments.

For your listening and reading exams, your teacher will enter you for either Foundation or Higher:
- If you do Higher, your grade for that skill will be from A* to E.
- If you do Foundation, your grade for that skill will be from C to G.

In your speaking and writing controlled assessments, you are not entered for Foundation or Higher. Your final mark in these controlled assessments depends on how well you do. This is called 'differentiation by outcome'.

Here are some guidelines on the length of the exams and controlled assessments:

Listening Foundation
An exam lasting 30–40 minutes.
Listening Higher
An exam lasting 40–50 minutes.
Reading Foundation
An exam lasting 30–40 minutes.
Reading Higher
An exam lasting 40–50 minutes.
Speaking
Two controlled assessments lasting four to six minutes each.
Writing
Two controlled assessments lasting about an hour each.

Individual exam boards' topic areas are shown opposite. You should revise all the topics relevant to your specification but it will help to build your vocabulary and improve your German if you also study the other topics.

AQA

Lifestyle
Health:
- Healthy and unhealthy lifestyles and their consequences
Relationships and choices:
- Relationships with family and friends
- Future plans regarding marriage/partnership
- Social issues and equality

Leisure
Free time and the media:
- Free time activities
- Shopping, money, fashion and trends
- Advantages and disadvantages of new technology
Holidays:
- Plans, preferences, experiences
- What to see and getting around

Home and environment
Home and local area:
- Special occasions celebrated in the home
- Home, town, neighbourhood and region; where it is and what it is like
Environment:
- Current problems facing the planet
- Being environmentally friendly within the home and local area

Work and education
School/college and future plans:
- What school/college is like
- Pressures and problems
Current and future jobs:
- Looking for and getting a job
- Advantages and disadvantages of different jobs

OCR

Topic area 1 – Home and local area
- Life in the home, friends and relationships
- Local area, facilities and getting around

Topic area 2 – Health and sport
- Sport, outdoor pursuits and healthy lifestyle
- Food and drink as aspects of culture and health

Topic area 3 – Leisure and entertainment (includes online)
- Socialising, special occasions and festivals
- TV, films and music

Topic area 4 – Travel and the wider world
- Holidays and exchanges
- Environmental, cultural and social issues

Topic area 5 – Education and work
- School life in the UK and in the target language country or community
- Work experience, future study and jobs, working abroad

Visit your awarding body's website for full course details or download your complete GCSE specifications.

your GCSE course

EDEXCEL

Speaking and writing
1. Media and culture
- Music/film/reading
- Fashion/celebrities/religion
- Blogs/Internet

2. Sport and leisure
- Hobbies/interests
- Sporting events
- Lifestyle choices

3. Travel and tourism
- Holidays
- Accommodation
- Eating, food, drink

4. Business, work and employment
- Work experience/part-time jobs
- Product or service information

5. Centre-devised option

Listening and reading
Out and about
- Visitor information
- Basic weather
- Local amenities
- Accommodation
- Public transport
- Directions

Customer service and transactions
- Cafés and restaurants
- Shops
- Dealing with problems

Personal information
- General interests
- Leisure activities
- Family and friends
- Lifestyle (healthy eating and exercise)

Future plans, education and work
- Basic language of the Internet
- Simple job advertisements
- Simple job applications and CVs
- School and college
- Work and work experience

WJEC

Personal and social life
- Self, family, friends, home life, shopping, meals, healthy living, illness and accidents, free time, fashion, relationships, future plans.

Local community
- Home town, school, education, local environment, pollution, recycling, local facilities, comparisons with other towns and regions, weather and seasons.

The world of work
- Work experience, part-time jobs, future careers, technology (sending messages, accessing information).

The wider world
- Travel and holidays, media, social issues (e.g. life of young people today, homelessness, crime, drugs, healthy living, religion, politics), life in the countries and communities where the language is spoken.

CCEA

Context 1: The individual – Students' lives, families, homes and interests, and those of others in German-speaking countries and communities
- Relationships: families and friends
- Local environment: advantages and disadvantages
- Activities: daily routine and leisure activities
- Health and lifestyle: diet, exercise and illness

Context 2: Citizenship – Lifestyles, attitudes and customs in students' own countries and communities, and in German-speaking countries and communities
- Social issues: problems in society and equality
- Travel and tourism: destinations and choices
- Environmental issues: attitudes to and responsibilities for litter, transport, energy, conservation and recycling
- Media and communications
- Celebrations: festivals and customs

Context 3: Employability – Education and employment in students' own countries and communities, and in German-speaking countries and communities
- School life
- Part-time jobs: advantages and disadvantages
- Future plans: choices and expectations

www.aqa.org.uk, www.ocr.org.uk, www.edexcel.com, www.wjec.co.uk, www.ccea.org.uk

A student's guide to the speaking and writing controlled assessments

How many controlled assessments do I have to do?
Two for speaking and two for writing.

When will I be doing my controlled assessments?
Anytime in Year 9, 10 or 11. Your teacher can choose the time.

How long are the controlled assessments?
Each speaking assessment will last four to six minutes (WJEC: four to seven minutes). The writing assessment will be a minimum of 200 words, spread over the two pieces, but you should aim for 400–600 words, spread over the two pieces, if you want at least a grade C. Each writing assessment must be done in an hour.

When do I start preparing?
There are three stages:

Stage 1: Your teacher will prepare you for the task. He/she cannot tell you at this stage what the task is.
Stage 2: The teacher gives you the task. After this, the teacher cannot give you any language guidance, but he/she can tell you that past tenses are to be used here and future tenses there, for example. Stage 2 can last for anything from a few days to most of a term, depending on the exam board:

AQA	Six hours including lesson time and homework time
OCR	Two hours
EDEXCEL	Speaking: two weeks and no more than six hours of contact time. Writing: No limit
WJEC	Two weeks
CCEA	Speaking: three to four hours. Writing: five to six hours

Stage 3: This is when you do the controlled assessment.

Can I ask my teacher to extend the deadline?
No.

What if I do an awful piece of controlled assessment?
Your teacher will let you do another one but it must be a different task.

> It is very clear that many GCSE candidates write less well using ICT. In particular, they tend to be less accurate and leave out more accents when they type. So use word-processing with care.

Can I use ICT?
In the controlled writing assessment, you can write your work on a computer but it will take place in exam conditions.

Can I use electronic translators?
No. In the controlled speaking assessment, you will have access to your cue card of 30–40 words. In the controlled writing assessment, you will have access to your cue card of 30–40 words and a dictionary. This can be an online dictionary.

> You should always take care to make all your work neat and easy to read.

Do I get marks for presentation?
No – if you write a brochure, for example, you will not get any marks for pictures and maps (even if you draw them yourself). Similarly, do not waste time on title pages, fancy borders, folders and so on.

Can I do the same piece of speaking or writing as other people in my class?
Yes, and you will probably use quite a lot of the same vocabulary and structures as well. But there will always be differences as you will be speaking or writing about your holiday or your work experience, for example.

Can I use a writing frame?

In Stage 1 and 2, yes. However, the more of your own ideas you write, the higher your marks are likely to be.

Can I use pieces of writing I have seen in books?

You must never, ever copy. However, you should try to use lots of interesting vocabulary and phrases you have learned from your worksheets and coursebooks.

Can I get other people to help me?

No – you and your teacher have to sign that this is your own, unaided controlled assessment. You will cover all of the language you need in class and you will be helped with your planning. Your teacher will have a good idea of the standard of writing you are capable of from your other work in class. If your teacher suspects you have not written a piece of controlled assessment yourself, he/she might...

- refuse to let you submit it at all
- make you rewrite the piece in exam conditions
- inform the exam board that you have been cheating.

> It is very easy for teachers and examiners to spot where a candidate has tried to write their own German and where they have copied, so don't do it. The Internet websites that advertise materials usually offer mistake-littered work.

Planning your study

Make sure that you have learned all the necessary words after you complete each topic. You could draw a mind map or create a database on your PC. During the topic try to learn 10 new words a day. Ask someone to test you on the words: you need to be able to spell the words properly, and use accents correctly, so remember to write them down when being tested.

- Each chapter in the book includes sample conversations. These conversations will help you to prepare for your controlled assessments in speaking. You might like to read the conversations with a friend and/or make a recording of the conversations. You could then listen to the conversations as part of your revision plan. This will boost your fluency.
- Practise the questions in the book. This will build your confidence and enable you to anticipate the type of questions that will occur in the GCSE examination.
- Decide if you know the topic thoroughly and if there are any weak areas: note them and look for ways to improve on them in the next topic, e.g. use of adjectives, use of the past tense.

How this book will help you

This Letts *Revise GCSE German Study and Revision Guide* will help you because...

- it contains the essential vocabulary and grammatical structures needed for the GCSE course.
- it contains progress checks as well as GCSE questions to help you to check and reaffirm your understanding.
- there are examples of controlled assessment tasks with model answers and advice from an examiner on how to get them right. Translations are provided on pages 154–156 to aid understanding.
- trying the exam practice questions will give you the opportunity to make use of the vocabulary that you have learned and will give you a measure of your progress.
- examiner's hints and key points are used throughout the chapters to help you. Use these as your signposts to guide you to success in your GCSE course.

40 points for improving your grade

Do not try to include all 40 points – 15 to 20 will be fine.

Speaking and writing

Listed below are 40 points that will help to improve the quality of language in your speaking and writing work and raise your grade in the controlled assessments. Try to include a good number of these points in your work. Examples of these points being used are shown where you see this icon on the 'Sample controlled assessment' pages throughout the book.

1 Try to include at least three uses of the present tense.

2 Try to include at least three past tenses.

3 Try to include at least three future tenses.

4 Make sure the word order is correct: the verb should be the second idea in a main clause but it comes at the end in a subordinate clause, e.g.:

Sie ist eine nette Frau, aber ich weiss, dass sie eine nette Frau ist.

5 Include at least three uses of **weil/da**.

6 Include at least two justified points of view, e.g.:

Ich brauche Deutsch weil ich in Europa arbeiten will.

I need to learn German because I want to work in Europe.

7 Use connecting words (connectives), e.g.:

der, die, das	who, which
während	while
wenn, wann, als	when

8 Use **um...zu** (in order to), e.g.:

Ich fuhr in die Großstadt, um Weihnachtsgeschenke zu kaufen.

I drove into the city, in order to buy Christmas presents.

9 Try to use impressive vocabulary, e.g.:

Reifenpanne	flat tyre
schmollen	to sulk

10 Use **seit** (for), e.g.:

Ich bin seit drei Jahren in dieser Schule.

I have been at this school for three years.

11 Use a **haben** structure, e.g.:

Ich habe Furcht.	I'm afraid.
Wir hatten Heimweh.	We were homesick.

12 Use negatives, e.g.:

niemand	no one, nobody
nie	never

13 Use **eben wollen** (to be about to), e.g.:

Ich wollte eben ausgehen. — I was about to go out.

14 Use a pluperfect tense after **nachdem**, e.g.:

Nachdem wir gegessen hatten,... After we had eaten,...

15 Use **so** + adjective/adverb, e.g.:

so langsam	so slow
so peinlich	so embarrassingly

16 Use **trotz** + the genitive (in spite of), e.g.:

trotz meines Erstaunens despite my astonishment

17 Use **dabei sein** (to be in the middle of), e.g.:

Sie war dabei, ihre Sachen auszupacken.

She was in the middle of unpacking her things.

18 Use exclamations, e.g.:

Dass ich nicht lache!	Don't make me laugh!
Das ist unglaublich!	That's unbelievable!

19 Use one or two adjectives in front of a noun, e.g.:

ein komischer Mensch	a strange person
mit der neuen Ärztin	with the new doctor

20 Try to reduce the number of simple verbs, e.g. **haben/sein/sagen**.

21 Use comparatives, e.g.:

Das ist eine bessere Idee.	That's a better idea.

22 Use superlatives, e.g.:

der längste Film	the longest film
das schlimmste Unglück	the worst bad luck

23 Use **bei** + a noun, e.g.:

bei unserer Ankunft	on our arrival

24 Use **bevor**, e.g.:

Bevor ich etwas dafür tun konnte...	Before I could do anything about it...

25 Try to include a conditional tense, e.g.:

Ich würde kommen	I would come

26 Try to include a mix of perfect and imperfect tenses.

27 Use **ohne** + the infinitive, e.g.:

ohne zu wissen	without knowing
ohne zu sprechen	without speaking

28 Use personal pronouns, e.g.:

Sie erklärte es mir.	She explained it to me.

29 Use **weiter machen** (to carry on doing), e.g.:

Sie sang weiter.	She carried on singing.

30 Use **sich entschliessen/den Entschluss machen**, e.g.:

Wir haben uns entschlossen, dahin zu gehen.
We have decided to go there.
Wir machten den Entschluss, nicht mit ihnen zu sprechen.
We made the decision not to talk to them.

31 Give full descriptions.

32 Try not to repeat a verb (see point 20 above).

33 Include a short piece of direct speech, between speech marks, plus inversion, e.g.:

>>Es tut mir Leid.<< sagte sie.	'I'm sorry,' she said.

34 Use **man**, e.g.:

Man weiß nie.	One never knows.

35 Include modal verbs (**können, müssen, dürfen, wollen**).

36 Include impersonal verbs, e.g.:

Es geht mir gut.	I'm doing well.
Es tut mir leid.	I'm sorry.
Es wundert mich nicht.	It doesn't surprise me.
Es gefällt mir.	It pleases me/I like it.

37 Use sayings, e.g.:

Morgen ist auch ein Tag!	Tomorrow is another day!

38 Use question words, e.g.:

wann? warum? was? wer? wie? wo? wozu?

39 Use the perfect tense with **sein**, e.g.:

Ich bin nie dahin gegangen.	I have never been there.

40 Try to include a subjunctive (**Konjunktiv**) phrase (this is not strictly needed for GCSE but it will earn extra marks if used), e.g.:

Wie wäre es, wenn...?	How would it be if...?
Wenn ich das nicht gemacht hätte.	If I hadn't done that.

In the piece of work below, the student has implemented a number of the 40 points. This piece of work would be worth an A*. The numbers in the text refer to the points outlined on pages 8 and 9.

Notice how the student has cleverly started the account with some general comments about the family holidays in the present tense, then narrated the main story-line in the past tense and used the last paragraph to look forward to next year, using the future tense.

Holidays

Jeden Sommer machen[1] meine Familie und ich Ferien in Kleinsee im bayerischen Alpenvorland nicht so weit von München, weil[5] die Eltern sich da total entspannt[9] fühlen[1] und wir Freunde am Campingplatz haben.[1]

Normalerweise[9] nehmen wir den Eurostar und reisen mit dem Zug und dem Taxi bis Kleinsee, aber letzten August haben wir, oder, besser[21] gesagt, hat Vati einen doofen Fehler gemacht![2] Er hat sich entschlossen,[2] mit der Fähre von Hull bis Brügge zu fahren, und die weiteren[21] siebenhundert Kilometer mit unserem alten[19] Wagen zu bereisen.[9/20] Das hätten[40] wir lieber nicht gemacht, da[5] unser alter[19] VW viel zu alt dafür ist.

Zweimal haben wir eine Panne unterwegs[9] gehabt. Die erste war eine Reifenpanne[9] auf dem Lande, wo[7] es niemand[12] gab, um uns zu helfen,[8] und die zweite Panne ist in der Mitte der Großstadt vorgekommen.[39] Vati hat zigmal[9] geflucht[9] und Mutti hat geschmollt![9]

Gegen Mitternacht sind wir endlich in den Campingplatz angekommen,[39] wo die Leute schon schliefen.[4] Wir mussten[35] alleine das Zelt aufstellen[9] und dieses Mal wurden alle beide[9] Eltern ärgerlich. Vati sagte, mein Bruder und ich sollten[35] »den Mund halten!«[18]

Aber morgen ist auch ein Tag[37] und alles ist wieder gut bis zum Ende des Urlaubes passiert.[39] Wir haben Wanderungen unternommen[9] und wir sind braun innerhalb und ausserhalb[2/9] des Sees geworden.[39] Wir haben auch viel mit deutschen Jugendlichen zu tun gehabt.[2]

Das Campingrestaurant war imponierend,[9] und wir haben Pizzas, Bratwurst und Wiener Schnitzel gegessen. Nächsten Sommer werden[3] wir wieder nach Kleinsee reisen[32] und ich freue mich darauf, besonders weil[5] meine Freunde auch dabei[9] sein werden,[3] und wir Ausflüge zusammen machen werden.[3/6]

The '40 points for improving your grade' are referenced in the passages on the 'Sample controlled assessment' pages in the same way as they appear in this example.

Tips for listening and reading

Make sure you read the questions carefully before starting to answer them, and highlight the question words. If there is a series of questions, look through the sequence and see if any of them will help you to answer questions from earlier on. Try to anticipate the answers, and note down possible words to look or listen for.

Devise a checklist to help you to remember what to look or listen for, e.g.
1. Numbers, 2. Dates, 3. Times, 4. Who does what, 5. The sequence of events, 6. Keywords to explain the passage.

Remember that the order of questions must follow the order of the passage, so you can be sure that, unless question 5 just requires an opinion, the material in the passage relating to it will come in between the material for questions 4 and 6.

1 Lifestyle and health

The following topics are covered in this chapter:

- Healthy and unhealthy lifestyles
- Food and drink
- Accidents and incidents
- Grammar

1.1 Healthy and unhealthy lifestyles

LEARNING SUMMARY	After studying this section, you should be able to:
	• describe how to keep fit and healthy
	• talk about your diet

Healthy lifestyles

AQA	✓
OCR	✓
EDEXCEL	✓
WJEC	✓
CCEA	✓

Health issues are a popular topic for both speaking and writing, so you may well choose them for a controlled assessment. You have the opportunity to use the three tenses in this topic: past, present and future. Show how thinking about your lifestyle (present) has made you change your (past) ways, so that (in future) you will eat and act differently. If you divide your piece of work into these three sections, you will give it a clear and organised structure. The vocabulary in the following statements will also help you in the listening and reading exams.

Using the three tenses will gain you a lot of credit.

Lifestyles

Here is a list of useful statements:

Bis jetzt habe ich zu viel Schokolade und Pommes Frites gegessen.
Up to now, I have eaten too much chocolate and chips.

In der Vergangenheit habe ich zu viel ferngesehen!
In the past, I watched too much television!

Ich war Sklave/Sklavin vom Computer!
I was a slave to the computer!

Ich ging nicht zu Fuß zur Schule.
I didn't use to walk to school.

Es ist höchste Zeit, meine schlechten Gewohnheiten zu ändern!
It's high time I changed my bad habits!

In der Zukunft werde ich unbedingt nicht rauchen.
In future, I shall definitely not smoke.

Von nun an, werde ich kein Alkohol trinken.

From now on, I will drink no alcohol.

Ich werde es vermeiden, zu viel Fett zu essen.

I will avoid eating too much fat.

Ich werde früher ins Bett gehen.

I will go to bed earlier.

Ich habe vor, Chips aufzugeben.

I intend to give up crisps.

Ich werde Süßigkeiten aufgeben!

I will give up sweets!

Ich werde meine Diät variieren.

I will vary my diet.

Ich will und ich werde gesund essen.

I want to and I will eat healthily.

Ich habe vor, gesunder zu essen.

I intend to eat more healthily.

Ich würde lieber weniger schnell essen.

I would like to eat more slowly.

Wie viele Früchte und Gemüse ich esse ist äußerst wichtig.

The amount of fruit and vegetables I eat is extremely important.

Ich werde fünf Portionen Frucht und Gemüse pro Tag essen.

I will eat five portions of fruit and vegetables per day.

Vielleicht sollte ich auch einige Vitamine schlucken.

Perhaps I should also swallow a few vitamins.

Ich werde es vermeiden, zu viel Fett zu essen.

I will avoid eating too much fat.

Ich werde so viel Zeit wie möglich in der freien Luft verbringen.

I will spend as much time as possible in the open air.

Ich werde regelmäßig Bewegung haben.

I will to get regular exercise.

Auch könnte ich wieder Sport für die Schule treiben/spielen.

I could also start playing sport for the school again.

Straßensport würde auch gesund sein.

Street sport would also be healthy.

Mir wird es auch Spaß machen, zum Fitnesscentre zu gehen.

It will also be fun for me to go to the gym.

Jetzt muss ich den Entschluß machen, weniger fernzusehen.

Now I have to make the decision to watch less television.

Ich werde nie mehr ein Couchpotato(e) sein!

I will never be a couch potato again!

Was das Internet betrifft, werde ich es stark begrenzen.

As far as the Internet is concerned, I will seriously limit it.

PROGRESS CHECK

Say or write the following in German:

1. I will eat healthily.
2. I will vary my diet.
3. I have eaten too much.
4. I intend…
5. In the past

1. Ich werde gesund essen.
2. Ich werde meine Diät variieren.
3. Ich habe zu viel gegessen.
4. Ich habe vor...
5. In der Vergangenheit

1.2 Food and drink

After studying this section, you should be able to:

- talk about food and drink
- say what you like and do not like to eat and drink

Eating and drinking

AQA	✓
OCR	✓
EDEXCEL	✓
WJEC	✓
CCEA	✓

The topic of food and drink frequently appears in the reading and listening exams. In your controlled speaking assessment, you might have to talk about food and drink and your likes and dislikes.

Meals (Mahlzeiten)

das Abendessen – tea, supper, dinner
das Essen – food, meal
das Frühstück – breakfast

Kaffee und Kuchen – afternoon coffee
das Mittagessen – lunch
das Picknick – picnic

Vegetables (Gemüse)

der Salat

die Erbse (-n) – pea
die grünen Bohnen – green beans
die Karotte (-n) – carrot
die Kartoffel (-n) – potato
der Kohl – cabbage

der Pilz (-e) – mushroom
die Pommes (frites) – chips
der Reis – rice
der Salat – salad, lettuce
die Zwiebel (-n) – onion

Fruit (Das Obst)

die Ananas (-) – pineapple
der Apfel (Äpfel) – apple
die Apfelsine (-n) – orange
die Banane (-n) – banana
die Birne (-n) – pear
die Brombeere (-n) – blackberry
die Erdbeere (-n) – strawberry

die Himbeere (-n) – raspberry
die Kirsche (-n) – cherry
die Melone (-n) – melon
der Pfirsich (-e) – peach
die Pflaume (-n) – plum, prune
die Stachelbeere (-n) – gooseberry
die Traube (-n) – grape

Meats (Fleischarten)

das Hähnchen

der Braten (-) – roast meat
die Ente – duck
das Fleisch – meat
die Frikadelle (-n) – rissole
das Hähnchen – chicken
das Kalbfleisch – veal
das Lammfleisch – lamb

die Pastete – pâté
das Rindfleisch – beef
der Rinderbraten – roast beef
der Schinken – ham
das Schweinefleisch – pork
das Steak – steak

die Kaffeekanne

On the table (Auf dem Tisch)

die Gabel – fork
das Glas – glass
die Kaffeekanne – coffee pot
der Löffel – spoon
das Messer – knife

der Pfeffer – pepper
das Salz – salt
die Schüssel – bowl
der Senf – mustard
die Soße – sauce, gravy
die Tasse – cup

der Tisch – table
das Tischtuch – table cloth
die Untertasse – saucer
der Zucker – sugar

Snacks (Imbisse)

die Bratwurst – fried sausage
die Bonbons – sweets
das Butterbrot – (slice of) bread and butter
die Chips – crisps

die Currywurst – curried sausage
das Omelett – omelette
die Schokolade – chocolate
der Toast – toast

die Krabbe

Fish and seafood (Fische und Meeresfrüchte)

die Auster – oysters
die Forelle – trout
der Hummer – lobster
der Kabeljau – cod

die Krabben – shrimps
der Krebs – crab
der Lachs – salmon
der Thunfisch – tuna

Desserts (Nachtische)

der Apfelkuchen – apple tart
das Eis – ice cream
das Feingebäck – pastries
das Kompott – stewed fruit
der Kuchen – cake, gateau

der Nachtisch – dessert
der Obstsalat – fruit salad
der Pudding – cold milk dessert
die Schwarzwälder – Black Forest gateau

der Honig

Breakfast (Das Frühstück)

der Aufschnitt – cold meats
das Baguette – French stick
das Brot – bread
das Brötchen – bread roll
die Butter – butter
die Cornflakes – cornflakes

die Getreideflocken – cereals
der Honig – honey
die Margarine – margarine
das Pfannengericht – fry-up
der Porridge – porridge

Drinks (Getränke)

das Bier – beer
das/die (Coca-) Cola – coke
der Eistee – ice tea
der Fruchtsaft – fruit juice
das Getränk – drink

der Kaffee (mit Sahne) – coffee (with cream)
die Limonade – lemonade
die Milch – milk
das Mineralwasser – mineral water

der Sprudel – sparkling mineral water
der Tee – tea

Conversation: Grade C

AQA ✓
OCR ✓
EDEXCEL ✓
WJEC ✓
CCEA ✓

Nimmst du dein Frühstück zu Hause oder in der Schule?

Ich nehme mein Frühstück zu Hause. Mit meiner Familie.

Und was isst du eigentlich?

Ich nehme Cornflakes und Toast und Marmelade.

Und isst man normalerweise gesund bei dir?

Ja, wir essen sehr gern Obst und Gemüse.

Und was für Obst und Gemüse isst du am liebsten?

Für Obst, Äpfel und Bananen und meine Lieblingsgemüse sind Karotten und grüne Bohnen. Aber, Brokkoli und Blumenkohl kann ich nicht leiden.

Und welche Fleischarten isst du gern?

Ich esse sehr gern Brathänchen und auch Rindfleisch.

Und welches Fleisch magst du nicht?

Ich mag nicht Schweinefleisch.

Und was für Snacks findest du gut?

Chips oder eine Tafel Schokolade.

Und was für Nachtisch isst du gern?

Das ist leicht. Schwarzwälderkirschtorte. Mit Schlag.

Das wundert mich nicht! Und was trinkst du gern?

Eine Cola, Orangensaft und auch Wasser!

Und mit deinem Frühstück?

Fruchtsaft oder eine Tasse Tee.

Und trinkst du gern Wein oder Bier?

Nein, ich hasse sie und ich bin noch zu jung!

In the restaurant (Im Restaurant)

Bedienung inbegriffen – service included
das Besteck – cutlery
Bitte zahlen! – The bill, please!
der Boss – boss
der Chef – chef, boss
die Flasche (-n) – bottle

das Gericht (-e) – dish
das Hauptgericht – main course
der Kellner – waiter
die Kellnerin – waitress
die Speisekarte – menu
das Trinkgeld – tip
die Toiletten – toilets

verbrannt

Adjectives and phrases

beiseite – apart from
billig – cheap
Es schmeckt! – It tastes good!
frisch – fresh
gefroren – frozen
Guten Appetit! – Enjoy your meal!
köstlich – delicious
lecker – tasty

prima – great
sauer – sour
schlecht – off, bad
teuer – dear, expensive
(zu) trocken – (too) dry
verbrannt – burnt
verkocht – over-cooked
zu kurz gekocht – under-cooked

sich streiten

Verbs

bedienen – to serve

sich beklagen – to complain

bestellen – to order

empfehlen – to recommend

essen – to eat

einen Fehler machen – to make
  a mistake

gratulieren – to congratulate

lieber essen – to prefer to eat

nehmen – to take, to have

probieren – to try

reservieren – to reserve

sich streiten – to argue

trinken – to drink

wechseln – to change

(be)zahlen – to pay

PROGRESS CHECK

Say or write the following in German:

1. Knife, fork and spoon
2. Afternoon coffee
3. Apart from chips!
4. Enjoy your meal!
5. ...is my favourite dessert
6. I will try the lamb.

1. das Messer, die Gabel, der Löffel 2. Kaffee und Kuchen 3. Pommes frites beiseite!
4. Guten Appetit! 5. ...ist mein Lieblingsnachtisch 6. Ich werde das Lammfleisch probieren.

1.3 Accidents and incidents

**LEARNING
SUMMARY**

After studying this section, you should be able to:

- describe your own or someone else's state of health
- refer to particular health problems
- explain how accidents happened
- describe incidents such as theft

Health

AQA	✓
OCR	✓
EDEXCEL	✓
WJEC	✓
CCEA	✓

The topic of health is frequently examined in the listening and reading papers. It may also figure in your controlled assessment for speaking and writing.

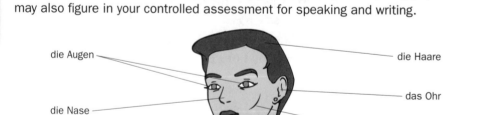

die Augen

die Nase

der Mund

die Haare

das Ohr

die Wange

der Hals

The body (Der Körper)

die Zähne

das **Auge** (-n) – eye	die **Kehle** – throat
das **Bein** (-e) – leg	das **Kinn** – chin
der **Bauch** – belly	das **Knie** (-n) – knee
das **Blut** – blood	der **Kopf** – head
die **Brust** – chest	die **Lippe** (-n) – lip
der **Ellbogen** (-) – elbow	der **Magen** – stomach
der **Finger** (-) – finger	die **Nase** – nose
der **Fuß** (¨e) – foot	das **Ohr** (-en) – ear
das **Fussgelenk** (-e) – ankle	der **Po** – bottom
das **Gehirn** – brain	der **Rücken** – back
das **Gesicht** – face	die **Schulter** (-n) – shoulder
die **Haare** – hair	die **Stimme** – voice
der **Hals** – neck	die **Wange** (-n) – cheek
die **Hand** (¨e) – hand	der **Zahn** (¨e) – tooth
die **Haut** – skin	die **Zunge** – tongue
das **Herz** – heart	

Health (Die Gesundheit)

das **Aspirin** – aspirin	die **Krankheit** – sickness
asthmatisch – asthmatic	das **Medikament** (-e) – medicine
sich ausruhen – to rest	das **Pflaster** (-) – plaster
die **Creme** – cream	die **Pille** (-n) – pill
dringend – urgent	das **Rezept** (-e) – prescription
der **Durchfall** – diarrhoea	die **Spritze** (-n) – injection
erkältet – having a cold	der **Stich** (-e) – sting
die **Erkältung** – cold	der **Termin** – appointment
das **Fieber** – high temperature	**Verletzte** – injured person, m/f
krank – ill, sick	die **Verletzung** – injury

der Stich

Fieber haben

Verbs and phrases

sich das Bein brechen – to break one's leg	**sich in den Finger schneiden** – to cut one's finger
im Bett bleiben – to stay in bed	**Halsschmerzen haben** – to have a bad throat
bluten – to bleed	**Magenschmerzen haben** – to have a bad stomach
sich erbrechen – to be sick	**stechen** – to sting
sich erholen – to recover	**sterben** – to die
eine Erkältung haben – to have a cold	**sich verletzen** – to injure, to hurt oneself
Fieber haben – to have a high temperature	

Conversation

AQA	✓
OCR	✓
EDEXCEL	✓
WJEC	✓
CCEA	✓

🗣 **Wie kann ich Ihnen helfen?**
🗣 Ich habe Halsschmerzen.
🗣 **Haben Sie andere Symptome?**
🗣 Ja, ich habe Fieber.
🗣 **Ja und noch etwas?**
🗣 Ich habe mich erbrochen.

Accidents and incidents

AQA	✓
OCR	✓
EDEXCEL	✓
WJEC	✓
CCEA	✓

Accidents and incidents (Unfälle und Vorfälle)

Dieb (in) – thief, m/f	**eine Panne** – breakdown
der Einbruch – burglary	**der Pkw/PKW** – private car
Einbrecher (in) – burglar, m/f	**eine Reifenpanne** – puncture
die Explosion – explosion	**stehlen** – to steal
Fahrer (in) – driver, m/f	**töten** – to kill
Feuer! – fire!	**die Versicherung** – insurance
die Gefahr – danger	**der Zusamenstoß** – collision
gefährlich – dangerous	

per Anhalter fahren

Verbs

per Anhalter fahren – to hitch-hike	**explodieren** – to explode
besser gehen – to get better	**holen** – to fetch
bremsen – to brake	**rutschen** – to slide, to skid
brennen – to burn	**umfahren** – to knock down
einbrechen – to burgle	**verlieren** – to lose
einem helfen – to help someone	**zusammenstoßen mit** – to collide with
ertrinken – to drown	

Conversation

AQA	✓
OCR	✓
EDEXCEL	✓
WJEC	✓
CCEA	✓

🗣 **Hast du den Zusammenstoß gesehen?**
🗣 Mehr oder minder aber ich kam um die Ecke.
🗣 **Waren die Fahrer verletzt?**
🗣 Ich glaube nicht. Es war nur ein leichter Zusammenstoß!

PROGRESS CHECK

Say or write the following in German:

1 I have a bad throat.
2 I have a temperature.
3 I had to rest.
4 The cars collided.
5 There were no injuries.
6 No one was killed.

1. Ich habe Halsschmerzen. 2. Ich habe Fieber. 3. Ich musste mich ausruhen. 4. Die Wagen sind zusammengestoßen. 5. Es gab keine Verletzungen. 6. Niemand war/wurde getötet.

1.4 Grammar

LEARNING SUMMARY	After studying this section, you should be able to understand:
	• grammatical terms
	• the indefinite article
	• the definite article

Grammatical terms

AQA	✓
OCR	✓
EDEXCEL	✓
WJEC	✓
CCEA	✓

In order to revise your grammar effectively, you will need to understand certain grammatical terms. Try to get into the habit of referring back to this section, whenever you feel the need.

First, read this sentence several times:

The weather never stays fine when we have a barbecue in the garden.

The	definite article
weather	noun (subject)
never	adverb
stays	verb
fine	adjective
when	subordinating conjunction
we	pronoun
have	verb
a	indefinite article
barbecue	noun (direct object)
in	preposition (= place word)
the	definite article
garden	noun

- The definite article is the grammatical name for the word 'the'.
- The indefinite article is the grammatical name for 'a' or 'an'.
- A noun is a person/animal/place/thing, e.g. Fred, dog, Berlin, DVD.
- A verb is an action word, e.g. tries, kicks, laughs, has, thinks.
- An adjective is a word that gives you information about a noun, e.g. small, red.
- An adverb is a word that gives you information about a verb, e.g. slowly, noisily.
- A preposition is a word placed before a noun or pronoun to indicate time, place or condition, e.g. on the table.
- A clause is a group of words containing a verb and subject.
- A main clause is a clause that can stand on its own and make sense as a sentence, however short it might be, e.g. 'The weather never stays fine.'
- A subordinate clause or relative clause is a clause that cannot exist on its own as a sentence. These clauses are called subordinate or relative, because they are subordinate to, or relate to, a main clause and depend on it to give them a meaning, e.g. 'when we have a barbecue in the garden' does not make sense on its own.
- A conjunction is a word that links two parts of a sentence, often two clauses, e.g. 'and' or 'but'.

- Subordinating conjunctions such as 'if/when', 'because', 'since', 'that' (in German, **wenn**, **weil**, **da**, **dass**) introduce subordinate clauses, e.g. when we have a barbecue in the garden. Notice once again, how, on its own, this clause does not make complete sense.
- A pronoun is a word taking the place of a noun. In the sentence on page 19, we could have replaced 'the weather' with 'it', provided the reader already knew we were talking about 'the weather'.
- A relative pronoun is a pronoun linking two parts of a sentence. The relative pronouns are 'that', 'which', 'who', 'whom', 'where' (in German, **der**, **die**, **das**, **wem**, **wo**).
- Words such as 'not', 'never', 'nothing', and 'nobody' are negatives. They show that an action is not happening or is unsuccessful.
- In German, the gender of a person, place, animal or thing tells you whether it is masculine, feminine or neuter.
- The person, place, animal or thing doing the action is called the subject of the sentence or clause, e.g. in 'the weather never stays fine', 'the weather' is the subject of the clause.
- The person, place, animal or thing that has the action done directly to it is called the direct object, e.g. in 'we have a barbecue', the direct object of the 'have' action is 'a barbecue'.

Word order

In German, the verb must be the second idea in a main clause and must come at the end of a subordinate clause, e.g.

main clause	subordinate clause
① ② ③	End

Der Regen kommt immer, wenn wir eine Grillparty im Garten haben.

PROGRESS CHECK

Look carefully at the following sentences from the sample piece of work on page 10 and find in each one **a)** a main clause **b)** a subordinate clause **c)** the subject and verb in each main clause **d)** the subject and verb in each subordinate clause.

① Jeden Sommer machen meine Familie und ich Ferien in Kleinsee, weil die Eltern sich da total entspannt fühlen.
② Das hätten wir lieber nicht gemacht, da unser alter VW viel zu alt dafür ist.
③ Die erste war eine Reifenpanne auf dem Lande, wo es niemand gab.

1. a) Jeden Sommer machen meine Familie und ich Ferien in Kleinsee b) weil die Eltern sich da total entspannt fühlen. c) meine Familie und ich machen d) die Eltern; fühlen
2. a) Das hätten wir lieber nicht gemacht, b) da unser alter VW viel zu alt dafür ist. c) hätten wir; gemacht d) unser alter VW; ist
3. a) Die erste war eine Reifenpanne auf dem Lande, b) wo es niemand gab. c) Die erste; war d) es; gab

---

The indefinite article

AQA	✓
OCR	✓
EDEXCEL	✓
WJEC	✓
CCEA	✓

In English, the indefinite article is the grammatical name for 'a', 'an' (singular) or 'some' (plural). In German, you take the basic form of **ein** (singular) or **einige** (plural) and add different endings, according to its gender and case.

ein Kind

Case	Masculine	Feminine	Neuter	Plural
Nominative [=Subject]	ein Mann	eine Frau	ein Kind	einige Leute
Accusative [=Direct object]	einen Mann	eine Frau	ein Kind	einige Leute
Genitive [=Possessive]	eines Mannes	einer Frau	eines Kindes	einiger Leute
Dative [=Indirect object]	einem Mann	einer Frau	einem Kind(e)	einigen Leuten

PROGRESS CHECK

Fill the gaps in the sentences below with the correct forms of **a) ein Mann b) eine Frau c) ein Kind**.

1 Ich sah .... am Bahnhof.

2 Ich gab..das Foto zurück.

3 ....ging ins Büro.

4 Ich fand ein Foto .... im Kino.

1. a) einen Mann b) eine Frau c) ein Kind 2. a) einem Mann b) einer Frau c) einem Kind
3. a) Ein Mann b) Eine Frau c) Ein Kind 4. a) eines Mannes b) einer Frau c) eines Kindes

The definite article

AQA	✓
OCR	✓
EDEXCEL	✓
WJEC	✓
CCEA	✓

In English, the definite article is the grammatical name for 'the'. In German, you take the basic form of **der** and add different endings, according to its gender and case.

die Leute

Case	Masculine	Feminine	Neuter	Plural
Nominative [=Subject]	der Mann	die Frau	das Kind	die Leute
Accusative [=Direct object]	den Mann	die Frau	das Kind	die Leute
Genitive [=Possessive]	des Mannes	der Frau	des Kindes	der Leute
Dative [=Indirect object]	dem Mann	der Frau	dem Kind(e)	den Leuten

PROGRESS CHECK

Fill the gaps in the sentences below with the correct forms of **a) der Mann b) die Frau c) das Kind**.

1 .... ging ins Büro.

2 Ich sah .... am Bahnhof.

3 Ich fand ein Foto .... im Kino.

4 Ich gab .... das Foto zurück.

1. a) Der Mann b) Die Frau c) Das Kind 2. a) den Mann b) die Frau c) das Kind
3. a) des Mannes b) der Frau c) des Kindes 4. a) dem Mann b) der Frau c) dem Kind

Sample controlled assessment

Speaking

1 You are going to have a conversation with your teacher about a trip to a rock concert in Germany that went badly wrong. Use the following pictures and prompts to help you.

From where and when did you leave for the stadium? ➡️ With whom did you go?

The journey ⬅️ How did you get there?

Getting into the stadium ➡️ Before the concert

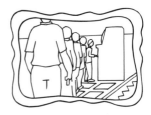

How the weather changed ⬅️ How the rock concert went

Two days later ➡️ The next morning

Sample controlled assessment

Student: Letztes Jahr befand ich[26] mich auf einem Schulaustauschbesuch bei meinem Freund am Rande des Schwarzwaldes. Am Mittwoch abend hatten alle Mitglieder des Austausches Eintrittskarten für das Rolling Bones Konzert in Freiburg, der Schwarzwälder Hauptstadt. Rolling Bones sind[1] eine Hardrockgruppe, für die[7] ich sehr schwärme.[1] Seit langem[10] freute ich mich auf dieses Konzert. Endlich ist der schöne Tag Ende April da. Es war ein ziemlich warmer Frühlingsabend, die Sonne schien und wir dachten, daß wir einen schönen Abend verbringen würden.

Teacher: Wo fand denn das Konzert statt und wie seid ihr dorthin gefahren?

Student: Wir sollten[26] vom Haus meines Austauschfreundes mit einem Schulbus zum Freiburger Stadion fahren. Der Bus sollte[35] uns um 18.00 Uhr abholen. So weit, so gut. Ich hatte den anderen gesagt, dass wir uns heute abend sehr gut amüsieren werden!

Teacher: Und wie war es im Bus?

Student: Ganz prima! Wir haben einen Film über die Rolling Bones gesehen und wir haben natürlich mitgesungen[2] und ein wenig getanzt. Doch das Tanzen hat den Lehrern nicht[12] gefallen![2] Die Reise hat eine Dreiviertelstunde gedauert und wir haben viel Spaß im Bus gehabt, ohne zu unartig vor den Lehrern zu sein. Wie immer!

Teacher: Interessant und seid ihr direkt im Stadion angekommen?

Student: Das ich nicht lache! Wir mußten anderthalb Stunden Schlange stehen und das am Eingang[9] des Stadions. Es war wie ein Probesingen für *X-Factor* in Manchester oder Liverpool! Doch als wir im Stadion selbst drin waren hatten wir[11] bessere Laune weil wir froh waren zusammen zu sein und die Vorbereitungen auf der Bühne sehen zu können. Es war[26] sehr spannend![18] Wir haben dreimal eine Bratwurst gegessen[26] und die mit Coca Cola heruntergespült.[9]

Teacher: So weit, so gut, hast du vorhin gesagt. Ab wann ist es denn dann schief gegangen?

Student: Es war wie in England! Plötzlich ist, wie oft bei uns, das Wetter umgeschlagen! Zwei Stunden lang hat es in Strömen geregnet und wir waren alle von Kopf bis Fuss nass.[37] Aber wir haben alle aus voller Kehle während des Konzerts mitgesungen.[26] Die Rolling Bones waren nicht so naß[21] wie wir und sie haben ihr Bestes getan, uns aufzuheitern.

Teacher: Und später, was ist später passiert?

Student: Zwei Tage danach bin ich krank geworden.[39] Mir[28] ging es gar nicht gut und ich bin zum Arzt gegangen. Ich hatte[11] unglaubliche[19] Kopfschmerzen, Nasen-, Hals- und Magenschmerzen und auch Fieber. Ich habe Zustände gekriegt![18] Der Arzt, nein, die Ärztin hat darauf bestanden, dass ich mich für 2 bis 3 Tage ins Bett lege, weil ich eine Grippe hatte.[26] Das habe ich auch gemacht – ich habe mir so leid getan![18] Die Lehrer hatten[26] kein Mitleid, die können so grausam sein!

Teacher: Das kann ich mir nicht vorstellen. Du übertreibst es!

Student: Vielleicht ein bisschen. Aber ich sage[1] Ihnen etwas, trotz[16] der Grippe werde ich[3] auf jeden Fall nächstes Jahr wieder mit der Schule in den Schwarzwald fahren. Hoffentlich erleben wir[1] nächstes Mal keine Katastrophe.

Teacher: Das hoffe ich auch, nächstes Mal komme ich mit!

Turn to page 154 for a translation of this passage.

Examiner's comments

The structure of the conversation is excellent. The student hasn't missed out any of the picture requirements and has dealt with them in an imaginative way.

This student has incorporated a number of the '40 points for improving your grade' from pages 8–9 and is on track for a top grade:

1   Several examples of the present tense

2   Examples of the past tense

3   An example of the future tense

7   'Die' is a good connecting word

9   Impressive vocabulary, e.g. 'Eingang', 'heruntergespült'

10 A 'seit' structure

11 'Haben' structures

12 An example of a negative

16 Use of 'trotz' + the genitive

18 Exclamations

19 An example of an adjective

21 A comparative

26 A mix of perfect and imperfect tenses

28 A personal pronoun

35 A modal verb ('sollen')

37 A nice saying ('wir waren alle von Kopf bis Fuss nass')

39 The perfect tense has been used with 'sein'

Sample controlled assessment

Writing

1 Write an imaginary magazine interview with a German-speaking, internationally-known pop star. You could include the following points:

- Introduce the star to your readers
- Her/his early career
- Her/his family and friends
- Training and keeping fit for singing
- Spare-time interests
- Social and political attitudes.

Interview mit Kris Ledermann - ein aufgehender Stern der Popwelt

Frauenpopmagazin: Liebe Leserinnen, Sie werden[3] schon von Kris Ledermann gehört haben, sowohl für seine männliche Schönheit als[21] auch für seine erstaunliche Musik. Sei recht herzlich willkommen bei *Frauen-Popmagazin*, Kris Ledermann.

Kris Ledermann: Ich bedanke[1] mich bei dir[28] und es macht mir[28] viel Freude hier zu sein. Aber eines muss[35] ich klären. Ich bin nicht unbedingt schön und oberflächliche Schönheit interessiert micht nicht.[12] Doch die innere Schönheit ist etwas ganz anders.

Frauenpopmagazin: Danke für die Berichtigung. Also, Kris, unsere Leserschaft, wird[3] Sie nach Ihrem Triumph beim Nixdorfer Popfestival letztes Jahr erkennen, wo Sie die Preise für den besten Sänger, den besten Lyriker und das beste neueste Talent gewonnen[2] haben. Es war das erste Mal, wo eine Persönlichkeit dreimal am Podium[9] gestanden ist.[39]

Kris Ledermann: Stimmt. Aber, ich hatte[11] viel Glück. Für mich war es eine peinliche Begegnung mit dem Starruhm gewesen. Ich bin ein politisch engagierter[19] Mensch und es wird eine bessere[19] Welt sein, wenn[7] wir Dinge wie Preise teilen können. Kein Mensch hat ein Recht auf mehr als einen Preis bei solchen Festivalen.[23] Das ist meine Meinung. Die guten Dinge dieser Erde sollten[35] wir so weit wie möglich teilen.

Frauenpopmagazin: Sprechen wir vielleicht von deiner Familie und deinem Freundenkreis.

Kris Ledermann: Ach, du duzt mich jetzt, wir machen Fortschritte.[9] Wir sind alle egal, nicht wahr?

Frauenpopmagazin: Würde ich auch sagen. Also, Familie und Freundenkreis?

Kris Ledermann: Also, meine Eltern, Gabi und Horst, haben einen erheblichen Einfluss auf mich ausgewirkt.[9] Mutti ist Musiklehrerin und Vati ist Müllwerker. Er ist der zivilisierteste[22] Mensch, den ich je gefunden habe. Die zwei sind total freigebig und sehr für Menschenrechte. Das bin ich auch gewesen[39] und zwar dank ihnen. Ich habe einen Bruder, Fred, mit dem ich Tennis und Squash regelmäßig spiele, um mich fit zu halten. Meine Freunde aus Harsewinkel meiner Heimatstadt sehe ich oft.

Frauenpopmagazin: Und was machst du sonst während deiner Freizeit?

Kris Ledermann: Ich spiele Gitarre und singe für die Patienten in den örtlichen Krankenhäusern, so oft ich kann.

Frauenpopmagazin: Das ist zu nett![18]

Kris Ledermann: Es ist eher[21] Pflicht. Wir geben den Leuten, was wir zu geben haben. Ich habe eine Gitarre und eine Stimme und werde[3] weiter für meine Mitmenschen arbeiten. Nie werde ich meine Karriere als mehr bedeutend als[21] andere Leute sehen.

Frauenpopmagazin: Kris, du bist eine Lehre für uns alle.

Turn to page 154 for a translation of this passage.

Examiner's comments

Remember that you will have to write two controlled assessments, each of up to 300 words. Here is a good example that uses a number of the '40 points for improving your grade' from pages 8–9:

1. An example of the present tense
2. The past tense has been used
3. Examples of the future tense
7. 'Wenn' is a connecting word
9. Impressive vocabulary, e.g. 'Podium', 'Fortschritte', 'ausgewirkt'
11. A 'haben' structure
12. A negative
18. An exclamation
19. Two examples of adjectives
21. Comparatives have been used
22. A superlative
23. 'Bei' + a noun
28. Personal pronouns
35. Modal verbs have been included ('müssen', 'sollen')
39. The perfect tense has been used with 'sein'

Sample controlled assessment

2 Write an e-mail from a hospital bed, telling your friend how you were involved in an imaginary fire. You could mention…

- how you noticed the fire
- what you tried to do to help
- why you ended up in hospital
- how you feel now.

Lieber Hansi,

Ich bin hier im Schöndorfer Krankenhaus. Ich war in einem Feuer. Ich sah das Haus von unserem Nachbarn, das brannte. Ich habe den Hund gehört. Er bellte oben neben dem Fenster eines Schlafzimmers. Ich hatte mein Handy und ich habe einen Krankenwagen und auch die Feuerwehr angerufen. Dann bin ich ins Haus gegangen und oben habe ich den Hund gefunden. Es gab viele Flammen. Ich ging mit dem Hund die Treppe hinunter aber ich habe mich ein bisschen verbrannt. Das war gestern. Jetzt geht es besser. Eine Journalistin kommt mit einem Fotograph nach dem Mittagessen und morgen bin ich in der Zeitung. Ich bin eine Heldin. Bis bald, Gisela

Now compare the version above with the one below.

Hallo Hansi!

Viele Grüsse aus dem Schöndorfer Krankenhaus, wo[7] ich jetzt Patientin bin! Keine Angst, keine Bange,[37] da es mir schon besser[21] geht und ich mich hier nur kurzfristig befinde.[1] Es war gleich nach der Schule und ich war[26] auf dem Weg nach Hause, um[8] mein Sportzeug auszusortieren, vor meinem Tennisspiel für die Grafschaft - schön wärs!

Plötzlich habe ich Rauch gerochen[2] und ich wusste,[26] dass es Feuer irgendwo gab. Du kennst mein Zuhause, das versteckt am Stadtrand und fast auf dem Lande liegt. Aus diesem Grund sieht man niemand in der Gegend während des Arbeitstages. Ich bin um meine Strassenecke gegangen[39] und zu meinem großen Erstaunen habe ich gesehen,[26] wie das Haus unseres einzigen[19] Nachbars schon brannte.[26]

Ich hatte mein Handy mit und wollte eben nach der Feuerwehr anrufen, als ich Schnappi, den bissigen[19] Hund unserer Nachbar am Schlafzimmerfenster erkannte, er bellte[9] und kratzte[9] am Glas der Scheiben. Deshalb habe ich nicht nur die Feuerwehr sondern auch einen Krankenwagen gerufen.[26] Was[38] sollte ich jetzt machen? Meine Eltern würden noch drei Stunden bei der Arbeit[23] sein und mein älterer Bruder, der nutzlos in solchen Lagen ist, schlief[26] vermutlicherweise neben seinen Schulbüchern im Garten. Es war nur Eines zu tun.

Ich habe Mut gefasst, bin aufs schnellste ins raucherfülle[9] Haus gegangen, bin die Treppe hinaufgestürmt, und bin mit Schwierigkeit bis zum Hund gelungen.[26/39] Klar wusste er, dass ich da war, um[8] ihm zu helfen und er hat nicht versucht mich zu beissen.

Während ich die Treppe mit Schnappi unter der Arm hinunterkletterte,[9] haben die Flammen mich ein wenig verbrannt, aber ich hatte es nicht bemerkt, bis ich mich später im Krankenwagen befand. Der bissige Hund war unverletzt und hat mir das Gesicht geleckt! Das war nicht Pflicht!

Morgen kommt eine Mannschaft von der Ortszeitung. Eine Journalistin wird[3] mich interviewen und ein Fotograph wird mich fotografieren. Diese Zeitung werde ich überhaupt nicht[12] kaufen, da du weisst, ich kann[35] es nicht leiden, Fotos von mir zu sehen! Bis bald, Gisela

Turn to page 154 for a translation of this passage.

Examiner's comments

The first piece of writing is much too short and you would probably be disappointed with your mark. To get a high grade, you need to write about 300 words.

In the second example, the candidate has used paragraphs, which will help the examiner to read it. Refer to pages 8–9 for the following mark-winning features of this piece:

1 Use of the present tense
2 The past tense has been used
3 The future tense
7 'Wo' is a connecting word
8 'Um…zu' structures
9 Impressive vocabulary, e.g. 'bellte', 'kratzte', 'rauchvolle', 'hinunterkletterte'
12 A negative
19 Adjectives have been used
21 A comparative has been included
23 'Bei' + a noun
26 A mix of perfect and imperfect tenses has been used
35 A modal verb ('können')
37 A saying ('Keine Angst, keine Bange')
38 'Was' is a question word
39 Examples of the use of the perfect tense with 'sein'

Exam practice questions

Listening

1 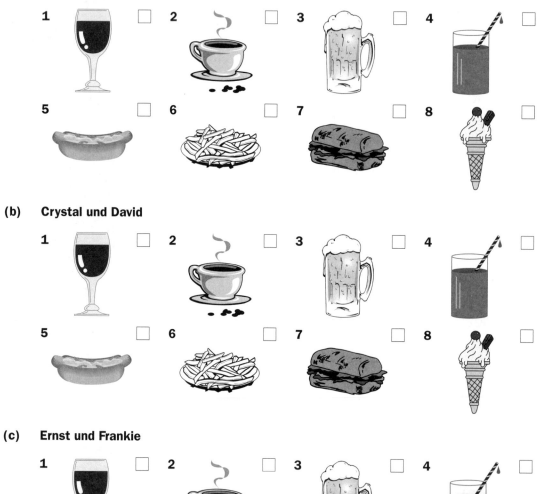 Track 3   What are the customers ordering to eat and drink? Put the customers' initials in the correct boxes (i.e. A for Alice, B for Benno, etc.).

(a)   Alice und Benno

1 ☐   2 ☐   3 ☐   4 ☐

5 ☐   6 ☐   7 ☐   8 ☐

(b)   Crystal und David

1 ☐   2 ☐   3 ☐   4 ☐

5 ☐   6 ☐   7 ☐   8 ☐

(c)   Ernst und Frankie

1 ☐   2 ☐   3 ☐   4 ☐

5 ☐   6 ☐   7 ☐   8 ☐

(12)

Exam practice questions

2   Track 4   A young woman is talking about how she has changed her lifestyle. Tick the correct boxes.

(a)   How many kilos did the doctor say she needed to lose?

A 15 ☐   **B** 25 ☐   **C** 30 ☐

(b)   What was her attitude to losing the weight?

A It would not be a problem   ☐

B She could not see the point   ☐

C She would do it, however hard   ☐

(c)   Why did she then start smoking?

A To comfort herself   ☐

B To help lose the weight   ☐

C Because her boyfriend had started   ☐

(d)   How many cigarettes does she smoke?

A Two or three a day   ☐

B Ten a day   ☐

C A packet a day   ☐

(e)   How did she lose weight?

A By joining a club   ☐

B By cutting out puddings   ☐

C By eating less fat and taking exercise   ☐

(f)   What happened when her boyfriend complained she was too thin?

A She started over-eating again   ☐

B She told him to find someone else   ☐

C She found a new boyfriend   ☐

(g)   What do we learn about her job?

A She has been promoted because of her positive attitude   ☐

B Things are just the same   ☐

C The management want to use her in their publicity material   ☐

(h)   What is the latest news of her old boyfriend?

A He has asked her out again   ☐

B She has refused to see him   ☐

C They are back together   ☐

(8)

Exam practice questions

3 🔵 Track 5 Two friends are playing football in the park. Listen to the conversation and tick the correct boxes.

(a) Fritz tripping Karl was...

    A an accident ☐   **B** deliberate ☐   **C** aggressive ☐

(b) Karl knows that Fritz is...

    A violent ☐   **B** aggressive ☐   **C** clumsy ☐

(c) Karl says he cannot...

    A stand up ☐   **B** walk ☐   **C** continue playing ☐

(d) Fritz thinks that Karl has...

    A twisted his knee ☐   **B** a slight injury ☐   **C** broken his leg ☐

(e) Fritz suggests they get Karl...

    A home to bed ☐   **B** to hospital ☐   **C** to the side of the pitch ☐   **(5)**

Reading

1 Read the statements and answer the questions that follow about people's likes and dislikes. There is one question that cannot be answered from the table, so leave this answer blank.

ANTJE	Ich esse gern alle Gemüse aber ich esse am liebsten grüne Bohnen.
BERT	Ich esse gern alle Früchte aber ich esse am liebsten Pflaumen.
CLAUDIA	Ich esse gern allerlei Fleisch aber ich esse am liebsten Brathähnchen.
ILSE	Ich esse gern allerlei Fleisch aber ich esse am liebsten Schinken.
SIGGI	Ich esse gern allerlei Fleisch aber ich esse am liebsten Lammfleisch.
GISELA	Ich esse gern alle Früchte ausgenommen Ananas.
SYLVIA	Ich esse gern allerlei Fleisch ausgenommen Rindfleisch.
WERNER	Ich esse gern alle Früchte aber ich kann Gemüse nicht leiden.
KNUD	Ich esse gern allerlei Gemüse ausgenommen Kohl.
KONRAD	Ich trinke gern alle Fruchtsäfte und ich kann Bier nicht leiden.
JULIA	Ich trinke gern Alkohol ausgenommen Bier.

(a) Who likes ham? .... **(1)**

(b) Who likes green beans? .... **(1)**

(c) Who likes most alcoholic drinks? .... **(1)**

(d) Who does not like beer? .... **(2)**

(e) Who likes all fruit except pineapple? .... **(1)**

Exam practice questions

(f)	Who likes roast chicken?	**(1)**
(g)	Who likes plums?	**(1)**
(h)	Who likes lamb?	**(1)**
(i)	Who especially likes beer?	**(1)**
(j)	Who cannot stand vegetables?	**(1)**
(k)	Who does not like beef?	**(1)**
(l)	Who likes nearly all vegetables?	**(1)**

2 Match the people to the statements. You will have to use names more than once.

TINA	Meine ganze Familie isst Schaschlik ziemlich gern aber für mich ist das mein Lieblingsessen. Das erste Mal, wo ich Schaschlik entdeckt habe, war in der Türkei. Ich liebe auch Turkish Delight!
BORIS	Wir Österreicher und Deutsche essen zu viel. Deshalb ist die Obesität in unseren zwei Ländern ein großes Problem. Die Lage würde nicht so schlecht sein, wenn wir keine Schlagsahne mit allen Nachtischen und mit dem Kaffee nähmen.
BRIGITTE	Vielleicht esse ich zu viel aber ich bin nicht sicher. Meistens esse ich gesund aber wir gehen oft ins Restaurant und, weil die Gerichte da normalerweise so lecker sind, nehme ich immer sehr große Portionen und auch drei oder vier Glas guten Weißweins damit! Nicht so klug.
ALDO	Für mich gibt es einen Unterschied zwischen Nord- und Süddeutschland, was das Essen betrifft. Im Norden essen wir viel gesunder, nicht so viel Fastfood und so weiter. Auch trinken wir viel weniger Bier.

(a)	The rest of the family likes kebabs, but not as much as I do.	
(b)	Our passion for cream makes things worse.	....
(c)	Eating out is when I get greedy.	....
(d)	I'm not sure whether I eat too much or not.	....
(e)	People eat and drink more in the South.	....
(f)	Being seriously overweight is a real problem for us.	....
(g)	I usually eat healthily.	....
(h)	The Germans overdo it as much as we Austrians.	....
(i)	Southern Germans eat more fast-food than we do.	....
(j)	I found my favourite food when I was abroad.	.... **(10)**

Exam practice questions

3 Read the bar and restaurant adverts and answer the questions that follow.

A
Imbiß Lecker!
die Gemütlichkeit des
alten Marktplatzes
in einem Schnell-Restaurant

Pizza und Dönner
Bratwurst, Nudeln
und Salate

Offen zwischen 10 und 24 Uhr.
Telefon: 06157 4680
Mittagessen Menus ab 8 Uhr

B
Ralfs Restaurant
Allerlei feine Kost
Unsere Bonus?
Nach dem Kauf von drei
Hauptgerichten ist das Vierte
kostenlos!

Reservierung notwendig
Für Ihre Reservation: Telefon:
06042 2879
Wir stehen Ihnen zur Verfügung
ab 18 bis 23 Uhr
Geschlossen: Montag

C
Violas Vegetarischer Palast am Nordstrand
Vegetarische Nusskoteletten?
Sicher, aber auch viel mehr
exotische Speisen!

Non-Vegetarierer können auch mitessen.

Menus 10–40 Euros.
Offen den ganzen Tag
ab 11 bis 24 Uhr.
Tanzen am Abend.
Um zu reservieren: Telefon
06924 5736

Write the letter of the restaurant that…

(a) serves meat and non-meat eaters ....

(b) offers snack meals ....

(c) is right next to the sea ....

(d) is in the market square ....

(e) has the most popular menus ....

(f) has lunch-time menus ....

(g) lets the fourth diner eat free ....

(h) is closed one day of the week ....

(i) requires you to reserve your table ....

(j) has dancing in the evening ....   **(10)**

4 Read this text message and answer the questions that follow.

> Sam, kannst du bitte bei der Schnellfix Werkstatt für mich anrufen? Ich habe eine Reifenpanne und das Benzin ist aus. Sag' nichts der Mutti, weil ich immer schimpfe*, wenn sie so etwas macht! Sag dem Mechaniker, dass ich auf dem Land 10 Kilometer weg bin. Ich bin auf der Strasse nach Bern. Kann der Mechaniker zu mir kommen, um mich zu retten? Ich sitze nicht im Wagen, weil das zu gefährlich ist. Ich stehe in einer kleinen Parkbucht 50 Meter vor dem Wagen. Danke, Vati.

(*schimpfen – to moan, to tell off)

(a) Why has the father sent a message? .... **(1)**

(b) What is wrong with the car? .... **(2)**

(c) Why shouldn't the son tell his mother? .... **(1)**

(d) What must Sam do? .... **(1)**

(e) Where is the father? .... **(2)**

(f) Where will the father be found and why? .... **(2)**

Exam practice questions

5 Read this text message and answer the questions that follow.

> Hallo!
>
> Ich texte Ihnen, um die Abwesenheit meiner Tochter, Irene, zu erklären. Sie hat schwere Magenschmerzen und liegt mit Fieber im Bett. Wir warten auf den Besuch vom Arzt, der glaubt, dass sie vielleicht unter Cholera leidet. Wie gesagt, sie hat viel hohes Fieber und schlechte Träume. Es tut mir Leid, dass ich nicht früher in Kontakt mit Ihnen gewesen bin, aber ich arbeite nachts und tags als Krankenschwester im Krankenhaus Ludwig Koch für tropische Medizin. Vielleicht hat meine schöne Tochter eine Infektion von mir bekommen. Hoffentlich nicht.
>
> Ich könnte zur Schule für ein Interview kommen, aber das wäre vielleicht eine schlechte Idee, weil ich auch infiziert sein könnte. Ich würde Sie nicht mit meinen schlechten Mikroben infizieren!, weil wir hier mit unheilbaren Krankenheiten wie Marburg- und Lhasafieber arbeiten. Wenn man Marburg- oder Lhasafieber hat, werden die Organe wie Wasser und man blutet an den Ohren und an der Nase, usw. Es ist nicht sehr appetitlich!
>
> Ich melde mich in vier oder fünf Tagen wieder um Ihnen Bescheid zu geben.* Noch Eines : ich schreibe nichts auf Papier, um Sie nicht zu infizieren.
>
> Mit besten Grüssen, Ulrike Egger.

(*Bescheid geben – to let know)

(a) Why has Mrs Egger sent this message?

.... (1)

(b) What do we learn about Irene's health? .... (2)

(c) What has the doctor suggested? .... (1)

(d) Why has Mrs Egger not been in contact earlier? .... (2)

(e) What does Mrs Egger hope has not happened?

.... (1)

(f) Why might it be a bad idea for Mrs Egger to come to school? .... (1)

(g) What three details does Mrs Egger give about Irene's symptoms?

    (i) ....

    (ii) ....

    (iii) .... (3)

(h) Give three reasons why we should be concerned about the fevers Mrs Egger mentions.

    (i) .... **(ii)** .... **(iii)** .... (3)

(i) When will Mrs Egger contact the school again? .... (1)

(j) Why has Mrs Egger not written on paper? .... (1)

(k) Who do you think wrote the text? .... (1)

Exam practice questions

6 Read this article on swine flu.

> Um die Chancen zu vermindern, durch Schweinegrippe infiziert zu werden, achten Sie auf diese Informationen:
>
> **Draußen**
> - Küssen Sie nicht Freunde und auch Verwandte
> - Geben Sie den Leuten Ihre Hand nicht
> - Husten Sie und niesen Sie in ein Papiertaschentuch
> - Werfen Sie den Tuch in den nächsten Mülleimer
> - Im Café und im Restaurant vermeiden Sie schmutziges Besteck
>
> **Zu Hause**
> Wenn Sie glauben, Sie könnten von Schweinegrippe infiziert sein...
> - Telefonieren Sie mit dem Doktor bzw der Doktorin in Ihrer Arztpraxis
> - Erklären Sie Ihre Symptome
> - Gehen Sie ins Bett und bleiben Sie da
> - Trinken Sie viel Wasser und gebrauchen Sie die normalen Medikamente gegen eine Grippe
> - Lassen Sie ein Mitglied der Familie zur Arztpraxis gehen, um Ihre Antiviraldrogen zu bekommen
> - Rufen Sie in die Praxis an, wenn Ihre Symptome sich verschlimmern

Complete the sentences below by choosing the correct words from the options given in this box.

> **fühlen   gegen   informieren   Besteck   Arztpraxis   holen   geben**
> **Zuhause   Symptome   von   befinden   Bett   nächsten   Papiertaschentuch**

Wenn Sie sich weg von Ihrem Zuhause **(a)** ...., sollten Sie Familie und Freunde

nicht küssen und die Hand nicht **(b)** .... Wenn Sie husten oder niesen,

gebrauchen Sie ein **(c)** ...., das Sie sofort wie möglich in den

(d) .... Mülleimer werfen sollten. Beim Essen und trinken im Café oder Restaurant,

sollten Sie verweigern, ein **(e)** .... zu gebrauchen, das nicht sauber ist.

Wenn Sie zu Hause sind und Sie Grippesymptome **(f)** ...., nehmen Sie per

Telefon oder Computerkontakt mit Ihrer **(g)** ...., auf erklären Sie Ihre Symptome

und befolgen Sie den Rat des Arztes bzw der Ärztin. Normalerweise sollten Sie sofort ins

(h) .... gehen. Sie können normale Medikamente **(i)** ....

Erkältungen und Grippen nehmen. Wenn Ihre Symptome stärker werden, sollte ein Verwandter zur

Arztpraxis gehen und Ihre Antiviraldrogen für Sie **(j)** .... Im schlimmsten Fall,

wenn Ihre Symptome noch schlimmer werden, **(k)** .... Sie sofort die Praxis und

wenn nötig das nächste Krankenhaus.   **(11)**

2 Relationships and choices

The following topics are covered in this chapter:

- Relationships with family and friends
- Future plans regarding marriage or partnership
- Social issues
- Equality
- Grammar

2.1 Relationships with family and friends

LEARNING SUMMARY

After studying this section, you should be able to:

- talk about your family, friends and pets
- describe your relationships with people

Relationships with family and friends

The following vocabulary and expressions will help you greatly in your listening and reading exams. You could also do a controlled assessment on relationships with family and friends.

Family

der Vater (Vati)

die Grossmutter (Oma)

die Mutter (Mutti)

der Grossvater (Opa)

die Schwester

der Bruder

Myself and my family (Ich und meine Familie)

das **Baby** – baby
die **Beziehung (zu)** – relationship (with)
der **Bruder (ü)** – brother
der **Cousin (-s)** – male cousin
die **Cousine (-n)** – female cousin
das **Einzelkind** – only child
die **Eltern** – parents
der **Enkel (-)** – grandson
die **Enkelin (-nen)** – granddaughter
das **Enkelkind (-er)** – grandchild
der **Erwachsene (-n)** – adult
die **Frau (-en)** – wife
geschieden – divorced
getrennt – separated
die **Großeltern** – grandparents
der **Halbbruder (ü)** – half-brother
die **Halbschwester (-n)** – half-sister
die **Kusine (-n)** – female cousin
ledig – single, unmarried
der **Mann (¨er)** – husband
die **Mutter (ü)** – mother
der **Neffe (-n)** – nephew
die **Nichte (-n)** – niece
die **Oma (-s)** – granny
der **Onkel (-)** – uncle

der **Opa (-s)** – grandpa
der **Schwager** – brother-in-law
die **Schwester (-n)** – sister
die **Schwiegermutter** – mother-in-law
der **Schwiegersohn** – son-in-law
die **Schwiegertochter** – daughter-in-law
der **Schwiegervater** – father-in-law
der **Sohn (¨e)** – son
die **Stiefmutter** – stepmother
der **Stiefsohn** – stepson
die **Stieftochter** – stepdaughter
der **Stiefvater** – stepfather
die **Tante (-n)** – aunt
unverheiratet – unmarried, single
der **Vater (ä)** – father
verheiratet – married
verlobt – engaged
Verlobte (-er) – fiancée, fiancé
die **Verlobung** – engagement
verwaist – orphaned
der **Verwandte (-n)** – relation
verwitwet – widowed
der **Vetter (-)** – male cousin
die **Zwillinge (pl)** – twins

die Zwillinge

die Einladung

Friends and visitors (Freunde und Besucher)

der **Austausch** – exchange
Austauschpartner (in) – exchange partner, m/f
der **Besuch (-e)** – visit
Besucher (in) – visitor, m/f
der **Brief (-e)** – letter
Brieffreund (in) – penfriend, m/f
die **Einladung (-en)** – invitation
der **Freund** – male friend

die **Freundin** – female friend
die **Gastfreundschaft** – hospitality
Kamerad (in) – school-friend, m/f
der **Kuss (¨e)** – kiss
die **Leute** – people
die **Liebe** – love
die **Partnerstadt** – twin-town
die **Party (-s)** – party
das **Treffen (-)** – meeting

Pets (Haustiere)

die Spinne

der (Gold)Fisch – (gold)fish	das Pferd – horse
der Hamster – hamster	die Ratte – rat
der Hund – dog	die Schildkröte – tortoise
das Kaninchen – rabbit	die Schlange – snake
die Katze – cat	die Spinne – spider
die Maus – mouse	der Vogel – bird
das Meerschweinchen – guinea pig	der Wellensittich – budgie

Verbs

lieben

mit einem aus-kommen – to get on with someone	lieben – to love
besuchen – to visit	nennen – to name
einladen – to invite	scheiden – to divorce
feiern – to celebrate	schreiben – to write
geboren sein – to be born	sich sehen – to see each other
Geschwister sein – to be brother and sister	sein – to be
hassen – to hate	sich streiten – to fall out, to quarrel
heiraten – to get married	tanzen – to dance
heißen – to be called	texten – to text
	sich trennen – to separate
	sich verloben – to get engaged

PROGRESS CHECK

Say or write the following in German:
1. I have a dog and three rabbits.
2. My uncle has written to me.
3. I was born in London.
4. We are celebrating Fred's birthday.

1. Ich habe einen Hund und drei Kaninchen.
2. Mein Onkel hat mir geschrieben.
3. Ich bin in London geboren.
4. Wir feiern Freds Geburtstag.

Controlled speaking assessment: family

Make sure you can answer these questions without thinking. Get someone to ask you the questions, so you can practise answering them without using the book.

Wie heißt du?	**Ich heiße…**
Wie alt bist du?	**Ich bin … Jahre alt.**
In welchem Jahr bist du geboren?	**Im Jahre…(neunzehnhundert-sechsundneunzig)…**
Wann hast du Geburtstag?	**Ich habe Geburtstag am…(zehnten Januar)…**
Wo bist du geboren?	**Ich bin in…(Leeds)…geboren.**
Wie groß bist du?	**Ich bin ein Meter…(siebzig)…**
Wie viele Personen sind in deiner Familie?	**Es sind … Personen.**
Wer sind sie?	**Sie sind mein Vater, meine Mutter, mein Bruder, meine Schwester und ich.**
Und dein Vater, was macht er von Beruf?	**Er ist…(Elektriker)…**
Und was macht deine Mutter von Beruf?	**Sie ist…(Doktorin)…**
Hast du Haustiere?	**Ja, ich habe eine Katze…(Fluff)…**
Hast du einen Freund/eine Freundin?	**Ja, er/sie heißt…(Sam)…**

> **KEY POINT**
>
> You will be assessed on your communication skills and on your quality of language. You will also be asked to show your knowledge of tenses. You should get at least a grade C if you can use the three tenses: past, present and future.

Follow these tips when preparing for the controlled speaking assessment:

- Try to use impressive vocabulary: make your own personal list of good, unusual words.
- Try to put enthusiasm into what you say.
- Avoid the temptation to answer with a pre-learned speech. You need to be able to talk for four to six minutes on each topic.
- You will become more familiar with the language if you record your answers and listen to them regularly.

1 You could expand here, with names, how you get on with the family individually, etc.

2 You have used a present tense. Now you can start thinking about the past and future tenses.

3 You have used two perfect tenses, one of them with 'sein'. Now, with the two uses of future tenses (6), you are on course for at least a grade C.

4 You get extra marks for a long list of extended family members.

5 You have given an opinion and justified it in some detail. Once more, this will gain you a lot of extra marks.

🔵 **Beschreib deine Familie.**

🔵 **Wir sind fünf zu Hause, meine Mutter, mein Vater, meine Schwester, mein Bruder und ich.[1] Wir haben auch einige Haustiere, einen Hund, eine Katze und drei Goldfische. Meine Mutter arbeitet[2] in der Großstadt als Bürochefin und mein Vater ist Verkäufer.**

🔵 **Und wie ist deine Mutter?**

🔵 **Sie ist gar nicht so groß und hat braune Augen. Sie ist zweiundvierzig Jahre alt und sie macht gern Aerobik.**

🔵 **Es gibt auch andere Mitglieder in deiner Familie?**

🔵 **Ich habe zwei Großmütter und einen Großvater. Der andere Großvater ist vor zwei Jahren gestorben.[3] Ich habe auch eine ganze Menge Tanten, Onkel, Cousins und Kusinen.[4]**

🔵 **Ausgenommen deine Katze und deine Goldfische, was sind deine Lieblingstiere?**

🔵 **Das würden die Pferde sein.**

🔵 **Und warum denn diese?**

🔵 **Sie sehen so ruhig aus, sind meistens sehr anhänglich und sie rennen auch so schön.[5] Eines Tages werde[6] ich mir ein Pferd kaufen.**

🔵 **Für deinen Geburtstag, was hast du für Geschenke erhalten?**

🔵 **Ich habe Sport-und Computerzeug, CDs, Bücher und auch ziemlich viel Geld erhalten.[3]**

🔵 **Und wie wirst du dieses Geld ausgeben?**

🔵 **Ich werde[6] etwas für meine Großeltern kaufen, da sie immer so nett zu mir und meinen Geschwistern sind.**

🔵 **Ausgezeichnet!**

Other useful sentences

Use the following phrases to help you in your exam or controlled assessment:

Das Familienleben in Großbritannien.
Family life in Great Britain.

Die Anzahl von ... steigt merklich.
The number of ... is increasing noticeably.

Es gibt Vorteile und Nachteile.
There are advantages and disadvantages.

Im Teenageralter war das Leben nie leicht.
Teenage life was never easy.

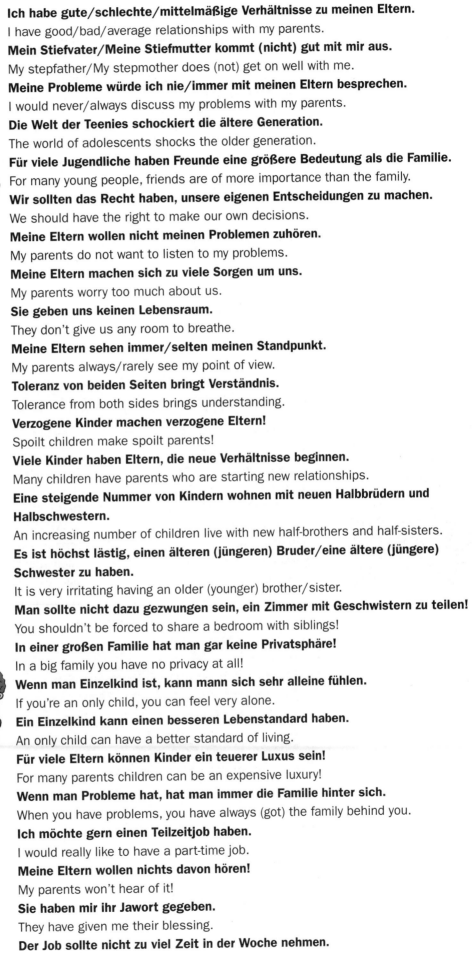

Ich habe gute/schlechte/mittelmäßige Verhältnisse zu meinen Eltern.

I have good/bad/average relationships with my parents.

Mein Stiefvater/Meine Stiefmutter kommt (nicht) gut mit mir aus.

My stepfather/My stepmother does (not) get on well with me.

Meine Probleme würde ich nie/immer mit meinen Eltern besprechen.

I would never/always discuss my problems with my parents.

Die Welt der Teenies schockiert die ältere Generation.

The world of adolescents shocks the older generation.

Für viele Jugendliche haben Freunde eine größere Bedeutung als die Familie.

For many young people, friends are of more importance than the family.

Wir sollten das Recht haben, unsere eigenen Entscheidungen zu machen.

We should have the right to make our own decisions.

Meine Eltern wollen nicht meinen Problemen zuhören.

My parents do not want to listen to my problems.

Meine Eltern machen sich zu viele Sorgen um uns.

My parents worry too much about us.

Sie geben uns keinen Lebensraum.

They don't give us any room to breathe.

Meine Eltern sehen immer/selten meinen Standpunkt.

My parents always/rarely see my point of view.

Toleranz von beiden Seiten bringt Verständnis.

Tolerance from both sides brings understanding.

Verzogene Kinder machen verzogene Eltern!

Spoilt children make spoilt parents!

Viele Kinder haben Eltern, die neue Verhältnisse beginnen.

Many children have parents who are starting new relationships.

Eine steigende Nummer von Kindern wohnen mit neuen Halbbrüdern und Halbschwestern.

An increasing number of children live with new half-brothers and half-sisters.

Es ist höchst lästig, einen älteren (jüngeren) Bruder/eine ältere (jüngere) Schwester zu haben.

It is very irritating having an older (younger) brother/sister.

Man sollte nicht dazu gezwungen sein, ein Zimmer mit Geschwistern zu teilen!

You shouldn't be forced to share a bedroom with siblings!

In einer großen Familie hat man gar keine Privatsphäre!

In a big family you have no privacy at all!

Wenn man Einzelkind ist, kann mann sich sehr alleine fühlen.

If you're an only child, you can feel very alone.

Ein Einzelkind kann einen besseren Lebenstandard haben.

An only child can have a better standard of living.

Für viele Eltern können Kinder ein teuerer Luxus sein!

For many parents children can be an expensive luxury!

Wenn man Probleme hat, hat man immer die Familie hinter sich.

When you have problems, you have always (got) the family behind you.

Ich möchte gern einen Teilzeitjob haben.

I would really like to have a part-time job.

Meine Eltern wollen nichts davon hören!

My parents won't hear of it!

Sie haben mir ihr Jawort gegeben.

They have given me their blessing.

Der Job sollte nicht zu viel Zeit in der Woche nehmen.

The job shouldn't occupy too much of the week.

Es gibt viele Gefahren für Jugendliche.

There are many dangers for young people.

Drogen, Alkohol, HIV, Angriff und Gewalttätigkeit figurieren unter den Bedeutendsten.

Drugs, alcohol, HIV, assault and rape figure amongst the most important of these.

Mädchen haben weniger Freiheit als Jungen.

Girls have less freedom than boys.

Es ist mir nicht erlaubt, mit Jungen auszugehen.

I am not allowed to go out with boys.

Ich soll immer um schlag zehn Uhr wieder zu Hause sein.

I have always to be home at ten o'clock on the dot.

Ich sollte das Recht haben, meine eigenen Freunde zu wählen.

I should have the right to choose my own friends.

Meine Eltern behandeln mich wie ein Kind.

My parents treat me like a child.

Meine Eltern interessieren sich nicht genug für mich.

My parents are not interested enough in me.

Aber die idealen Eltern existieren nicht.

But, the ideal parents don't exist.

Ist das Sein oder Schein?

Appearances can be deceptive.

Describing people (Um die Leute zu beschreiben)

geduldig

aggressiv – aggressive	**grausam** – cruel
arrogant – arrogant	**hilfsbereit** – helpful
die Arroganz – arrogance	**laut** – loud, noisy
bescheiden – modest	**neidisch** – envious
(un)ehrlich – (dis)honest	**nett** – nice
die Geduld – patience	**praktisch** – down to earth
geduldig – patient	**reizbar** – irritable
gelassen – calm, quiet	**snobistisch** – snobby
gemein – nasty	**tolerant** – tolerant
gesprächig – talkative	**verständnisvoll** – understanding

PROGRESS CHECK

Say or write the following in German:

1. The number is increasing noticeably.
2. My parents always see my point of view.
3. My mother worries about me.
4. There are advantages and disadvantages.
5. Appearances can be deceptive.

1. Die Anzahl steigt merklich.
2. Meine Eltern sehen immer meinen Standpunkt.
3. Meine Mutter macht sich Sorgen um mich.
4. Es gibt Vorteile und Nachteile.
5. Ist das Sein oder Schein?

2.2 Future plans regarding marriage or partnership

LEARNING SUMMARY

After studying this section, you should be able to:

- explain your plans or other people's plans for marriage or partnership
- give views on marriage and parenthood

Marriage and partnership

AQA	✓
OCR	✓
EDEXCEL	✓
WJEC	✓
CCEA	✓

The following statements are about future plans, marriage and partnership.

Ich hoffe, ich werde mein Leben führen, wie ich gewählt habe.

I hope I will lead my life as I have chosen.

Ich werde meine erwünschte Zukunft beschreiben.

I will describe the future I hope to have.

Ich werde mit fünfundzwanzig (Jahren) heiraten.

I will get married when I'm twenty-five.

Ich werde nicht vor meinem dreißigsten Geburtstag heiraten.

I will not get married before my thirtieth birthday.

Hoffentlich werde ich zwei Kinder haben.

Hopefully, I will have two children.

Wenn alles so vorkommt, werde ich sehr glücklich sein.

If everything turns out like that, I will be very happy.

Ich werde ein Luxusleben mit einem Luxushaus haben.

I will have a luxury life with a luxury house.

Ich werde einen Millionär/eine Millionärin heiraten.

I will marry a millionaire.

Mein(e) Partner(in) wird ein Star von Bühne und Leinwand sein.

My partner will be a star of stage and screen.

Ich werde mir einen lieben Partner/eine liebe Partnerin finden.

I will find myself a kind partner.

Ich werde Hausfrau/Hausmann sein.

I will be a housewife/house husband.

Mein(e) Partner(in) wird arbeiten, während ich zu Hause bleibe.

My partner will work, while I stay at home.

Ich werde für die Gesellschaft und nicht für mich arbeiten.

I will work for society and not for myself.

Wenn ich reich werde, werde ich Geld für wohltätige Zwecke spenden.

If I become rich, I will donate money to charity.

Ich werde mein Leben wohltätigen Organisationen in Afrika widmen.

I will dedicate my life to charitable organisations in Africa.

KEY POINT

There are many opportunities for you to use the future tense in this topic but don't forget to include some past and present tenses as well.

Nachdem ich die Schule verlassen habe, werde ich...

After I have left school, I shall...

Nachdem ich meine Prüfungen fertiggemacht habe, werde ich...

After I have finished my exams, I will...

Nachdem ich die Universität besucht habe, werde ich...

After I have been to university, I shall...

> **KEY POINT**
>
> The examples above include the word **nachdem** at the start of the sentence. This is a good framework for using the past tense.

Ich werde heiraten, um den Kindern ein wenig Stabilität zu geben.

I shall get married to give the children a little stability.

Ich habe keine Ahnung, warum die Leute heiraten.

I have no idea why people get married.

Ich werde die Kinder zu Hause beaufsichtigen.

I shall look after the children at home.

Die Ehe ist wichtig für die Beziehung(en) des Ehepaars.

Marriage is important for the couple's relationship.

Die Ehe bindet die zwei Personen aneinander.

Marriage binds the two people together.

Die Ehe hat keine wirkliche Bedeutung für die Beziehung der Partner.

Marriage has no real importance for the partners' relationship.

Was bedeutend ist ist einander zu lieben.

What's important is to love each other.

Ich bin weder für noch gegen die Ehe.

I am neither for nor against marriage.

Ich habe Furcht vor der Idee, Kinder zu haben.

I am frightened of the idea of having children.

Eines Tages möchte ich gern heiraten.

I would really like to get married one day.

Heiraten ist in meinem Aktionsprogramm!

Getting married is in my plan of action!

Ich schwärme dafür, Kinder zu haben.

I am really enthusiastic about having children.

Der Gedanke, Kinder zu haben, sagt mir nichts.

The idea of having children does nothing for me.

Bloß der Gedanke macht mir Todesangst!

The very idea frightens me to death!

Das wird nach einigen Jahren kommen, wenn ich reif genug dazu bin!

That will come after some years, when I'm mature enough for it!

> **PROGRESS CHECK**
>
> Say or write the following in German:
> 1. I am really enthusiastic about it.
> 2. After I have left school
> 3. I will work for society.
>
>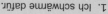
>
> 3. Ich werde für die Gesellschaft arbeiten.
> 2. Nachdem ich die Schule verlassen habe
> 1. Ich schwärme dafür.

2.3 Social issues

After studying this section, you should be able to:

- talk about homelessness, drugs, crime and smoking
- give views on social issues

Social issues

AQA	✓
OCR	✓
EDEXCEL	✗
WJEC	✓
CCEA	✓

You may wish to do your controlled speaking or writing assessment on social issues. This topic may also appear in your listening and reading exams. The following vocabulary and phrases should help you.

obdachlos

Homelessness (Die Obdachlosigkeit)

ausländische Arbeitnehmer – immigrant workers

die Einwanderer – immigrant population

einwandern – to immigrate

ohne festen Wohnsitz – without fixed abode

Immigrant (in) – immigrant, m/f

immigrieren – to immigrate

die Menschenrechte – human rights

obdachlos – homeless

die Obdachlosen – the homeless

der Rassenhass – racial hatred

das Vorurteil (-e) – prejudice

Es gibt Unterkunft in offiziellen Unterkunftszentren.
There is accommodation in official accommodation centres.

Die Betten sind rationiert.
The beds are rationed.

Diese Zentren sind oft von Kirchorganisationen geleitet.
These centres are often managed by church organisations.

Die Obdachlosen befinden sich oft in einem Teufelskreis.
The homeless often find themselves in a vicious circle.

Im Vereinigten Königreich gibt es 20 000 Obdachlosen.
In the United Kingdom, there are 20 000 homeless.

Einige überleben durch den Verkauf vom *Big Issue*.
Some survive by selling the *Big Issue*.

Viele sterben anonym.
Many die in anonymity.

In Deutschland verlassen viele junge Leute ihr Zuhause zur Zeit der Staatsprüfungen.
In Germany, many young people leave their homes at the time of the State examinations.

Es gibt viel Stress in den Schulen durch den Druck immer erfolgreich zu sein.
There is a lot of stress in schools through the pressure to succeed all the time.

Die Ausreißer befinden sich ohne Freunde oder Familie.
The runaways find themselves without friends or family.

Zu Obdachlosen gehören nicht nur Jugendliche, sondern auch Alte, Einwanderer und Mütter mit jungen Kindern.
Amongst the homeless are not only adolescents, but also old people, immigrants and mothers with young children.

Die größte Anzahl davon leben auf der Straße.

The largest number of them live on the street.

Einige leiden unter Geisteskrankenheiten.

Some suffer from mental illnesses.

der Dieb

Crime (Das Verbrechen)

der Diebstahl — theft

der Dieb (-e) – male thief

die Diebin (-nen) – female thief

Einbrecher (in) – burglar, m/f

der Einbruch (¨e) – burglary

ins Gefängnis gehen – to go to jail

das Urteil – sentence

Verbrecher (in) – criminal, m/f

verbrecherisch – criminal (adj.)

Nachts habe ich zu viel Angst, auszugehen.

At night, I am too frightened to go out.

Man sieht überall Gruppen von Rowdys.

You see groups of troublemakers everywhere.

Sie beobachten einen auf eine drohende Weise.

They watch you in a threatening way.

Solche junge Leute sollte man verhaften.

Such young people should be arrested.

Oft kann man nichts dagegen tun, weil sie unter sechszehn (Jahren) sind.

You often cannot do anything because they are under sixteen.

Messerverbrechen ist ein erhebliches Problem, besonders in benachteiligten Wohnsiedlungen.

Knife crime is a considerable problem, particularly in disadvantaged housing estates.

Man investiert zu wenig/nicht genug in der Infrastruktur unserer Gesellschaft.

Too little/Not enough is invested in the infrastructure of our society.

Wir sollten mehr Polizisten auf der Strasse haben.

We should have more police on the streets.

Die Gesellschaft erntet, was sie gesät hat!

Society reaps what it has sown!

Ich war Zeuge/Zeugin eines Vorfalls im Stadtzentrum.

I witnessed an incident in the town centre.

Jemand hat die Polizei informiert.

Someone informed the police.

Drugs (Drogen)

die Tabletten

die Dosis – dose

Drogen einnehmen – to take drugs

das Ecstasy – ecstasy

die Einspritzung – injection

der Entzug – detox

auf Entzug sein – to be in detox

der Gruppenzwang – peer pressure

die harte (-n) Droge (-n) – hard drug

das Haschisch – cannabis

das Heroin – heroin

das Kokain – cocaine

das Marihuana – cannabis

Süchtige (-n) – addict, m/f

die Süchtigkeit – habit, addiction

die Tablette (-n) – tablet

der Verbrauch – consumption

verlocken – to tempt

die weiche (-n) Droge (-n) – soft drug

In meiner Stadt sind Drogen ein ungeheueres Problem.

In my town, drugs are a massive problem.

Drogenabhängigkeit verursacht mehr als die Hälfte aller Verbrechen.

Dependence on drugs causes more than half of all crimes.

Drogenabhängigkeit ist die Ursache von der Mehrheit der Verbrechen unter der Gruppe 15–25.

Drug addiction is the cause of the majority of crime(s) amongst the 15–25s.

Süchtige müssen stehlen, um ihren Fix kaufen zu können.

Drug addicts have to steal in order to be able to buy their fix.

In meiner Stadt werden die Drogen ein erhebliches Problem.

In my town, drugs are becoming a considerable problem.

Sie liegen vielen Problemen zugrunde.

They are at the root of many problems.

Die Jugendlichen sind verlockt, weil Drogen gefährlich sind.

Young people are tempted because drugs are dangerous.

Deshalb scheint es cool, wie die anderen zu tun.

And so it seems cool, to do like the others.

Es hat auch mit dem Gruppenzwang zu tun.

It also has to do with group pressure.

Wenn junge Leute so viel Stress in der Schule haben, scheinen Drogen einen Ausweg anzubieten.

When young people have so much stress in school, drugs seem to offer a way out.

Für Familienprobleme scheinen Drogen auch eine Lösung anzubieten.

For family problems, also, drugs seem to offer a solution.

Es ist genau das Gegenteil!

It is the exact opposite!

Wenn man Süchtiger ist, wird jedes Mitglied der Familie davon betroffen.

When one is addicted, every member of the family becomes affected by it.

Die langfristigen Folgen sind unbekannt.

The long-term consequences are unknown.

rauchen

Smoking (Das Rauchen)

einen Krebs bekommen – to get cancer

das Nikotin – nicotine

das Nikotinpflaster – nicotine patch

das passive Rauchen – passive smoking

rauchen – to smoke

das Rauchverbot – smoking ban

die Sozialkosten – social costs

der Tabak – tobacco

verbieten – to ban

das Werbungsverbot – ban on advertising

die Zigarettenhersteller – cigarette producers

Die Tabakhersteller versuchen, die jungen Leute anzureizen.

The tobacco producers try to attract young people.

Die multinationalen Firmen ermutigen die Jugendlichen zum Rauchen.

The multinationals encourage young people to smoke.

Sie verteilen kostenlose Zigaretten.

They distribute free cigarettes.

Die Zigaretten können den Raucher entspannen.

Cigarettes can calm the smoker.

Die letzten Zahlen erschrecken einen.

The latest figures are frightening.

Jetzt rauchen mehr Mädchen als Jungen.

Now, more girls than boys smoke.

Die Tabakwerbung ist verboten worden.

Tobacco advertising has been banned.

… ein Mädchen in zehn raucht.

… girl(s) in every ten smoke.

Viele junge Leute rauchen, um mehr erwachsen zu scheinen.

Many young people smoke to appear more adult.

Ich bin nikotinsüchtig.

I am addicted to nicotine.

Das passive Rauchen beängstigt mich.

Passive smoking worries me.

Es beschädigt die Lungen des passiven Rauchers.

It damages the lungs of the passive smoker.

Er/sie sie verdient es nicht.

He or she doesn't deserve it.

Mit Hilfe der Nikotinpflaster habe ich Zigaretten aufgegeben.

With the help of nicotine patches I have given up cigarettes.

Ich würde nie wieder rauchen.

I would never smoke again.

Früher rauchte ich regelmäßig.

Before I smoked regularly.

Für Werbung existiert jetzt ein Fernsehverbot.

There is now a TV ban on advertising.

Das Rauchen ist äußerst gesundheitsschädlich.

Smoking is exceptionally bad for your health.

Nachdem ich einen Film über die Gefahren, die das Rauchen verursacht, gesehen habe…

After seeing a film on the dangers caused by smoking…

Mein Cousin, der Asthmatiker ist, ist Opfer des passiven Rauchens geworden.

My cousin, who is asthmatic, became a victim of passive smoking.

Der Tabak enthält Substanzen, die das Herz, die Adern, die Haut und besonders die Lungen beschädigen.

Tobacco contains substances that damage the heart, veins, skin and particularly the lungs.

Heutzutage kann ich nicht verstehen, warum die Leute mit dem Rauchen anfangen.

Nowadays, I cannot understand why people begin smoking.

Eines Tages, wird niemand Rauchen.

One day, no one will smoke.

Eines Tages, wird eine neue Generation sich fragen, warum die Leute der Altzeit ein so giftiges Substanz wie das Nikotin in den Körper einnahmen.

One day, a new generation will wonder why people from the old days took such a poisonous substance as nicotine into their bodies.

> When you look at all the expressions in this section, you will see why a controlled assessment on smoking can be a good choice. It allows you to use powerful arguments and emotions and gives you the opportunity to use a mix of past, present and futures tenses.

Ich habe keinen Wunsch wieder anzufangen.

I have no wish to start again.

Niemand hat das Recht, den anderen weh zu tun.

No one has the right to harm others.

Die Zigarettenhersteller finanzieren das Motorrennen.

The cigarette manufacturers finance motor racing.

Der Tabak stinkt!

Tobacco stinks!

Das Haar und die Kleidung von Rauchern riechen schlecht.

Smokers' clothing and hair stink.

Raucher haben braune Zähne und gelbe Finger.

Smokers have brown teeth and yellow fingers.

Gewisse Leute finden das Rauchen entspannend und befriedigend.

Certain people find smoking relaxing and satisfying.

Zigaretten kämpfen gegen den Stress.

Cigarettes combat stress.

PROGRESS CHECK

Say or write the following in German:

1. I would never smoke again.
2. You see groups of troublemakers everywhere.
3. One day, no one will smoke.
4. The greatest number live on the streets.
5. It has to do with group pressure.

5. Es hat mit dem Gruppenzwang zu tun.
3. Eines Tages, wird niemand rauchen. 4. Die Mehrheit leben auf der Strasse
1. Ich würde nie mehr rauchen. 2. Man sieht überall Gruppen von Rowdys.

2.4 Equality

LEARNING SUMMARY	**After studying this section, you should be able to:** • talk about and give views on equality

Equality

AQA	✓
OCR	X
EDEXCEL	X
WJEC	X
CCEA	✓

Equality (Die Gleichheit)

die Behinderten – the disabled

die sexuelle Gleichheit – sexual equality

die Gleichberechtigung – equal rights

die Lage der Frau – the position of women

ein Behinderter

The following expressions will help you in the listening and reading exams, and in the controlled assessment.

Ich finde das (un)recht.

I find that (un)just.

Gleiche Arbeit, gleicher Lohn.

Equal work for equal pay.

Das ist Menschenrecht.

That's human rights.

Man sollte Zugangsrechte haben.

One should have rights of access.

Die Regierung sollte die Gleichheit der Gelegenheiten fördern.

The Government should promote equality of opportunity.

Frauen sollten mit den Männern konkurrieren.

Women should compete with men.

Man sollte die Frauen auf Gleichheitsbasis behandeln.

Women should be treated on a basis of equality.

Sie ist Feministin geworden.

She became a feminist.

Er ist ein Chauvinistenschwein.

He is a male chauvinist (pig).

Mädchen haben normalerweise kein Recht auszugehen, während Jungen machen können, was sie wollen.

Normally, girls don't have the right to go out, while boys can do what they like.

Frauen haben noch nicht alles erreicht, was zu erreichen ist.

Women have not yet achieved everything that is to be achieved.

> It would be unwise for boys to write or speak against sexual equality in their controlled assessment, even if in humour, because they may come across as being prejudiced.

PROGRESS CHECK

Say or write the following in German:
1. She became a feminist.
2. Girls don't have the right to go out.
3. Women have not yet achieved everything.
4. Boys can do what they like.

1. Sie ist Feministin geworden. 2. Mädchen haben kein Recht auszugehen.
3. Frauen haben noch nicht alles erreicht. 4. Jungen können machen, was sie wollen.

2.5 Grammar

LEARNING SUMMARY	After studying this section, you should be able to understand: • the present tense

The present tense

AQA	✓
OCR	✓
EDEXCEL	✓
WJEC	✓
CCEA	✓

Regular verbs in the present tense

Ninety percent of verbs in German are regular and cause no problems. Just remove the **-en** or **-n** ending of the infinitive and add the endings **-e**, **-st**, **-t**, **-en**, **-t**, **-en**, **-en** to the stem.

For example:

sagen

sagen	to say
ich sage	I say
du sagst	you say (informal singular)
er/sie/es/man sagt	he/she/it/one says
wir sagen	we say
ihr sagt	you say (informal plural)
Sie sagen	you say (formal, plural and singular)
sie sagen	they say

KEY POINT

The **wir** (we), **Sie** (you) and **sie** (they) forms are the same as the infinitive.

Irregular verbs in the present tense

Here are some important points to remember about irregular verbs in the present tense in German:

1. There is usually a change in vowel in singular persons (**du**, **er**, **sie**, **es**, **man**).
2. For most irregular verbs, the **ich** form of the present tense is exactly the same as you would expect of a regular verb, i.e. the stem of the infinitive + **-e**, e.g. **fahre**, **habe**, **lese**, **sehe**.
3. Except for the verb **sein**, all irregular verbs in the plural forms **wir**, **Sie** and **sie** are the same as the infinitive, e.g. **wir müssen**, **Sie sprechen**, **sie tragen**.
4. The **ihr** form just adds **-(e)t** to the stem of the infinitive, e.g. **ihr trefft**, **ihr tragt**, **ihr fallt**. The verb **sein** is the only odd one out.

Here are some examples:

brechen

	brechen (to break)	**fahren** (to go, to drive)	**fallen** (to fall)
ich	breche	fahre	falle
du	brichst	fährst	fällst
er/sie/es/man	bricht	fährt	fällt
wir	brechen	fahren	fallen
ihr	brecht	fahrt	fallt
Sie	brechen	fahren	fallen
sie	brechen	fahren	fallen
	haben (to have)	**halten** (to hold)	**helfen** (to help)
ich	habe	halte	helfe
du	hast	hältst	hilfst
er/sie/es/man	hat	hält	hilft
wir	haben	halten	helfen
ihr	habt	haltet	helft
Sie	haben	halten	helfen
sie	haben	halten	helfen

lesen

	können (to be able/can)	lesen (to read)	mögen (to like)
ich	kann	lese	mag
du	kannst	liest	magst
er/sie/es/man	kann	liest	mag
wir	können	lesen	mögen
ihr	könnt	lest	mögt
Sie	können	lesen	mögen
sie	können	lesen	mögen
	müssen (to have to)	nehmen (to take)	schlafen (to sleep)
ich	muss	nehme	schlafe
du	musst	nimmst	schläfst
er/sie/es/man	muss	nimmt	schläft
wir	müssen	nehmen	schlafen
ihr	müsst	nehmt	schlaft
Sie	müssen	nehmen	schlafen
sie	müssen	nehmen	schlafen
	schlagen (to hit)	sehen (to see)	sein (to be)
ich	schlage	sehe	bin
du	schlägst	siehst	bist
er/sie/es/man	schlägt	sieht	ist
wir	schlagen	sehen	sind
ihr	schlagt	seht	seid
Sie	schlagen	sehen	sind
sie	schlagen	sehen	sind
	sprechen (to speak)	stehlen (to steal)	tragen (to carry, to wear)
ich	spreche	stehle	trage
du	sprichst	stiehlst	trägst
er/sie/es/man	spricht	stiehlt	trägt
wir	sprechen	stehlen	tragen
ihr	sprecht	stehlt	tragt
Sie	sprechen	stehlen	tragen
sie	sprechen	stehlen	tragen
	treffen (to meet)	treten (to step)	vergessen (to forget)
ich	treffe	trete	vergesse
du	triffst	trittst	vergisst
er/sie/es/man	trifft	tritt	vergisst
wir	treffen	treten	vergessen
ihr	trefft	tretet	vergesst
Sie	treffen	treten	vergessen
sie	treffen	treten	vergessen

schlagen

treffen

werfen

	waschen (to wash)	**werden** (to become)	**werfen** (to throw)
ich	wasche	werde	werfe
du	wäschst	wirst	wirfst
er/sie/es/man	wäscht	wird	wirft
wir	waschen	werden	werfen
ihr	wascht	werdet	werft
Sie	waschen	werden	werfen
sie	waschen	werden	werfen

	wissen (to know)	**wollen** (to want, to wish)
ich	weiß	will
du	weisst	willst
er/sie/es/man	weiß	will
wir	wissen	wollen
ihr	wisst	wollt
Sie	wissen	wollen
sie	wissen	wollen

PROGRESS CHECK

Say or write the following in German:
1. I like German.
2. You (**du**) can speak French?
3. She has a lot of friends.
4. Grandpa gives wonderful Christmas presents.
5. You (**ihr**) drive too fast, both of you!
6. Why do you break so many glasses?
7. She always tells the truth.
8. Hans is becoming really tall.
9. She always steps on the gas!
10. We get (**treten**) in touch.
11. I help as often as I can.
12. Do you (**du**) see the problem, or not?
13. He sleeps too deeply.
14. The clock strikes three.
15. We are too lazy!
16. We are hungry.
17. He steals to buy his drugs.
18. You (**du**) break your arm every summer!
19. Does she take coffee?
20. They don't like beef.

1. Ich mag Deutsch. 2. Du kannst Französisch (sprechen)? 3. Sie hat viele Freunde.
4. Opa gibt wunderbare Weihnachtsgeschenke. 5. Ihr fahrt zu schnell, alle beide!
6. Warum brichst du so viele Gläser? 7. Sie spricht immer die Wahrheit.
8. Hans wird wirklich groß. 9. Sie tritt immer auf das Gas! 10. Wir treten in Kontakt.
11. Ich helfe, so oft ich kann. 12. Siehst du das Problem oder nicht? 13. Er schläft zu tief.
14. Die Uhr schlägt drei. 15. Wir sind zu faul! 16. Wir haben Hunger.
17. Er stiehlt, um seine Drogen zu kaufen. 18. Du brichst den Arm jeden Sommer!
19. Nimmt sie Kaffee? 20. Sie mögen Rindfleisch nicht.

Sample controlled assessment

Speaking

1 **Track 6** You are going to have a conversation with your teacher about smoking. You could discuss the following:

- whether you smoke or have smoked in the past
- your opinion on smoking
- the negative effects of smoking.

Teacher: Kann es sein, dass du rauchst?

Student: Ja, ich habe in der Vergangenheit geraucht[2] aber ich würde[25] nie[12] mehr rauchen und dafür gibt es drei Gründe. Erstens hat das Rauchen angefangen[2] meine Gesundheit zu beeinflussen.[9] Ich bin Sportlerin und vertrete die Schule und die Grafschaft beim Tennis und Basketball. Mir[28] ist aufgefallen, dass ich beim Laufen mehr gehustet habe. Das war nicht gut und hatte eine schlechte[19] Auswirkung auf mein Selbstbewusstsein.

Teacher: Und was war der zweite Grund?

Student: Ah, es kostete[26] unheimlich viel![18] Ich rauchte ein Päckchen pro Tag und das hat mehr als[21] tausend Pfund im Jahr gekostet.[26] Ich hatte[26] zu der Zeit auch noch einen Teilzeitjob. Den Großteil[21] meines Geldes habe ich für Zigaretten, kleine Zigarren und Schnupftabak ausgegeben![2/26]

Teacher: Was ist denn Schnupftabak?

Student: Es ist ein braunes oder rotbraunes Puder, das[7] aus getrockneten und gemahlenen Tabakblättern gemacht wird. Man kann[35] es ein bißchen mit Kokain vergleichen, weil[5] es die Nase stark beschädigt und Krebs verursachen kann.

Teacher: Ich verstehe! Und warst du davon abhängig?

Student: Ich glaube[1] eher[21] von den Zigaretten. Aber was ich weiß, ist, daß es höchste Zeit war, mein Geld zu sparen und auf meine Gesundheit zu achten! Ich habe es mit Nikotinpflastern, einer ganzen Menge Nikotinpflastern, geschafft.[26] Glücklicherweise hat das geklappt![18]

Teacher: Geklappt?

Student: Ja, es war erfolgreich und hat gut funktioniert.[9] Mein Freund Jason hat mir sehr viel dabei geholfen. Wir gingen nicht zusammen aus aber wir waren und werden immer sehr gute Freunde sein. Er hat zur selben Zeit dieses Gift aufgegeben und wir haben unseren Entzug zusammen gemacht. Nicht leicht! Ich würde[25] so etwas nicht zum zweiten Mal machen.

Teacher: Wußten deine Eltern, dass du geraucht hast?

Student: Das kann ich nicht sagen. Wenn ja, dann waren sie sehr geduldig und einfühlsam. Das war auch vielleicht ein Grund, warum ich aufgehört habe. Meine Eltern sind so gut[15] zu mir gewesen. Ich bin der Meinung, dass ich es ihnen schuldig war aufzuhören.

Teacher: Und der dritte Grund?

Student: Das hatte[26] mit einem Jungen zu tun und auch dabei hat Jason mir geholfen. Er kann[35] sehr ehrlich mit mir sein und er hat mir auf eine einfühlsame[9] Weise erklärt, wie meine Kleidung und meine Haare nach Tabak gerochen haben. Ich verspreche[1] Ihnen etwas, ich werde[3] nie mehr nach Tabak stinken. Für eine junge Frau wie mich war das genug!

Teacher: Und genug ist genug. Danke für ein äußerst interessantes und lebendiges Gespräch.

Student: Ich bedanke[1] mich auch!

Turn to page 154 for a translation of this passage.

Examiner's comments

Many candidates will choose to do a controlled speaking assessment on smoking. It is often a very good choice, because it allows you to speak with enthusiasm and emotion. Put simply, it gives you the opportunity not to sound boring.

This student has produced an excellent piece of work by including many of the '40 points for improving your grade' on pages 8–9:

1   The present tense has been used
2   Examples of the past tense
3   An example of the future tense
5   Use of 'weil'
7   'Das' is a connecting word
9   Impressive vocabulary, e.g. 'beeinflussen', 'funktioniert', 'einfühlsame'
12 'Nie' is an example of a negative
15 'So' + an adjective
18 Exclamations
19 An example of an adjective
21 Comparatives have been used
25 The conditional tense has been used
26 A mix of perfect and imperfect tenses has been used
28 A personal pronoun
35 A modal verb ('können')

Sample controlled assessment

Writing

1 Write about your future plans regarding marriage or partnership. You could…
- mention any past experiences and relationships
- state any lessons you feel you may have learned from a previous relationship
- say what your plans are for the next few years
- explain whether you think of yourself as a modern or old-fashioned person
- say whether or not you feel it is too early to consider having long relationships.

Vor zwei Jahren glaubte[26] ich, dass ich nie heiraten würde,[25] weil meine Freundin mich im Stich gelassen hatte[4] aber jetzt bin ich anderer Meinung. In der Zwischenzeit bin ich mit einigen Mädchen ausgegangen[2/39] und habe gute Beziehungen zu ihnen gehabt.[2/26] Ich bin ein sehr geselliger Mensch und brauche die Gesellschaft von anderen Menschen sehr.

Aber als Ehemann oder Lebensgefährte[9] zu leben, das liegt[1] lange in der Zukunft. Mit sechzehn Jahren bin ich[1] viel zu jung, um an eine Hochzeit oder so etwas zu denken. Ich werde[3] noch zwei Jahre in meiner Gesamtschule studieren und werde[3] danach hoffentlich drei oder vier weitere Jahre an der Universität verbringen. Auch habe ich noch nicht eine Person gefunden,[2] die mir[28] die Erde zu beben macht,[37] wie man[34] in den Schlagern[9] sagt!

Was ich behaupten kann,[1/35] ist, dass ich kein Chauvinistenschwein bin , obgleich ich Rugbyspieler bin und wir in dem Ruf stehen, extrovertierte[9] Schickimickis* zu sein. Ich würde[25] auch bestätigen, dass ich für Frauenrechte und auch für Chancengleichheit[9] bin. Wenn meine Zukunftspartnerin besser[21] qualifiziert als ich wird,[3] bessere[19/21] Jobprospekte hat oder nur einen mehr interessanten Beruf als ich hat, werde ich dazu bereit sein, Hausmann[9] zu sein und die Kinder zu pflegen, vorausgesetzt, dass meine Partnerin genug Geld verdient,[1] für unseren[19] Unterhalt aufzukommen.

Was ich gelernt habe, ist das meine Zukunftsfrau bzw -Partnerin nicht nötigerweise äußerst schön sein wird, weil die bedeutendste[22] Schönheit innerlich ist, und wenn ich mir eine Person finde,[4] die[7] ein grosses Herz hat, mich[28] zum Lachen bringt und Mitleid mit den Armen dieser Welt hat,[11] wird das für mich[28] genug sein.

(*extrovertierte Schickimickis - hooray Henries)

Turn to page 155 for a translation of this passage.

Examiner's comments

This fine piece of work features a number of the 40 mark-winning points from pages 8–9:

1. At least three uses of the present tense
2. At least three past tenses
3. Examples of the future tense
4. Confident use of word order
7. Good use of a connecting word
9. Impressive vocabulary, e.g. 'Lebensgefährte', 'Schlagern', 'extrovertierte', 'Chancengleichheit', 'Hausmann'
11. A 'haben' structure
19. Use of adjectives in front of a noun
21. Comparatives have been used
22. Use of the superlative
25. The conditional tense has been used
26. A mix of perfect and imperfect tenses
28. Confident use of personal pronouns
34. Use of 'man'
37. A well-known saying
39. An example of the perfect tense being used with 'sein'

Exam practice questions

Listening

1 🔵 **Track 7** Günther is talking about his family. Answer the questions by filling in the gaps **in English**. There are **two** sections.

Section 1

(a) Günther no longer lives with his .... , whose place has been taken by

.... **(2)**

(b) The children do not .... and get on .... **(2)**

Section 2

(c) They all went to a .... to celebrate. **(1)**

(d) Alex's favourite present was a new .... **(1)**

(e) Günther will be .... in .... and wants to

go to an .... to celebrate. **(3)**

2 🔵 **Track 8** Millie Mosel is a famous, young German film star. Listen to her speaking about her adolescence. Answer the questions by filling in the gaps **in English**.

(a) Millie spent an .... adolescence in .... , where she

did not get on with Sylvia, her .... , who had .... her.

(b) Millie had later .... home and was spotted in a ....

by a .... , who offered her a ....

(c) For Millie, Heike Linz has become a sort of .... figure, since Millie's own

mother, whom she will never .... , passed away ....

ago. Perhaps Millie's loss explains why she has a talent for .... roles. **(12)**

3 🔵 **Track 9** Listen to the discussion about four new soap characters and then tick the correct boxes to complete the following sentences.

(a) Willi Herder is...

    A   chatty and loud   ☐

    B   patient but chatty   ☐

    C   loud and unsnobby   ☐

Exam practice questions

(b) Carla Heinrich is also...

    A   too chatty   ☐

    B   too loud   ☐

    C   too snobby   ☐

(c) Carla would be a good person to have around in...

    A   a party   ☐

    B   an accident   ☐

    C   a bar quiz   ☐

(d) Ulrike Diederich is...

    A   positive   ☐

    B   not so positive   ☐

    C   not at all positive   ☐

(e) As a character, Ulrike is likely to be...

    A   a great success   ☐

    B   not very successful   ☐

    C   a total failure   ☐

(f) Ulrike has a side to her that is...

    A   sarcastic   ☐

    B   cruel   ☐

    C   gruesome   ☐

(g) For a minister of religion, Siegfried Siedler seems to have...

    A   the right character   ☐

    B   too much to say   ☐

    C   need of help   ☐

(h) Siegfried is...

    A   helpful, but impatient   ☐

    B   down-to-earth   ☐

    C   calm and helpful   ☐   **(8)**

Exam practice questions

Reading

1 Read the magazine article below, in which young people explain their parents' attitudes to them going out and the results. Answer the questions that follow.

Ausgehen oder zu Hause bleiben müssen? Vier junge Personen erklären wie es zu Hause ist.

Für mich ist es schwierig, besonders weil meine Eltern Lehrer sind! Sie glauben, meine Schulaufgaben sind viel bedeutender als meine Freunde. Schule ist alles für sie und sie vergessen, dass wir junge Leute ein Leben ausserhalb der Prüfungen haben müssen. **Bernd, 16 Jahre**

Ich habe Glück, weil meine Eltern sehr verständnisvoll sind. Sie erlauben mir auszugehen, so oft ich will, vorausgesetzt, dass ich kein Alkohol trinke und vor elf Uhr zu Hause bin. Aber wenn ich zu einer Party gehe, muss mein Freund mit mir kommen, sonst gehe ich nicht. **Brigitte, 17 Jahre**

Ich soll nicht ausgehen und so ist es! Meine Eltern verbieten total alle Ausflüge und Jungen dürfen mich nicht anrufen! Es ist so schlecht geworden, dass ich jetzt schlechte Verhältnisse zu Mutter und Vater habe! Ich glaube, ich werde mein Zuhause verlassen. **Susi, 15 Jahre**

Für mich ist es teils gut, teils schlecht. Während der Arbeitswoche habe ich keine Chance auszugehen, was peinlich ist. Aber am Wochenende kann ich immer ausgehen, wenn ich meine Hausaufgaben fertig gemacht habe! Mit Jungs kann ich auch ausgehen, vorausgesezt, dass sie kein Haschisch einnehme und ich nie betrunken nach Hause komme. **Karli, 16 Jahre**

(a) Why does Bernd find things particularly difficult? .... **(1)**

(b) What do Bernd's parents feel about school work? .... **(1)**

(c) What do Bernd's parents forget? .... **(1)**

(d) Why is Brigitte lucky? .... **(1)**

(e) When out, what must Brigitte do? Give two details.

   (i) ....   **(ii)** .... **(2)**

(f) How is going to a party different for Brigitte?

   .... **(2)**

(g) How is the position different for Susi?

   .... **(3)**

(h) What is Susi considering doing? .... **(1)**

(i) Are things good or bad for Karli? .... **(1)**

(j) When is Karli not allowed to go out? .... **(1)**

(k) What must Karli do at the weekend? .... **(1)**

(l) What two things must Karli remember at weekends?

   (i) ....

   (ii) .... **(2)**

Exam practice questions

2 Danny has written this e-mail to his German girlfriend Antje, after she told him she has started smoking. There are **five** gaps for you to fill in using the words in the box below. **Write the correct word** next to each letter in the answer spaces below.

Hallo Antje!

Ich schreibe **(x)** am schnellsten nach unserem Telefongespräch, weil ich jetzt sehr ängstlich bin. Du kennst meine Meinung über das Zigarettenrauchen und ich werde jetzt versuchen, dich zu überreden, nicht **(a)** zu rauchen.

Ich weiß nicht, ob es der Gruppenzwang sei, oder Stress in der Schule, oder... Aber ich kann den Gedanke nicht leiden, dass du **(b)** bekommst.

Du weißt, dass Nikotin Krebs verursachen kann. **(c)** Prozent von allen Rauchern sterben an Nikotinkrankheiten.

Noch etwas, du riechst so gut mit deinem schönen Parfüm. Willst du, dass vielleicht deine Kleidung nach Tabak **(d)**? Ich sage dir was, wenn du das Rauchen aufgibst, werde ich auch Schokolade aufgeben, um so **(e)** wie du zu werden!

Schreib mir bitte sofort.

Dein Danny.

Choose your answers from this box:

mir	dick	dir	mehr	Krebs	halb
schlank	stinkt	uns	fünfzig	spricht	

Write your answers here:

Example: (x) dir

(a) ....

(b) ....

(c) ....

(d) ....

(e) ....

(5)

Exam practice questions

3   Read this letter from Farida and answer the questions by ticking the correct boxes.

> Ich wohne seit drei Jahren in der Nähe von Frankfurt aber ich stamme aus Istanbul in der Türkei. Ich bin Schülerin im Gymnasium Ludwig Koch in Kühlstein, bin sechzehn Jahre alt und nächstes Jahr gehe ich in die Unterstufe. Mein Leben hier ist gut und ich mache viele Fortschritte mit meiner Schularbeit. Wir sind fast hundert Muslims hier in diesem großen Gymnasium und haben keine Probleme, weil wir versuchen, uns zu integrieren. Während der ersten zwei Jahre, musste ich zusätzliche Deutschklassen besuchen, damit ich Deutsch gut verstehen und sprechen konnte. Jetzt aber bin ich deutschsprachig und ich habe viele deutsche Freunde. Meine Religion ist auch kein Problem, weil die Frankfurter sehr tolerant sind. Ich gehe regelmäßig in die örtliche Moschee und die Schüler im Gymnasium interessieren sich für Islam. Es gibt auch einige, die versuchen ein wenig Arabisch zu lernen. Komischerweise hat das meine Mutter ermuntert und sie geht zweimal in der Woche zu deutschen Abendkursen in meiner Schule, und jetzt spricht sie viel besser Deutsch als am Anfang.

(a)   How long has Farida been living in Germany?

     A   Three months ☐   **B**   Three years ☐   **C**   13 years ☐   **(1)**

(b)   How do we know Farida has made a lot of progress? Next year she is going…

     A   into the Sixth Form ☐   **B**   on exchange ☐   **C**   on work experience ☐   **(1)**

(c)   How many Muslims are there in the school?

     A   Almost 100 ☐   **B**   100 exactly ☐   **C**   More than 100 ☐   **(1)**

(d)   What had helped the Muslims avoid problems with Frankfurt people? Frankfurters…

     A   work hard ☐   **B**   ignore them ☐   **C**   are tolerant ☐   **(1)**

(e)   What did Farida do to improve her German?

     A   She went on exchange   ☐

     B   She went to extra German classes   ☐

     C   She found a German boyfriend   ☐   **(1)**

(f)   Why does she not have to put up with racial prejudice from Frankfurters?

     A   They are cheerful ☐   **B**   They ignore them ☐   **C**   They are tolerant ☐   **(1)**

(g)   Give two examples of local pupils' positive approach towards Muslims. Tick two boxes.

     A   They show an interest in Islam ☐   **B**   Some try to learn a little Arabic ☐

     C   Some visit Turkey ☐   **D**   Some come to the mosque ☐   **(2)**

(h)   Give two examples of how this affected Farida's mother. Tick two boxes.

     A   She joined the PTA ☐   **B**   She goes to acting classes ☐

     C   She was encouraged ☐   **D**   She goes to German evening classes ☐   **(2)**

Exam practice questions

4 Read this account of part of Angelina Jolie's life and answer the questions that follow.

Angelina Jolie und ihre Eltern

Der amerikanische Filmstar, Angelina Jolie figuriert in der Glamourwelt von vielen Jugendlichen, nicht wahr? Alle haben schon von ihrer Benefizarbeit und ihrem Mann, Brad Pitt, gehört. Leider, hat man auch von dem Streit zwischen den zwei gehört.

Unheimlich reich, mit einem der schönsten Männer der Welt, sollte Angelina ein sehr frohes Leben haben. Aber alles ist nicht, wie es scheint. Ihr Privatleben hat ihre schwarze Seite gehabt. Vielleicht hat ihre Obsession mit einem gesunden Leben und einer gesunde Diät mit den Tragödien in ihrem persönlichen Leben zu tun.

Sie ist im Jahre 1975 in Los Angeles geboren. Ihre Mutter, Marcheline Bertrand, war Französin und ihr Vater, John Voight, wie Angelina, ist ein berühmter amerikanischer Filmstar, deren Familie aus Deutschland kam. Als junges Kind hat Angelina den Streit zwischen ihren Eltern gesehen und nach dem Ehebruch zwischen Marcheline und John, hat sie den Kontakt mit ihrem Vater fast verloren. Jetzt sollen die Dinge zwischen Tochter und Vater viel besser gehen.

Vor ein paar Jahren ist Marcheline an Krebs gestorben und Angelina wurde sehr stark davon affektiert. Wenn wir solche Details aus den Leben der Stars wissen, können wir diese berühmten Personen ein wenig besser verstehen und ihre Charakter nicht so streng urteilen*.

(*urteilen – to judge)

(a) What does everybody know about Angelina? Give two details.

(i) .... (ii) .... **(2)**

(b) What should she have and why?

.... **(2)**

(c) What is it useful to learn about her life?

.... **(1)**

(d) What may the tragedies in her life partly explain?

.... **(2)**

(e) Of what mixed blood is she?

.... **(2)**

(f) What caused the lack of contact with her father?

.... **(1)**

(g) How is the relationship between Angelina and her father now?

.... **(1)**

(h) How did her mother die and what was the effect?

.... **(2)**

3 Leisure, free time and the media

The following topics are covered in this chapter:

- **Free time activities**
- **Shopping, money, fashion and trends**
- **Advantages and disadvantages of new technology**
- **Grammar**

3.1 Free time activities

After studying this section, you should be able to:

- talk about your interest in sport and your hobbies
- give reasons why you like or dislike various sports
- talk about your favourite films and TV programmes
- talk about music and whether you play musical instruments

Sport and leisure

AQA ✓
OCR ✓
EDEXCEL ✓
WJEC ✓
CCEA ✓

Sport and leisure is a favourite topic with examiners. It is likely that you will be asked about your sporting interests in the controlled speaking and writing assessments. You should make sure that you can talk about your favourite sports and be able to say which you like and which you dislike. You must be able to say how you spend your free time, how you spent your free time (for example, last weekend) and how you will spend your free time (for example, next weekend). You will also find the following vocabulary of considerable help for the listening and reading exams.

Sports (Sportarten)

das Tischtennis

das Angeln – fishing
der Basketball – basketball
der Fußball – football
der Handball – handball
das Hockey – hockey
das Klettern – climbing
die Leichtathletik – athletics
das Pferdereiten – horse riding
das Radfahren – cycling
das Rugby – rugby

das Schwimmen – swimming
das Segeln – sailing
das Skateboardfahren – skateboarding
das Tennis – tennis
das Tischtennis – table tennis
der Volleyball – volleyball
das Wasserskilaufen – waterskiing
das Windsurfen – windsurfing
der Wintersport – winter sports

der Meister

Sports vocabulary

der Ball (¨e) – ball
die Mannschaft (-en) – team
Meister (in) – champion, m/f
Radfahrer (in) – cyclist, m/f

das Spiel (-e) – match
Spieler (in) – player, m/f
der Wettbewerb (-e) – competition
Zuschauer (in) – spectator, m/f

Sports verbs

angeln – to fish
applaudieren – to applaud
fangen – to catch
fischen – to fish
Fußball spielen – to play football
gern haben – to like a lot

gewinnen – to win
sich interessieren für – to be interested in
klettern – to climb
laufen – to run
rennen – to run
Rollschuh laufen – to

(roller) skate
Schlittschuh laufen – to (ice) skate
schwimmen – to swim
teil-nehmen – to take part
verlieren – to lose
zu-schauen – to spectate

Sängerin

Leisure (Die Freizeit)

die Angelrute (-n) – fishing rod
der Badeanzug (¨e) – swimming costume
der Café – café
die Clique – the gang
das Computerspiel – computer game
der Garten (ä) – garden
gern (-e) – with pleasure
das Hobby (-s) – hobby, pastime
der Jugendklub – youth club
die Kassette (-n) – cassette
das Kegeln – bowling
das Kino (-s) – cinema
der Klub – club
das Konzert (-e) – concert
das Lied (-er) – song
das Mountainbike – mountain bike
der Nachtklub – night club

die Party (-s) – party
das Rad – (bi)cycle
der Rollschuh (-e) – roller skate
der Rucksack – rucksack, back-pack
Sänger (in) – singer, m/f
das Schach – chess
der Schlittschuh – skate
der Spaziergang – walk
das Spiel (-e) – game
das Spielzeug (-e) – toy
das Sportzentrum – sports centre
der Stadion – stadium
der Tanz (¨e) – dance
das Videospiel (-e) – video game
das Wochenende – weekend
der Zirkus (-se) – circus
der Zoo – zoo

wandern (gehen)

Leisure verbs

aus-gehen – to go out
die Gartenarbeit machen – to do the gardening
Karten spielen – to play cards
lieber machen/spielen – to prefer doing/playing
Musik spielen – to play music
plaudern – to chat
Schach spielen – to play chess

schwimmen gehen – to go swimming
sich amüsieren – to have a good time
sich baden – to bathe
sich sonnen – to sunbathe
singen – to sing
spazieren gehen – to go walking
tanzen – to dance
wandern (gehen) – to go hiking
(zu)hören – to listen

PROGRESS CHECK

Say or write the following in German:

1. I play tennis at the weekend.
2. I prefer playing football.
3. You (**du**) will never play in the rain!
4. We are going out on Friday evening.
5. They cannot dance.
6. I hate playing cards.

1. Ich spiele Tennis am Wochenende.
2. Ich spiele lieber Fußball.
3. Du wirst nie im Regen spielen!
4. Wir gehen Freitagabend aus.
5. Sie können nicht tanzen.
6. Ich hasse Kartenspielen.

Conversation

AQA	✓
OCR	✓
EDEXCEL	✓
WJEC	✓
CCEA	✓

You are likely to be asked questions such as the following in your controlled speaking assessment. Practise these questions and answers with a partner.

Was ist dein Lieblingshobby?

Ich spiele sehr gern Tischtennis, Hockey, Basketball und auch Karten. Ich gehe auch gern spazieren und am Wochenende gehe ich mit Freunden aus. Lesen ist auch ein Lieblingshobby.[1]

Wo spielst du denn Tennis?

In der Sporthalle im Winter und draußen im Sportzentrum im Sommer.

Mit wem spielst du?

Mit meinen Freunden und Schulkameraden und von Zeit zu Zeit mit meinem Onkel.

Gehst du auch Ins Kino oder ins Theater?

Ich gehe ins Kino, so oft ich Geld dazu habe aber ich gehe nie ins Theater, weil ich glaube, es ist mehr für Erwachsene. Aber, vielleicht sollte ich meine Meinung über das Theater ändern.

Du magst die Gartenarbeit?

Ich kann es nicht leiden. Besonders weil ich dazu von den Eltern gezwungen bin!

Und was ist dein Lieblingssport?

Das würde der Fußball sein aber ich spiele nicht momentan, da ich mir das Bein beim Spielen gebrochen habe!

Und was für andere Hobbys hast du?

Allerlei Dinge. Erstens, all die Sportarten, die ich schon erwähnt habe plus Rugby. Ich bin auch ein großer Fernsehfan und ich lese eine ganze Menge Bücher aber ich gehe am liebsten mit meinen Freunden aus.

Was liest du am liebsten?

Historische Liebesgeschichten und Biographien, auch Sportmagazine. Mode interessiert mich nicht!

Während der Woche, was machst du abends, nachdem du deine Haus-aufgaben fertig gemacht hast?

Ich habe lange Unterhaltungen im Net und das zwar mit meinen besten Freunden. Auch lese ich und ich sehe ein wenig fern. Wenn ich das Haus satt habe, dann gehe ich zu Freunden und verbringe eine Stunde oder so etwas bei Ihnen.[2]

Und was hast du letzten Abend nach deinen Schulufgaben gemacht?

Dies und das. Ich habe ein bißchen ferngesehen. Ich habe auch Musik gehört und habe eine halbe Stunde bei meinem Freund verbracht. Ich bin zu Fuß gegangen und leider hat es geregnet![3]

1 Notice how the candidate gives a whole list of hobbies. This is a good example to follow. Always try to give extra detail when you can.

2 This is your chance to use as many present tenses as possible.

3 This is your opportunity to use as many past tenses (see pages 70–73) as you can.

🔵 **Armer Teufel! Was wirst du heute abend machen, das heißt, nach deiner Arbeit für die Schule?**

🔵 **Es hängt davon ab. Vielleicht, wenn es nicht regnet, will ich ein bißchen Sport draußen treiben. Ich werde auch mit meinen Freunden telefonieren oder mit ihnen durch Facebook sprechen. Dann, werde ich ein wenig fernsehen, bevor ich ins Bett gehe.[4]**

> **4** This is your opportunity to use a good number of future tenses (see page 91).

PROGRESS CHECK

Say or write the following in German:

1. I like playing basketball and computer games.
2. I will go to the cinema next weekend.
3. I have forgotten to go to the theatre with Boris!
4. I shall go out with the gang.

1. Ich spiele gern Basketball und Computerspiele. 2. Ich werde nächstes Wochenende ins Kino gehen. 3. Ich habe vergessen, zum Theater mit Boris zu gehen! 4. Ich werde mit der Clique ausgehen.

Cinema and TV

AQA	✓
OCR	✓
EDEXCEL	✓
WJEC	✓
CCEA	✓

Film and TV could be a topic for your controlled speaking and writing assessments. You might well be asked about your favourite kind of film or TV programme. In the reading exam, you may be given a TV or film schedule and asked questions about the programmes or films shown and the times they are on.

Cinema and TV (Kino und Fernsehen)

der Liebesfilm

die Aufführung (-en) – performance
die CD (-s) – CD
die DVD (-s) – DVD
deutsche Fassung – German version
originelle Fassung – undubbed
der Horrorfilm – horror film
die Komödie – comedy
der Krimi – detective film
der Liebesfilm – romantic film
die Nachrichten – news
der Schauspieler – actor

die Schauspielerin – actress
der Schirm – screen
die Seifenoper – soap
die Sendung – programme
die Serie – series
der Star – star
die Tagesschau – news magazine
der Trickfilm – cartoon
hat den Untertitel – is subtitled
die Videokassette – video cassette
der Western – western (film)

Conversation

AQA	✓
OCR	✓
EDEXCEL	✓
WJEC	✓
CCEA	✓

> Here, you will get credit for expressing and justifying opinions.

🔵 **Was für Filme hast du gern?**

🔵 **Ich habe Abenteuerfilme sehr gern. Die Liebesgeschichten habe ich gar nicht so gern, weil sie zu sentimental sind. Die Horror- und Kriegsfilme sind zu nervig.**

Music and musical instruments

AQA	✓
OCR	✓
EDEXCEL	✓
WJEC	✓
CCEA	✓

If your teacher knows that you like music or play an instrument, you may be asked about music in your controlled speaking assessment. You need to be able to talk about your likes, dislikes and preferences. You might like to choose a famous musician for your presentation, if you are doing one, or for your controlled writing assessment. Music may also appear in the listening and reading exams.

die Diskothek

Musical terms

die Diskothek – disco(theque)
die Hi-Fi Anlage – hi-fi (system)
der Jazz – jazz
die klassische Musik – classical music

Klavier spielen – to play the piano
der Musiker – male musician
die Musikerin – female musician
das Orchester – orchestra, band
die Popmusik – pop music

Musical instruments (Die Musikinstrumente)

die Blockflöte – recorder
die Geige – violin
die Gitarre – guitar

das Instrument – instrument
das Klavier – piano
die Trompete – trumpet

Conversation

AQA	✓
OCR	✓
EDEXCEL	✓
WJEC	✓
CCEA	✓

🔊 **Kannst du ein (musikalisches) Instrument spielen?**
🔊 Ich kann die Klarinette spielen.
🔊 **Was für Musik magst du am liebsten?**
🔊 Ich höre am liebsten Pop(musik).

3.2 Shopping, money, fashion and trends

LEARNING SUMMARY

After studying this section, you should be able to:

- talk about shops and shopping
- talk about the post office, bank and money
- describe clothes, fashion and trends

Shops and shopping

AQA	✓
OCR	✓
EDEXCEL	✓
WJEC	✓
CCEA	✓

Adjectives and phrases

berühmt – famous
billig – cheap
blutig – rare (steak)

durchgebraten – well-done (steak)
frisch – fresh

Haupt – main
kühl – cool
laut – noisy
lecker – tasty

bestellen

Verbs

auf-wärmen – to warm up (food)

bedienen – to serve

bestellen – to order

empfehlen – to recommend

essen – to eat

einen Fehler machen – to make
a mistake

gratulieren – to congratulate

lieber essen/trinken – to prefer to

sich beklagen – to complain

sich streiten – to argue

trinken – to drink

vor-ziehen – to prefer

wechseln – to (ex)change

Shops (Läden)

in der ... abteilung – in the ...
department

in der Apotheke – at the chemist's

in der Bäckerei – at the bakery

in der Bank – at the bank

in der Boutique – at the boutique

in der Buchhandlung – at the bookshop

in der Drogerie – at the drugstore

in der Fleischerei – at the butcher's

im Friseursalon – at the hairdresser's

in der Gemüsehandlung – at the
greengrocer's

im Geschäft – at the shop

im Kaufhaus – at the department store

im Kiosk – at the kiosk

in der Konditorei – at the cake shop
/confectioner's

im Laden – at the shop

auf dem Markt – at the market

in der Modeboutique – at the fashion
boutique

im Supermarkt – at the supermarket

an der Tankstelle – at the petrol station

Shopping (Einkaufen)

der Korb

im Ausverkauf – at the sales

billig – cheap

Das ist alles – That's all

geschlossen – closed

der Korb – basket

kostenlos – free (of charge)

Was kostet das? – What does it cost?

der Kunde/die Kundin – customer, m/f

Noch etwas? – Anything else?

offen – open

das Parfüm – perfume

der Preis – price

das Sonderangebot – special offer

im ersten Stock – on the first floor

das Stück – piece

teuer – dear, expensive

die Tüte – bag

im Untergeschoss – in the basement

Conversation

AQA	✓
OCR	✓
EDEXCEL	✓
WJEC	✓
CCEA	✓

Wann gehst du einkaufen?

So oft ich kann, das heisst, wenn ich Geld habe.

Machst du gern die Besorgungen?

Absolut nicht. Ich mache sie, wenn ich muss.

The post office

AQA ✓
OCR ✓
EDEXCEL ✓
WJEC ✓
CCEA ✓

At the post office (Im Postbüro)

der Brief (-e) – letter
der Briefkasten – letterbox
die Briefmarke (-n) – stamp
Briefträger (in) – post(wo)man
erste(r) Klasse – first class

das Paket (-e) – packet, parcel
die Post – post, mail
die Postkarte (-n) – postcard
zweite(r) Klasse – second class

Banks and money

AQA ✓
OCR ✓
EDEXCEL ✓
WJEC ✓
CCEA ✓

die Münzen

At the bank (In der Bank)

die Bank – bank
in Euros – in euros
das Geld – money
der Identitätsnachweis – proof of identity
die Kasse – till, cash point
das Kleingeld – change
die Kreditkarte (-n) – credit card

die Münze (-n) – coin
in Pfund Sterling – in pounds sterling
der Reisescheck – traveller's cheque
die Sparkasse – savings bank
Wechsel – Foreign Exchange
der Wechselkurs – exchange rate
ein Zwanzigeuroschein – a twenty-euro note

Bank verbs

an-nehmen – to accept
ein Formular aus-füllen – to fill in a form
unterschreiben – to sign

unterzeichnen – to sign
wechseln – to (ex)change
zahlen – to pay
zählen – to count

Conversation

AQA ✓
OCR ✓
EDEXCEL ✓
WJEC ✓
CCEA ✓

🗨 **Legst du Geld auf die Seite/beiseite?**

🗨 Von Zeit zu Zeit spare ich fünf oder zehn Pfund in meiner Sparkasse (ein), mehr wenn ich Weihnachtsgeld bekomme oder einen Teilzeitjob habe.

🗨 **Und wie gibst du dein Geld aus?**

🗨 Das kommt darauf an. Für Geburtstage, Weihnachten und so weiter kaufe ich Geschenke aber für mich persönlich kaufe ich die normalen Dinge, DVDs, CDs, Kleidung, Eintrittskarten für Konzerte und Spiele. Wenn ich ein wenig übrig habe, gebe ich es dem Bettler auf der Strasse oder den Strassenmusikern.

Say or write the following in German:
1. What does it cost?
2. Anything else?
3. Credit card
4. I go to the cinema or the theatre.
5. I go shopping as often as I can.

5. Ich gehe einkaufen, so oft ich kann.
4. Ich gehe ins Kino oder ins Theater.
3. die Kreditkarte
2. Sonst noch etwas?
1. Was kostet das?

Fashion and trends

AQA	✓
OCR	✓
EDEXCEL	✓
WJEC	✓
CCEA	✓

The following vocabulary will help you when you need to speak or write about clothes, fashion and style. It will also be useful for the listening and reading exams.

Clothes and accessories (Kleider und Zubehörteile)

der Schlips

der Anorak (-s) – anorak
der Anzug (¨e) – man's suit
der Badeanzug – swimsuit
die Badehose (-n) – swimming trunks
der Bikini (-s) – bikini
bunt – colourful
dunkel – dark
eng – narrow, tight
farbig – colourful
gestreift – striped
die Größe – size
Welche Größe? – What size (is it)?
Größe 36, 38, 40, 42, 44 – size 10, 12, 14, 16, 18 (equiv.)
günstig – good value, worth it
der Gürtel (-) – belt
der Handschuh (-e) – glove
hell – light (colour)
das Hemd (-en) – shirt
die Hose (-n) – (pair of) trousers
der Hut (¨e) – hat
die Jacke (-n) – coat, jacket
das Kleid (-er) – dress

die Krawatte (-n) – tie
der Mantel (ä) – (over)coat
die Mode – fashion
das Nachthemd (-en) – nightdress
pleite – broke, short of cash
preiswert – good value
der Pullover (-) – pullover
der Regenmantel (ä) – raincoat
der Rock (¨e) – skirt
der Schal (-s) – scarf
der Schlafanzug (üge) – pyjamas
der Schlips (-e) – tie
der Schuh (-e) – shoe
der Slip (-s) – pants
die Socke (-n) – sock
der Stiefel (-) – boot
die Strumpfhose (-n) – tights
das Sweatshirt (-s) – sweatshirt
das T-Shirt (-s) – T-shirt
der Trainer (-s) – trainer
der Trainingsanzug (üge) – tracksuit
die Unterhose (-n) – underpants

Materials (Materiale)

aus Baumwolle – (made of) cotton
aus Denim – (made of) denim
aus Kunststoff – (made of) synthetic
  material
aus Leder – (made of) leather

aus Metall – (made of) metal
aus Nylon – (made of) nylon
aus Plastik – (made of) plastic
aus Seide – (made of) silk
aus Wolle – (made of) wool

aus Schottenstoff

Style (Der Stil)

altmodisch –
  old-fashioned
ausgebeult – baggy
  (trousers)
einfach – plain, simple
eng – tight
gestreift – striped
Goth- – goth(ic)

Karo – check
kurz – short
lang – long
die Nummer Eins –
  number one, top of
  the range
ohne jeden Schick –
  frumpy

(der) Rap – rap
Rasta – rasta
Rock – rock
aus Schottenstoff –
  tartan
mit...(blauen)...Tupfen
  – (blue-)spotted
weit – baggy

Out shopping

Welche Größe hast du, Anna?
What dress size are you, Anna?
Ich habe Größe 38.
I'm size 12.
Welche Schuhgröße haben Sie?
What shoe size are you?
Ich habe Größe 38.
I'm a size 5 (shoes).
Diese Jacke aus Seide passt dir gut.
This silk jacket suits you (nicely).
Ich suche ein Hemd aus Denim.
I'm looking for a denim shirt.
Du brauchst ein Paar Sportschuhe.
You need a pair of trainers.
Darf ich diesen Rock/diese Hose anprobieren?
May I try this skirt/these trousers on?
Es tut mir Leid, aber sie sind aus.
I'm sorry, but they're sold out.
Bitte, wo finde ich den Ankleideraum?
Please, where can I find the fitting room?
Für meine Arbeit im Büro werde ich mir einen eleganten/smarten Anzug kaufen.
For working in the office, I shall buy myself a smart suit.
Ich habe oft aus den wohltätigen Secondhand Läden gekauft.
I have often bought second-hand from the charity shops.
Wirst du deine neue Jacke tragen?
Will you be wearing your new jacket?
Für Hochzeiten, trage ich normalerweise helle Kleider und große, gelbe hochhackige Schuhe.
For weddings, I normally wear light-coloured clothes and big, yellow high-heels.
Die Zwillinge tragen bunte T-Shirts mit (dazu) passenden Hosen.
The twins wear brightly-coloured T-shirts with matching trousers.

Conversation

AQA ✓
OCR ✓
EDEXCEL ✓
WJEC ✓
CCEA ✓

🔵 **Ist es dir bedeutend, modisch zu sein?**

⚪ Ja und nein. Ich bin ziemlich modisch, aber es kostet so viel!

🔵 **Würdest du für Kleider ausgeben, nur weil sie die Nummer Eins sind?**

⚪ Es kommt darauf an. Wenn ich genug Geld habe, mache ich das von Zeit zu Zeit. Aber, wenn ich pleite bin, kaufe ich billig.

🔵 **Also, du bist modisch aber nur zu einem gewissen Grade?**

⚪ Ich würde sagen. Es gibt Dinge, die mehr Bedeutung haben. Meine Eltern haben genug Geld, aber sie sind nicht reich. Wir geben mehr Geld für Bücher aus, weil wir gut informiert sein möchten.

🔵 **Und, das ist ein sehr guter Grund! Ich danke dir!**

⚪ Ich auch.

3.3 Advantages and disadvantages of new technology

LEARNING SUMMARY	After studying this section, you should be able to: • talk about computers, mobile phones and other machines • explain the advantages of new technology • explain the disadvantages of new technology

New technology

AQA ✓
OCR ✓
EDEXCEL ✓
WJEC ✓
CCEA ✓

You will find the following vocabulary and sentences useful for the listening and reading exams, and for the controlled speaking and writing assessments.

der Laptop

ICT (Informatik)

ab-melden – to sign off	**das Ikon** – icon
die Anlage – attachment	**das Internet** – Internet
an-melden – to sign in	**die Kamera** – (cine-) camera
aus-loggen – to log off	**klicken** – to click
das Breitband – broadband	**der Laptop** – laptop
der Browser – browser	**das Menü** – menu
die Datei – file	**das Mobiltelefon** – mobile (phone)
die Datenbank – database	**der MP3-player** – MP3 player
ein-loggen – to log on	**der Ordner** – folder
der Fotoapparat – (still) camera	**der Papierkorb** – recycle bin
herunter-laden – to download	**senden** – to send
das Handy – mobile (phone)	**speichern** – to save
die Homepage – homepage	**suchen** – to search

die Tastatur

die **Suchmaschine** – search engine
im Internet surfen – to surf the Internet
die **Tastatur** – keyboard
die **telefonische Nachricht** –
   telephone message
der **Telefonvertrag** – phone contract
der **Text** – text

texten – to text
verfassen – to compose
im Voraus bezahlt – pre-paid
die **Webseite** – webpage
die **Website** – website
das (WorldWide) Web – the Web

The advantages of new technology

Das Internet in der Schule, das ist prima, weil es uns erlaubt, Daten über passende Berufe zu suchen.
The Internet in school is great because it allows us to search for data about suitable jobs/careers.

Wir haben unsere eigene Site in der Schule.
We have our own site at school.

Internet ist eine ausgezeichnete Weise, uns in Kontakt mit der ganzen Welt zu bringen.
The Internet is an excellent way of putting us in contact with the whole world.

Ich surfe gern im Internet, weil das meine Kenntnisse und Freundeskreis erweitert.
I like surfing the Internet because it widens my knowledge and circle of friends.

Durch Internet habe ich mir Freunde/Kontakte überall in der Welt gemacht.
Through the Internet, I have made friends/contacts all over the world.

Internet erlaubt mir auch meine Fremdsprachen zu praktizieren.
The Internet also allows me to practise my foreign languages.

Meine Freunde und ich bereiten unsere eigene Site vor.
My friends and I are preparing our own site.

Es macht mir Freude, das Netz zu navigieren.
It gives me pleasure to navigate the Net.

Es ist äußerst praktisch und wir können die nötigen Informationen ohne Schwierigkeit finden.
It is extremely practical and we can find the necessary information without any difficulty.

Das Handy beruhigt die Eltern, die immer wissen wollen, wo wir uns befinden.
The mobile phone calms (down) parents who always want to know where to find us.

Mit dem Handy kann man Nachrichten senden, die man sonst nie bekommen würde.
With the mobile phone you can send messages, which you would otherwise never get.

Im Notfall kann das Handy unentbehrlich sein.
In an emergency the mobile phone can be indispensable.

The disadvantages of new technology

Mit dem Computer...	With the computer...
geht man weniger aus.	you go out less.
hat man weniger Bewegung.	you have less exercise.
treibt man weniger Sport.	you play less sport.
kann man Computersüchtig werden.	you can become a computer addict.
wird die Realität durch eine virtuelle Wirklichkeit ersetzt.	reality will be displaced by virtual reality.
riskiert man sich die Augen zu beschädigen.	you risk damaging your eyes.
verlieren Freunde ihre Bedeutung.	friends lose their importance.

Der Computer…	The computer…
macht die Hausaufgaben für die Studenten.	does the homework for the students.
wird eine falsche Realität für einen.	becomes a false reality for you.
führt zum Überverbrauch von ungesundem Fastfood.	leads to over-consumption of unhealthy fast-food.
kann einen von den anderen Menschen trennen.	can cut you off from other people.
Mit dem Handy…	With the mobile phone…
kann man nie alleine sein.	you can never be alone.
wird man zu leicht zu kontaktieren.	you become too easy to contact.
verbringt man zu viel Zeit beim Texten.	you spend too much time texting.
wird die Familie ängstlich, wenn man nicht zu kontakt(ier)en ist.	the family gets anxious if you cannot be reached.
kann der Autofahrer Verkehrsunfälle verursachen.	the motorist can cause accidents.
können die Rechnungen astronomisch sein!	the bills can be astronomical!
hat man selten genug Kredit um den Eltern zu antworten!	you rarely have enough credit to answer the parents!
Mit dem MP3…	With your MP3…
wird man ein wandelnder Sklave/ eine wandelnde Sklavin der Technologie.	you become a walking slave to technology.
kann man die Außenwelt total vergessen.	you can completely forget the outside world.
kann man total in seiner privaten Welt leben.	you can live completely in your own private world.

PROGRESS CHECK

Say or write the following in German:

1 Friends lose their importance.
2 It is extremely practical.
3 I like surfing the Internet.
4 The bills can be astronomical!
5 One gets less exercise.
6 I have made friends everywhere.

1. Freunde verlieren ihre Bedeutung.   2. Es ist äußerst praktisch.
3. Ich surfe gern im Internet.   4. Die Rechnungen können astronomisch sein!
5. Man hat weniger Bewegung.   6. Ich habe mir Freunde überall gemacht.

3.4 Grammar

LEARNING SUMMARY

After studying this section, you should be able to understand:

- the imperfect tense
- the perfect tense

The imperfect tense

AQA	✓
OCR	✓
EDEXCEL	✓
WJEC	✓
CCEA	✓

The imperfect is a simple past tense, which you need to be able to use reasonably confidently in your controlled speaking and writing assessments. In German, the imperfect tense covers three English tenses.

For example: **ich spielte Tennis** =

1. I was playing tennis
2. I used to play tennis
3. I played tennis (regularly)

> Students can get away with just using the imperfect, but this is not advisable, since it will limit the grade you achieve. To get a high grade, you should also use the perfect tense (see pages 72–73).

KEY POINT

The imperfect tense is normally used as the basic past tense in reports, stories, novels, etc. However, when you are relating events of a personal nature, as in your GCSE work, where you use 'I, me, we, us' in English, you would expect to use the perfect tense.

How to form the imperfect tense

Regular verbs

To form the imperfect tense with regular verbs, you need to add the following endings to the stem of the infinitive: **-te, -test, -te, -ten, -tet, -ten, -ten**. You find the stem of the infinitive by cutting off the **-(e)n**.

For example:

ich machte

Machen	to make
ich machte	I made
du machtest	you made (informal singular)
er/sie/es/man machte	he/she/it/one made
wir machten	we made
ihr machtet	you made (informal plural)
Sie machten	you made (formal, plural and singular)
sie machten	they made

With verbs whose infinitive stem ends in **t** (e.g. **antworten**, **warten**) you put an **-e** between the **t** and the imperfect endings, e.g. **ich antwortete**, **du wartetest**.

Irregular verbs

You need to be able to handle the irregular verbs on page 71 reasonably confidently in order to achieve well at GCSE. Although all these verbs are irregular, you only need to remember the **ich** form to be able to work out all the other persons in this tense, since these verbs follow the same pattern as all the regular ones.

Remember these points when forming the imperfect tense with irregular verbs:

- The **ich** and the **er/sie/es/man** forms will be identical.
- Add **-st** to the **ich** form to get the **du** form.
- Add **-en** to all the plural forms, except for **ihr** (you), where you just add **-t**.

For example: **ich begann, du begannst, er/sie/es/man begann, wir begannen, ihr begannt, Sie begannen, sie begannen.**

ich brach

ich las

Infinitive	Imperfect	Meaning
ankommen	**ich kam...an**	I arrived
anrufen	**ich rief...an**	I phoned
aufstehen	**ich stand...auf**	I got up
ausgeben	**ich gab...aus**	I spent
beginnen	**ich begann**	I began
bekommen	**ich bekam**	I got
bringen	**ich brachte**	I brought
halten	**ich hielt**	I stopped
bleiben	**ich blieb**	I stayed
brechen	**ich brach**	I broke
kommen	**ich kam**	I came
essen	**ich aß**	I ate
fahren	**ich fuhr**	I travelled/drove
fallen	**ich fiel**	I fell
fangen	**ich fing**	I caught
finden	**ich fand**	I found
fliegen	**ich flog**	I flew
frieren	**ich fror**	I froze
geben	**ich gab**	I gave
gehen	**ich ging**	I went
gewinnen	**ich gewann**	I won
haben	**ich hatte**	I had
helfen	**ich half**	I helped
kennen	**ich kannte**	I knew
lassen	**ich ließ**	I left
laufen	**ich lief**	I ran
lesen	**ich las**	I read
liegen	**ich lag**	I was lying down
nehmen	**ich nahm**	I took
rennen	**ich rannte**	I ran
rufen	**ich rief**	I called
scheinen	**ich schien**	I seemed
schreiben	**ich schrieb**	I wrote
schwimmen	**ich schwamm**	I swam
sehen	**ich sah**	I saw
sein	**ich war**	I was
sitzen	**ich saß**	I was seated
tragen	**ich trug**	I wore/carried
treten	**ich trat**	I stepped

The perfect tense

AQA	✓
OCR	✓
EDEXCEL	✓
WJEC	✓
CCEA	✓

You would normally use the perfect tense in your controlled speaking and writing assessments to describe your past actions.

How to form the perfect tense

To form the perfect tense, follow these steps:

- Use the correct personal form of the present tense of **haben** as the helper verb.
- Add to it the past participle of the verb (with regular verbs, the past participle is formed by surrounding the stem of the infinitive by **ge...t**, e.g. **gekauft**, **gemacht**).
- Remember to put the past participle at the end of the verb phrase.

Here are some examples:

Ich habe gekauft.	I have bought.
Ich habe drei CDs im Supermarkt gekauft.	I bought three CDs in the supermarket.

> **KEY POINT**
>
> Once again, German has one tense to cover three English ones. For example, **ich habe gekauft** = I have bought, I did buy, I bought.

Irregular past participles

The following common verbs all have irregular past participles, which you need to learn.

Sie haben gewonnen

Infinitive	Pronoun + 'haben'	Past participle	Meanings
beginnen	ich habe	begonnen	I have begun, I began, I did begin
bekommen	du hast	bekommen	you have got, you got, you did get
bringen	er hat	gebracht	he has brought, he did bring, he brought
denken	sie hat	gedacht	she has thought, she did think, she thought
essen	es hat	gegessen	it has eaten, it did eat, it ate
fangen	man hat	gefangen	one has caught, one did catch, one caught
finden	wir haben	gefunden	we have found, we did find, we found
geben	ihr habt	gegeben	you have given, you did give, you gave
gewinnen	Sie haben	gewonnen	you have won, you did win, you won
helfen	sie haben	geholfen	they have helped, they did help, they helped
lassen	ich habe	gelassen	I have left, I did leave, I left
sehen	sie hat	gesehen	she has seen, she did see, she saw
tragen	man hat	getragen	one has worn, one did wear, one wore
treffen	wir haben	getroffen	we have met, we did meet, we met
trinken	ihr habt	getrunken	you have drunk, you did drink, you drank
vergessen	Sie haben	vergessen	you have forgotten, you did forget, you forgot
verlieren	sie haben	verloren	they have lost, they did lose, they lost
waschen	ich habe	gewaschen	I have washed, I did wash, I washed

The perfect tense with 'sein'

There are a number of verbs in German that use the present tense of **sein** instead of the present tense of **haben**. Again, you need to familiarise yourself with these and become confident when you use them.

> **KEY POINT**
>
> You do not need to know the reason why some verbs use **sein** in the perfect tense.

Below is a list of the most common verbs that use **sein** in the perfect tense:

man ist eingeschlafen

Infinitive	Pronoun + 'sein'	Past participle	Meanings
ankommen	ich bin	angekommen	I have arrived, I did arrive, I arrived
abfahren	du bist	abgefahren	you have left, you did leave, you left
aufwachen	du bist	aufgewacht	you have woken up, you did wake up, you woke
aufstehen	sie ist	aufgestanden	she has got up, she did get up, she got up
bleiben	es ist	geblieben	it has stayed, it did stay, it stayed
einschlafen	man ist	eingeschlafen	one has fallen asleep, one did fall asleep, one fell asleep
fahren	wir sind	gefahren	we have travelled, we did travel, we travelled
fallen	ihr seid	gefallen	you have fallen, you did fall, you fell
geschehen	es ist	geschehen	it has happened, it did happen, it happened
kommen	Sie sind	gekommen	you have come, you did come, you came
laufen	sie sind	gelaufen	they have run, they did run, they ran
Rad fahren	du bist	Rad gefahren	you have cycled, you did cycle, you cycled
reisen	er ist	gereist	he has travelled, he did travel, he travelled
reiten	ich bin	geritten	I have ridden, I did ride, I rode
schwimmen	sie ist	geschwommen	she has swum, she did swim, she swam
segeln	es ist	gesegelt	it has sailed, it did sail, it sailed
sein	man ist	gewesen	one has been, one was
Ski fahren	wir sind	Ski gefahren	we have ski-ed, we did ski, we ski-ed
wachsen	ihr seid	gewachsen	you have grown, you did grow, you grew
werden	Sie sind	geworden	you have become, you did become, you became

wir sind Ski gefahren

Sample controlled assessment

Speaking

① **Track 10** You are going to have a conversation with your teacher about what you like doing in your free time. You could...

- give a list of several things you like doing
- say which is your favourite pastime
- talk about one or two of your other pastimes
- say if you intend to make a career out of any of your pastimes.

Teacher: Was machst du gerne in deiner Freizeit?

Student: Es kommt darauf an, es hängt vom Wetter ab. Ich bin[1] eine große Sportfreundin und bin sehr gerne an der frischen Luft. Aber ich habe[1] auch andere Interessen und Hobbys, die ich drinnen betreiben kann.[4]

Teacher: Also, fangen wir mit deinem Sport an. Was für eine Sportart magst du?

Student: Ich spiele[1] Frauenfußball für die Schule und für die Grafschaft und Tischtennis für unseren Jugendklub. Ich habe die Stadt beim Tennis repräsentiert[2/26] und bis letzten Sommer habe ich auch Leichtathletik im Hundert-und Zweihundertmetersprint für den Bezirk gemacht.[2/26] Das Sprinten habe ich aufgegeben,[9/26] weil[5] ich zu viel zu tun hatte.[26] Es war[26] ein guter Entschluß. Was mich am meisten[22] interessiert,[4] ist nicht Leistungssport[9] sondern Straßenhockey, was ziemlich unorganisiert ist.[4] Wenn ich auf der Straße mit meinen Freunden spiele, kann[35] ich mich total entspannen. Das ist nicht der Fall beim Leistungssport! Ich bin nicht[12] daran interessiert, berühmt zu werden.

Teacher: Das ist imponierend. Sport bei Seite, was sind deine Hobbys?

Student: Ich habe das Internet und das Fernsehen gerne aber ich schwärme für stille, gelassene[19] Dinge wie Lesen und Schach. Ich spiele Schach mit meinem Vater und das ist eine Art von Verbindung zwischen uns beiden geworden.[39] Wir spielen oft stundenlang und Mutti kann nicht verstehen, wie wir so lange im Wohnzimmer sitzen können,[4] ohne[27] zu sprechen![18]

Teacher: Und könntest du vielleicht eine Karriere aus einem deiner Hobbys machen?

Student: Ich würde[25] gern Sportlehrerin werden aber ich würde[25] studieren müssen, bis ich 22 bin und das ist zu lang. Ich werde vielleicht an die Uni gehen und, da[5] ich Bücher so gerne habe, könnte ich auch Bibliothekarin werden. Aber das dauert auch zu lange. Vielleicht werde ich[3] im Jugenddienst in unserer Stadt arbeiten. Ich könnte vielleicht zum Jugendsportprogramm beitragen.

Teacher: Prima! Zumindest hast du viele Möglichkeiten.

Student: Ja, das würde ich auch sagen.

Turn to page 155 for a translation of this passage.

Examiner's comments

This student is on course for a good grade having implemented a number of the 40 points from pages 8–9:

1 The present tense has been used

2 Examples of the past tense

3 The future tense has been used

4 The student has shown good knowledge of word order

5 'Weil' and 'da' have been used

9 Impressive vocabulary, e.g. 'aufgegeben', 'Leistungssport'

12 A negative has been included

18 An exclamation

19 An adjective has been used

22 'Am meisten' is an example of the superlative

25 Examples of the conditional tense

26 A mix of perfect and imperfect tenses has been used

27 'Ohne' + the infinitive

35 A modal verb ('können')

39 The perfect tense has been used with 'sein'.

Sample controlled assessment

Writing

1 Write about the advantages and disadvantages of modern technology.
You could...

- give a list of the items of modern technology (e.g. a mobile phone) on which you rely
- explain how these machines help you personally
- explain the negative side of modern technology
- comment on the dangers of criminal activity in relation to the Internet, etc.
- say how you feel about the cost of modern technology
- put down any thoughts you may have about the future of such technologies.

Ich weiß[1] nicht, was ich ohne mein Handy, meinen MP3 und mein Internet tun würde.[25] Ich darf[35] mein Internet sagen, weil meine Webseite und auch mein Facebook es für mich personalisiert haben. Aber, fangen wir mit meinem Handy an.

Es ist mehr[21] ein guter Freund als[21] ein Stück Technologie, weil[5] es mir und meiner Familie eine Art Sicherheit bringt.[6] Bevor[24] ich mein persönliches Mobiltelefon hatte, wussten meine Eltern nicht, wo ich war,[2] um wieviel Uhr ich nach Hause kommen würde, was ich zum Essen möchte und so weiter. Und, weil[5] Vati und Mutti ängstliche Leute sind,[4] habe ich jetzt die Freiheit Dinge zu machen, die[7] ich früher nicht machen konnte. Zum Beispiel, es ist mir erlaubt,[36] öfter auszugehen als vor einem Jahr, besonders, weil ich ein zuverlässiges Handy habe.

Meine Facebook und meine Webseite haben mir[28] die Welt geöffnet. Dadurch habe ich so viele neue Kontakte und Freunde, dass meine Aussichten[9] sich immer mehr erweitern. Ich fühle, ich habe mehr Verständnis für individuelle Personen, weil[5] ich jetzt so viele Leute kenne.[6]

Aber ich muss[35] zugeben, dass die neue Technologie eine andere, negative Seite hat. Als Beispiel nehmen wir mein MP3. Die Eltern sagen, dass ich die ganze Zeit mit meinem Kopfhörer auf dem Kopf verbringe und, dass es fast unmöglich ist, ein Gespräch mit mir zu Hause zu führen.[9] Das ist nicht total richtig, aber sie haben ein wenig recht![18]

Aber was Pornographie und Pädophilen betrifft, gebe ich[1] meinen Eltern hundert Prozent recht! Facebook and Chatrooms werden[3] geisteskranken[9] Fremden die Gelegenheit anbieten, einen Eintritt zu unserem persönlichen Leben und Freundenkreis[9] zu bekommen. Deshalb werden meine Freunde und ich äußerst vorsichtig sein.[3/6]

Ein anderer[19] Nachteil für mich sind die Rechnungen! Technologie wird[3] nie[12] sehr billig sein und eines Tages müssen meine Freunde und ich lernen, unser Internet- und Handyverbrauch zu vermindern. Vielleicht wird[3] ein Wissenschaftler oder Informatiker eine Weise erfinden, worauf wir unsere neue Technologie fast kostenlos benutzen können.[35] Wir können alle träumen!

Turn to page 155 for a translation of this passage.

Examiner's comments

This student's performance has been enhanced by including a good number of the 40 points from pages 8–9:

1 The present tense has been used

2 The past tense

3 Examples of the future tense

4 This student has shown a good understanding of word order

5 'Weil' has been used

6 Justified points of view

7 'Die' is a connective

9 Impressive vocabulary has been used, e.g. 'Aussichten', 'führen', 'geisteskranken'. 'Freundenkreis'

12 An example of a negative

18 An exclamation

19 An example of an adjective

21 The comparative

24 'Bevor' has been used

25 An example of the conditional tense

28 A personal pronoun

35 Modal verbs ('dürfen', 'müssen', 'können')

36 An impersonal verb

Exam practice questions

Listening

1 *Track 11* Listen to the answer-phone message that Rudi has left for Mira. Fill in the blanks.

Heute abend können wir nicht zum .... gehen. Die Eintrittskarten sind

.... Aber für morgen gibt es Karten und ich habe welche ....

Ruf mich an, wenn du nicht .... kannst. Ich schlage vor, wir

.... uns vor dem Theater eine .... Stunde vor der

.... , das heißt, um .... sieben Uhr.   **(8)**

2 *Track 12* Listen to this German mobile phone company's automatic helpline. Which button must you press if you wish to do the following:

(a)   Take out a new contract   ....

(b)   Install a new phone   ....

(c)   Top-up your credit   ....

(d)   Make a complaint   ....

(e)   If none of the above options is the right one, what should the caller do?   ....   **(5)**

3 *Track 13* Listen to these radio announcements. In each case, choose the correct description from the options given and write it in the space provided.

Interview with important politician	**A sporting victory**	**Tail-back on major motorway**
Musicians on tour	**German leader flies abroad**	**Bad weather casualties**

(a)   ....

(b)   ....

(c)   ....

(d)   ....

(e)   ....

(f)   ....   **(6)**

Exam practice questions

4 **Track 14** Two friends are talking about their likes and dislikes. Tick three boxes for each person.

		Manni	Doro
A	hat kein Interesse für Fussball	☐	☐
B	hat Liebesfilme sehr gern	☐	☐
C	ist Fanatiker für Schach und Tanzen	☐	☐
D	verliert Geld in Kartenspielen	☐	☐
E	tanzt im Jugendklub	☐	☐
F	interessiert sich für das Theater	☐	☐
G	geht ziemlich gern ins Kino	☐	☐

(6)

5 **Track 15** Listen to this TV film promotion and complete the information.

(a) Title of film:

....

(b) Year the film appeared:

....

(c) Name of the prize it won:

....

(d) Max Müller's nationality:

....

(e) Cost of subscription:

....

(f) Phone number:

....

(6)

Exam practice questions

6 🎵 **Track 16** Listen to these radio adverts. In which places are the management looking for new staff? Tick the correct box for each advert.

(a) A Doctor's surgery ☐ B Old people's home ☐

    C Hospital ☐ D Chemist's ☐

(b) A Fashion boutique ☐ B Department store ☐

    C Bookshop ☐ D Garden centre ☐

(c) A Delicatessen ☐ B French restaurant ☐

    C Wine bar ☐ D Frankfurter stall ☐ **(3)**

7 🎵 **Track 17** A German athlete is describing his normal training day. Fill in the correct letter for each time of day in the activity grid.

A Physiotherapy
B Lunch
C Sprinting
D Breakfast
E Running
F Boxing
G The first shower
H Walking
I The second shower
J Gymnastics

Time	Activity
6.30	
7.00	
8.00	
10.00	
11.00	
12.00	
13.00	
13.30	
14.30	
16.30	

(10)

Exam practice questions

Reading

1 Read this advert from the Bavarian Alpenvorland and then tick the six correct boxes.

> ## Recht herzlich willkommen im Bayerischen Alpenvorland!
> ### Wir halten Sie auf Trab!
>
> Hier kann man...
> - reiten gehen
> - Höhlenfahrten machen
> - Autorennsport machen
> - Handball spielen
>
> - Klettern gehen
> - Fallschirm springen
> - Tennis spielen
> - Paragliding machen
>
> - Rad fahren
> - rudern gehen
> - Ski fahren
> - Wind surfen

You can:

A ☐ B ☐ C ☐

D ☐ E ☐ F ☐

G ☐ H ☐ I ☐

J ☐ K ☐ L ☐

(6)

Exam practice questions

2 Read this article about Marlene Dietrich from the magazine, *Filmgeschichte*, and answer the questions.

Marlene Dietrich

Marlene Dietrich, eine Schauspielerin und Sängerin war eine der ersten Sexsymbols in der Welt der Filme. Sie ist 1901 in Schöneberg in Deutschland geboren und ihr wirklicher Name war Maria Magdelena Dietrich von Losch.

Schön, schlank und blond, sie interpretierte zwischen den 20er und 40er Jahren des zwanzigsten Jahrhunderts eine ganze Serie Frauen, die so attraktiv für schwache Männer waren, dass sie die Macht hatten, diese Männer zu ruinieren. Ihr bekanntester Film war *Der Blaue Engel* (1930), wo sie eine *femme fatale* spielte.

Aber dieses Image hatte nichts mit der wirklichen Dietrich zu tun. Heutzutage glauben die Filmkritiker, dass ihr Regisseur, Josef von Sternberg, ihr eine falsche Personalität gegeben hatte. In der Realität war sie keine wirkliche *femme fatale*, sondern eine relativ kalte, reservierte Person, die den Starruhm* nicht suchte.

Trotzdem hat Marlene ihr Image behalten und während des Zweiten Weltkrieges war sie an der Spitze der Hitparade mit ihrem Hit, *Unter der Laterne* (*Underneath The Lamplight*), in Deutschland und in den englischsprachigen Ländern. In ihren späteren Jahren lebte sie ein stilles, geschlossenes Leben in einer kleinen Wohnung in Paris, wo sie alleine war und fast nichts mit den Leuten zu tun hatte. Ein trauriges Ende.

Wenn Ihr Urgroßeltern noch leben, fragen Sie sie, >>Wer war Marlene Dietrich?<<.

(*der Starruhm – stardom)

Example: Where was Marlene Dietrich born? In Schöneberg, in Germany.

(a) As well as acting, what else did Dietrich do? .... **(1)**

(b) Describe how Dietrich looked. Give three details.

    (i) .... **(ii)** .... **(iii)** .... **(3)**

(c) When was Dietrich at the top as an actress?

    .... **(1)**

(d) What was her apparent effect on the main male characters?

    .... **(2)**

(e) For what is von Sternberg criticised?

    .... **(1)**

(f) Describe Marlene's real personality. Give three details.

    (i) ....

    (ii) ....

    (iii) .... **(3)**

(g) What was special about her song, *Unter der Laterne*?

    .... **(1)**

(h) What was sad about the end of her life?

    .... **(1)**

Exam practice questions

3 Look at the television schedule below.

Im Fernsehen heute abend

19.00   **Nachrichten**

19.20   **Kulturschau**
Retrospektive : Einen Blick auf die Lieder von Dietrich

20.00   **Finanzielles**
Großeltern im Altheim. Sind die Sozialkosten zu viel ?

20.30   **Sie leben nur zweimal!**
Abenteuerfilm mit 007

22.30   **Tagesschau**
Aktuelles im Tagesschau

23.00   **Pause zur Reflexion**
Christen, Juden und Muslims sprechen zusammen

For what time would you set the recorder for the following programmes?

Example: News   19.00

(a)   Adventure film   ....

(b)   Religious discussion   ....

(c)   Economics report   ....

(d)   News magazine   ....

(e)   Songs   ....

(5)

Exam practice questions

4 These young people are talking about their pocket money.

> Ich benutze mein Taschengeld, um Klamotten zu kaufen aber ich kaufe auch Blumen für meine Mutter und meinen Vater daraus.
> *Rita*

> Meine Eltern sind freigebig und ich bekomme 30 Euro pro Woche. Ich gebe 20 Euro für Eintrittskarten zur Kegelbahn und zu den Rockkonzerten aus, und ich spare den Rest in unserer Bank.
> *Siggi*

> Ich bekomme kein Taschengeld, weil ich einen Teilzeitjob habe, wo ich 65 Euro pro Woche verdiene. Ich gebe das Ganze für Kleinigkeiten aus.
> *Uschi*

> Kleider, Kleider und immer mehr Kleider. Mein Taschengeld verschwindet in Modeboutiques.
> *Gabriela*

> Ich bekomme 40 Euro von meinen Eltern und Großeltern. Aber ich könnte nicht sagen, wo das hingeht, ausgenommen, ich gehe gern mit meinen Freunden aus. Das muss es sein! *Ricki*

> Ich schwärme für klassische Musik und ich kaufe allerlei klassische CDs und DVDs. Am Ende der Woche bleibt nichts übrig.
> *Peter*

> Wie ich mein Geld ausgebe? Das ist leicht zu beantworten. Für Schmuck und mein Pferd Schwarzi. Die zwei gehen nicht gut zusammen, nicht wahr? Ich bekomme 300 Euro pro Monat. Also sagen wir 30 Prozent für den Schmuck, der Rest geht für Schwarzi.
> *Antonia*

Write the name of the correct person in each answer space.

(a) Buys clothes only ....

(b) Doesn't forget the parents ....

(c) Spends money on jewellery and a horse ....

(d) Saves a third of his or her pocket money ....

(e) Probably spends money on going out ....

(f) Spends money on the great composers ....

(g) Spends the money (s)he earns on little things .... **(7)**

Exam practice questions

5 Read this e-mail and answer the questions that follow.

Tschüß Joanna!

Du hast mich gefragt, was wir für Fitnesstraining machen können, wenn du zu uns kommst, essen beiseite! Da haben wir Glück. Meine Eltern sind, wie du weißt, Sportlehrer, und haben Zugang zu vielen Sportmöglichkeiten.

Erstens können wir zum Sportzentrum gehen, und Raketensportarten wie Tennis, Squash oder Badminton spielen. Wenn du gern und oft im Freien bist, können wir im Wald und am Strand wandern gehen. Und, weil wir neben dem Meer wohnen, könnten wir auch jeden Tag schwimmen und später ein alkoholfreies Bier im Strandcafé trinken!

So etwas wäre so viel besser als zu Hause mit meinen jüngeren Bruder und Schwester zu bleiben. Sie sind Sklaven vom Computer und vom Fernsehen und scheinen den ganzen Tag zu verbringen, sich über die Computerspiele und die Fernsehprogramme zu streiten!

Weisst du was, wir könnten auch kegeln gehen, das wäre aber nett! Sag mir Bescheid*, welche Dinge dich am meisten interessieren, und wir können diese einprogrammieren! Bis nächste Woche. Ich kann nicht warten!

Uli.

(* Sag mir Bescheid – let me know)

(a) Why is Joanna in luck?

.... **(2)**

(b) Where could they play racket sports?

.... **(1)**

(c) In which two areas could they go walking?

(i) .... **(ii)** .... **(2)**

(d) What could they do at the seaside?

....

.... **(3)**

(e) Why are they better off in the fresh air?

.... **(2)**

(f) What else does Uli particularly like doing?

.... **(1)**

(g) What else does Uli suggest?

.... **(2)**

(h) When will they finally meet and how does Uli feel about it?

.... **(2)**

Exam practice questions

6 Read this e-mail Corinne sent to her exchange partner, Al, about a visit to the Europa-Park near her home and answer the questions that follow.

Hallo Al

Es freut uns zu hören, dass deine Eltern dich zu uns bringen können. Emmendingen, unsere kleine Stadt, ist ganz in der Nähe von Freiburg und, wenn Ihr die A5 (Eurostrasse 35), Ausfahrt 60, nehmt, dann sind wir nur 5–10 Minuten weg. Wir sind auch sehr froh, dass deine Eltern bei uns übernachten können. Und mein Vater hat einen sehr guten Vorschlag gehabt, was nicht normal ist!

Der Europa-Park ist auch ganz in der Nähe und weil deine Eltern den nächsten Tag mit uns verbringen werden, könnten wir alle den Europa-Park besuchen. Es ist ein ganz moderner Freizeitpark, wo man sich äußerst gut amüsieren kann.

Die Fahrten sind Furcht erregend*, es gibt auch ruhige Achterbahnen** für die Eltern und eine ganze Menge gute Restaurants und Imbißstuben, wo man ganz gut essen und trinken kann.

Sag mir so schnell wie möglich, ob so ein Park deinen Eltern gefallen würde und, wenn ja, dann wird Mutti die Eintrittskarten reservieren. Auch von Nutzen für deine Eltern, der Europa-Park ist auf dem Wege nach ihrem Reiseziel in Frankreich.

Bis bald, Corinne.

(*Furcht erregend – frightening, **ruhige Achterbahnen – gentle roller coasters)

(a) What are the directions for Al's family to get to Emmendingen?

.... **(1)**

(b) Why does Corinne praise her father?

.... **(2)**

(c) What is Corinne's father's suggestion?

....

.... **(3)**

(d) Give five advantages of the Europa-Park.

(i) ....

(ii) ....

(iii) ....

(iv) ....

(v) .... **(5)**

(e) What does Al now need to do?

.... **(2)**

(f) What will the mother then do? .... **(1)**

(g) What is helpful for Al's parents?

.... **(1)**

4 Holidays

The following topics are covered in this chapter:

- Holidays and accommodation
- Transport
- Grammar

4.1 Holidays and accommodation

LEARNING SUMMARY

After studying this section, you should be able to:

- talk about past and future holidays
- understand information about booking holidays and booking accommodation
- write about experiences abroad

Holidays and accommodation

AQA	✓
OCR	✓
EDEXCEL	✓
WJEC	✓
CCEA	✓

The holiday topic is a topic that lends itself to different tenses. It is the favourite topic for many students in the speaking and writing controlled assessments. The vocabulary sections are particularly important because they are very likely to be tested in the listening and reading exams.

Your controlled speaking assessment must last between four and six minutes. It is a long time to talk about one topic, so why not put two topics together? Your title could be 'The things I like doing'. You could spend two or three minutes speaking about your holidays and two or three minutes speaking about your hobbies (refer to Chapter 3 – Leisure, free time and the media).

Holidays (Die Ferien/Der Urlaub)

das Andenken (-) – souvenir

die Ansichtskarte – picture postcard

der Aufenthalt (-e) – stay

der Ausflug (-̈e) – excursion

die Auskunft – information

das Auskunftsbüro – information office

im/ins Ausland – abroad

Ausländer (in) – foreigner, m/f

die Aussicht (-en) – view

die Broschüre (-n) – brochure

die Fahrt (-en) – journey

der Film (-e) – film

der Fotoapparat (-e) – camera

die Führung (-en) – guided tour

die Gegend (-en) – area

Gute Reise! – Safe journey!

die Grenze (-n) – border

das Informationsbüro – information office

die Landkarte (-n) – map

der Paß (-̈sse) – passport

Passagier (in) – passenger, m/f

die Pauschalreise (-n) – package holiday

der Plan (-̈e) – plan

die Postkarte (-n) – postcard

die Reise (-n) – journey

der Reiseführer (-) – guidebook

Reiseleiter (in) – guide, m/f

reservieren – to book, to reserve

die Reservierung – booking, reservation

die Rundfahrt (-en) – tour

Schöne Ferien! – Happy holidays!

Schönes Wochenende! – Enjoy your weekend!

die Sonderfahrt (-en) – special excursion

das Souvenir (-s) – souvenir

die Stadtführung (-en) – guided tour

der Stadtplan (-̈e) – town map

die Überfahrt (-en) – crossing

die Unterkunft – accommodation

das Verkehrsamt – tourist office

die Verspätung – delay

das Verkehrsamt

die Landkarte

Verbs

sich (gut) amüsieren – to enjoy oneself

sich aus-kennen – to know one's way around

aus-packen – to unpack

sich aus-ruhen – to relax, to rest

besichtigen – to see the sights

besuchen – to visit

ein-packen – to pack

sich entspannen – to relax

faulenzen – to laze around

sich freuen auf (+Akk) – to look forward to

los-fahren – to set off

organisieren – to organise

packen – to pack

planen – to plan

reiten – to ride

segeln – to sail

übernachten – to stay overnight

in Urlaub fahren – to go on holiday

sich verirren – to get lost

vor-haben – to have on (plan)

Camping (Das Camping)

das Camping

Camper (in) – camper, m/f

der Campingplatz (¨e) – campsite

der Fahrradverleih – bicycle hire

das Klo (-s) – toilet

der Spielplatz (¨e) – games area

der Strom – electricity

das Trinkwasser – drinking water

die Wäscherei (-en) – launderette

der Waschraum (¨e) – washroom

das Zelt (-e) – tent

zelten – to camp, to pitch a tent

das Zelten – camping

der Zeltplatz (¨e) – campsite

At the beach (Am Strand)

baden – to bathe

das Boot (-e) – boat

ertrinken – to drown

das Freibad – open-air pool

der Liegestuhl (¨e) – deckchair

das Meer – sea

die See – sea

sich sonnen – to sun oneself

die Sonnenbrille (-n) – sunglasses

die Sonnencreme – sun cream

die Sonnenmilch – suntan lotion

das Sonnenöl – suntan oil

der Strand (¨e) – beach

tauchen – to dive

At the hotel/youth hostel (Im Hotel/in der Jugendherberge)

der Schlafsack

ab-waschen – to wash up

die Bettwäsche – bed linen

das Büro (-s) – office

die Decke (-n) – blanket

das Doppelzimmer (-) – double room

das Einzelzimmer (-) – single room

der Empfang – reception

das Erdgeschoss – ground floor

das Esszimmer – dining room

der Fahrstuhl (¨e) – lift

der Gast (¨e) – guest

der Gasthof (¨e) – hotel

die Gaststätte (-n) – hotel

die Halbpension – half-board

die Herbergsmutter – female hostel warden

der Herbergsvater – male hostel warden

das Hotel (-s) – hotel

die Jugendherberge (-n) – youth hostel

die Küche – kitchen

die Mülltonne – rubbish bin (large)

der Personalausweis – personal ID

der Schlafraum (¨e) – dormitory

der Schlafsack (¨e) – sleeping bag

der Spielraum (¨e) – games room

die Vollpension – full-board

das Wohnzimmer – sitting room

Conversation

AQA	✓
OCR	✓
EDEXCEL	✓
WJEC	✓
CCEA	✓

🗣 **Wo warst du letztes Jahr im Urlaub?**

🗣 Ich bin nach Deutschland gefahren.

🗣 **Und wo in Deutschland?**

🗣 Wir sind nach den Ostfriesischen Inseln gefahren.

🗨 **Und wo genau liegen diese Inseln?**

🗨 Sie liegen neben der Nordküste in der Nähe von Holland.

🗨 **Und mit wem warst du auf Urlaub?**

🗨 Ich war mit meiner Familie und unseren Nachbarn.

🗨 **Und wieviele Personen machte das alle zusammen?**

🗨 Wir sind zu neun gereist.

🗨 **Imponierend! Und hat das dir gefällt?**

🗨 Sicher. Wir werden wieder dahin fahren.

4.2 Transport

LEARNING SUMMARY

After studying this section, you should be able to:

- deal with controlled speaking assessments about transport
- answer listening and reading questions about how to get to places
- include references to transport in your controlled writing assessments

Travel

AQA	✓
OCR	✓
EDEXCEL	✓
WJEC	✓
CCEA	✓

The following vocabulary will help you in the listening and reading exams, and in the controlled assessment.

By public transport (Mit den öffentlichen Verkehrsmitteln)

die Bushaltestelle

das Flugzeug

der Zug

aus-steigen – to get off/out
die Bahn (-en) – railway
der (Haupt)Bahnhof (¨e) – (main) railway station
der Bahnsteig (-e) – platform (railway)
der Busbahnhof (¨e) – bus station
die Bushaltestelle (-n) – bus stop
die einfache Fahrt – single ticket
ein-steigen – to get on/in
die Endstation (-en) – terminus
die Fahrkarte (-n) – ticket
der Fahrkartenautomat – ticket machine
der Fahrkartenschalter (-) – ticket office
der Fahrpreis (-e) – fare
der Flughafen – airport
das Flugzeug (-e) – (aero)plane
das Gepäck – baggage
die Gepäckrückgabe – baggage (re)claim
hin und zurück – return

kontrollieren – to check
die Linie (-n) – line, route
nehmen – to take (bus, train)
pünktlich – on time
das Reiseziel – destination
die S-bahn – (sub)urban railway
der Schlafwagen (-) – sleeping car
der Schnellzug (¨e) – express train
die Tageskarte (-n) – day ticket (rover)
der TEE-Zug – Trans-European Express
die U-bahn – underground, tube
die U-Bahnstation (-en) tube station
um-steigen – to change (bus, train, etc.)
die Verbindung (-en) – connection
verpassen – to miss (bus, train, etc.)
verspätet – late (adj)
die Verspätung (-en) – delay
der Warteraum (¨e) – waiting room
das Ziel (-e) – destination
der Zug (¨e) – train
der Zuschlag (¨e) – supplement

By car (Mit dem Wagen)

ADAC – German equivalent of the AA
die Ausfahrt (-en) – motorway exit
das Auto (-s) – car
die Autobahn (-en) – motorway
das Benzin – petrol
die Bremse (-n) – brake
der Diesel – diesel
die Einbahnstraße – one-way street
der Fahrgast (̈e) – passenger
der Führerschein (-e) – driving licence
die Geldstrafe – on-the-spot fine
gesperrt – closed to traffic
gestattet – allowed, permitted

das Glatteis – ice
der Gürtel (-) – seatbelt
die Hauptstraße (-n) – main road
hupen – to use the horn
der Kofferraum (̈e) – boot
die Landstraße (-n) – country road
das Lenkrad (̈e) – steering wheel
der Motor (-en) – engine
die Parkuhr (-en) – parking meter
das Parkverbot – no parking
einen Platten haben – to have a flat (tyre)
der Rasthof (̈e) – service station

Countries and nationalities (Länder und Nationalitäten)

Österreich

Frankreich

Großbritannien

Europa

Deutschland

die Vereinigten Staaten

Amerika (n) – America
Australien (n) – Australia
Belgien (n) – Belgium
Dänemark (n) – Denmark
Deutschland (n) – Germany
England (n) – England
Europa (n) – Europe
Frankreich (n) – France
Griechenland (n) – Greece
Großbritannien – Great Britain
Holland (n) – Holland
Irland (n) – Ireland
Italien (n) – Italy
Japan (n) – Japan
Kanada (n) – Canada
Luxemburg (n) – Luxembourg
Neuseeland (n) – New Zealand
die Niederländer (f, pl) – Netherlands
Nordirland (n) – Northern Ireland
Norwegen (n) – Norway
Österreich (n) – Austria
Portugal (n) – Portugal
Russland (n) – Russia
Schottland (n) – Scotland
Schweden (n) – Sweden
Spanien (n) – Spain
das Vereinigte Königsreich – the United Kingdom
die Vereinigten Staaten (m, pl) – the United States
Wales (n) – Wales

amerikanisch – American
australisch – Australian
belgisch – Belgian
dänisch – Danish
deutsch – German
englisch – English
europäisch – European
französisch – French
griechisch – Greek
britisch – British
holländisch – Dutch
irisch – Irish
italienisch – Italian
japanisch – Japanese
kanadisch – Canadian
luxemburgisch – of Luxembourg
neuseeländisch – of New Zealand
niederländisch – Dutch
nordirländisch – Northern Irish
norwegisch – Norwegian
österreichisch – Austrian
portugisisch – Portuguese
russisch – Russian
schottisch – Scottish
schwedisch – Swedish
spanisch – Spanish
britisch – British

amerikanisch – American

walisisch – Welsh

Verbs

an-kommen – to arrive
aus-geben – to spend (money)
bedauern – to regret
sich beschwerden – to complain
besuchen – to visit
bezahlen – to pay for
fotografieren – to photograph
Heimweh haben – to be homesick
kosten – to cost
mieten – to hire, to rent
schicken – to send
vermieten – to rent, to let out
warten (auf + Akk) – to wait (for)
wechseln – to change

zahlen – to pay
Zeit verbringen – to spend time
zurück-gehen – to go back, to return
zurück-kehren – to go back, to return

Conversation

AQA	✓
OCR	✓
EDEXCEL	✓
WJEC	✓
CCEA	✓

> **KEY POINT**
>
> Most of the following questions are predictable so make sure you have prepared an answer for each one.

🔊 **Warst du schon einmal in Deutschland?**

🔊 Ich bin letzten Sommer mit dem Schulaustausch nach Deutschland gefahren. Es hat zehn Tage gedauert und wir haben allerlei interessante Dinge gemacht.

🔊 **Und was hast du eigentlich gemacht?**

🔊 Wir waren in Büdingen in Mittelhessen, nicht so weit von Frankfurt und wir haben den Frankfurter Flughafen besucht. Wir sind ins Gebirge gegangen, wo wir ein wenig Klettern versucht haben und wir haben Ausflüge überall in der Büdinger Gegend gemacht.

🔊 **Und gefällt dir Deutschland gut?**

🔊 Ich finde Deutschland und die Deutschen ganz toll, weil das Leben ziemlich ähnlich ist und die Leute sehr gastfreundlich sind.

🔊 **Und wie war das Wetter in Büdingen?**

🔊 Ich würde sagen, es war gemischt, teils sonnig teils regnerisch, wie hier in England.

🔊 **Seid ihr mit dem Flugzeug gereist oder...?**

🔊 Nein, wir hatten einen Reisebus von Lindseytours und wir sind mit der Fähre über den Kanal gereist. In Deutschland haben wir den Reisebus immer gebraucht.

🔊 **Wohin wirst du nächstes Jahr fahren und was wirst du machen?**

🔊 Ich werde noch einmal nach Deutschland fahren aber dieses Mal mit meiner Familie, da meine Austauschpartnerin Steffi und ihr Bruder Markus uns eingeladen haben. Wir werden die Seen besuchen, klettern gehen und meine Eltern werden die berühmte Weinstraße mit Steffis Eltern entdecken!

🔊 **Wie werdet ihr nach Deutschland fahren?**

🔊 Wir werden mit der Fähre und unserem PKW fahren. Hoffentlich werden wir keine Panne haben!

4.3 Grammar

LEARNING SUMMARY	**After studying this section, you should be able to understand:** ● the future tense ● the definite article, indefinite article and adjectival endings

The future tense

AQA	✓
OCR	✓
EDEXCEL	✓
WJEC	✓
CCEA	✓

The future tense is used to say what you will do in the future, e.g. I will go to Germany and I shall stay with friends.

The future is the easiest of all the tenses to form and you will find there are no exceptions. This should give you confidence to use it.

Like in English, German uses a helper (auxiliary) verb + the infinitive to give the idea of the future. English uses 'will' or 'shall' and German uses **werden**.

For example:

> If you know the present tense of 'werden', you can form any future action you want, provided you use the correct vocabulary.

ich werde **reisen**	I will travel
du wirst **übernachten**	you will stay overnight
er/sie/es/man wird **ankommen**	he/she/it/one will arrive
wir werden **abfahren**	we will leave
ihr werdet **fliegen**	you will fly
Sie werden **landen**	you will land
sie werden **warten**	they will wait

KEY POINT

As with the perfect and imperfect tenses, German has one future tense to cover three English ones. For example, **ich werde reisen** = I will travel, I shall travel and I will/shall be travelling.

The definite article, indefinite article and adjectival endings

AQA	✓	
OCR	✓	
EDEXCEL	✓	
WJEC	✓	
CCEA	✓	

When **der, die, das, ein, eine, einige** and adjectives are used in front of nouns, they usually change their endings. This can seem very haphazard and can be very frustrating for students. There is only one way to deal with the difficulty and that is to learn the tables below. Try chanting them out loud, recording them on to your MP3 player and listening back to them, or simply write down the things you find the most difficult.

	Masculine the good father	Feminine the good mother	Neuter the good child	Plural the good children
Nominative	der gute Vater	die gute Mutter	das gute Kind	die guten Kinder
Accusative	den guten Vater	die gute Mutter	das gute Kind	die guten Kinder
Genitive	des guten Vaters	der guten Mutter	des guten Kind(e)s	der guten Kinder
Dative	dem guten Vater	der guten Mutter	dem guten Kind	den guten Kindern

KEY POINT

- In the shaded parts of the table, the adjectival ending is always **-en**. Remember that adjectives never add an ending if they come after the noun.
- Except for in the dative plural, the feminine 'the' word is always **die** or **der**.

	Masculine a good father	Feminine a good mother	Neuter a good child	Plural (some) good children
Nominative	ein guter Vater	eine gute Mutter	ein gutes Kind	einige gute Kinder
Accusative	einen guten Vater	eine gute Mutter	ein gutes Kind	einige gute Kinder
Genitive	eines guten Vaters	einer guten Mutter	eines guten Kind(e)s	einiger guten Kinder
Dative	einem guten Vater	einer guten Mutter	einem guten Kind	einigen guten Kindern

KEY POINT

- In the shaded parts of the table, the adjectival ending is always **-en**.
- In the nominative and accusative singular, the adjectival endings after an **ein** word closely mimic **der, die, das**, etc., i.e.:

der	die	das	den	die	das
guter	gute	gutes	guten	gute	gutes

Sample controlled assessment

Speaking

1 **Track 18** You are discussing last year's holiday with a German friend. Your teacher will play the role of your friend. You could discuss the following:

- What you did for your holidays last year and what you might do next year
- What good and bad experiences you had
- What your reactions were to your last holiday
- If any serious, dramatic, humorous or other interesting events took place
- Why these events may have affected your decision where to go and what to do on your next holidays.

Student: Letzten Sommer hatten[26] meine Familie und ich ein schlechtes[19] Erlebnis während unserer Ferien in der Türkei. Deshalb werden[3] wir diesen August nach Südfrankreich fahren. Mit ein wenig Glück erleben wir nächstes Jahr nicht wieder[12] so eine Katastrophe wie im letzten Urlaub.

Teacher: Es wäre sehr interessant deine Geschichte zu hören.

Student: Wo soll[35] ich denn anfangen![18] Also, beginnen wir mit dem Flughafen in der Türkei. Wir sind aus dem Flugzeug gestiegen[39] und mit dem Bus zur Gepäckhalle gefahren. So weit, so gut. Keine Probleme weder[12] mit der Polizei noch mit den Zollbeamten. Dann haben wir entdeckt,[2] dass meine Schwester, Anita, den falschen Koffer hatte. Als wir zum Ausgabeband zurück gegangen sind,[39] haben wir entdeckt,[2] daß Anitas Koffer verschwunden war.[4] Die Fluglinie hat uns den richtigen Koffer drei Tage später in unser Hotel gebracht.[26]

Teacher: Und was waren die anderen Katastrophen?

Student: Ach ja. Die Busreise zum Hotel war ohne weiteres herrlich. Die Sonne schien,[26] es war[26] sehr warm und die Landschaft und das Meer glänzten[26] so schön,[15] dass die Passagiere sehr guter Laune waren. Als wir im Hotel Hercules angekommen sind hat sich die Laune schnell geändert.

Teacher: Erzähl mir genau, was geschehen ist.

Student: Das Hercules war nicht wirklich ein Hotel, mehr eine Baustelle. Wir hatten[11] kein fließendes Wasser im Badezimmer, eine Fensterscheibe fehlte[9] im Wohnzimmer und wir hatten Insekten in den Betten! Vati hat sich bei der Hotelleitung[23] beschwerdt.[9] Wir haben dann eine andere Wohnung bekommen aber die war schlimmer[21] als die erste!

Teacher: Was habt ihr denn dann gemacht?

Student: Sie kennen meinen Vater nicht! Er hat von Zeit zu Zeit doofe Ideen und dies war einer dieser Zeiten! Er hat ein Zelt gekauft und wir haben während der ganzen Ferien gezeltet.[9] Flexitours haben uns die Kosten erstattet aber unser Urlaub war ruiniert. Aus diesem Grund freue ich mich auf die nächsten Ferien in Frankreich.[6] Es wird[3] so viel besser werden!

Teacher: Das hoffe ich auch!

Turn to page 155 for a translation of this passage.

Examiner's comments

Refer to pages 8–9 to see why this student has improved his or her chances of a high grade:

2 Examples of the past tense

3 Use of the future tense

4 This student has shown a good understanding of word order

6 A justified point of view

9 Impressive vocabulary has been used, e.g. 'fehlte', 'beschwerdt', 'gezeltet'

11 An example of a 'haben' structure

12 Negatives have been used

15 'So' + an adjective

18 An exclamation

19 An example of an adjective

21 A comparative

23 'Bei' + a noun

26 A mix of perfect and imperfect tenses has been used

35 A modal verb ('sollen')

39 Examples of the perfect tense with 'sein'

Sample controlled assessment

Writing

1 Write about a recent holiday. You could…

- say where you went on holiday and in what sort of accommodation you stayed (campsite, hotel, etc.)
- describe what the place was like and how you felt about the people you met
- mention how the weather may have affected your holiday for good or bad
- give details of the things you did to amuse yourself and of the places you visited
- explain what you may do and where you may go for your next holidays.

Ich möchte[35] Ihnen meine Sommerferien in Cornwall beschreiben. Sie haben in der Stadt St Ives stattgefunden[2] und wir haben uns tagein tagaus wirklich gut amüsiert.[26] Dieses Teil von Cornwall hat den Spitznamen, "das Englische Riviera" und dank dem extra schönen Wetter kann[35] ich das verstehen.

Mutti hat zwei Zimmer im Voraus in einem winzigen Gasthof mit Übernachtung und Frühstück reserviert,[2] was eine sehr gute Wahl vom Anfang an schien[4] und das wegen der Freundlichkeit und des Professionalismus der Gastwirtin.[6] Es ist richtig, dass sie uns extrem große Portionen zum Essen gab, aber das war[26] nur eine Seite ihrer Gastfreundlichkeit. Sie war nie zu beschäftigt, um[8] den Gästen zu helfen. Als, zum Beispiel, einer der Gäste eine Reifenpanne hatte, hat sie das Gasthof verlassen[2] und ihm[28] den Reifen gewechselt!

Wir hatten[11] so viel Glück während dieser Ferien, meistens dank dem fantastischen[19] Wetter! Die Sonne schien[26] so oft und das Meer war so blau, dass ich kapiert habe,[4/6] warum es so viele Maler und Malerinnen in diesem Teil von Cornwall sind. Während des Tages haben wir die ganze Zeit am Strand verbracht,[26] wo[7] wir uns gebadet und gesonnt haben.[2]

Am Abend war es ganz anders, da wir eine Disko am Ende des Piers gefunden haben, wo wir stundenlang tanzten[26] und wir uns neue Freunde gemacht haben,[4] insbesondere Maxi und Maria, mit denen ich regelmäßig[9] telefonisch und durch das Internet korrespondiere.

Nächstes Jahr werden wir[3] alle drei nach Spanien ohne die Eltern fahren und wir werden[3] ohne weiteres uns gut amüsieren, weil[5] wir uns so gut verstehen.[6] Für diese Gelegenheit bin ich Mutti und Vati sehr dankbar, weil[5] sie so verständnisvoll gewesen sind.[39] Viele Eltern würden mir den Besuch verboten haben. Ich kann Ihnen nicht erklären, wie viel ich mich auf diesen Urlaub schon freue! Dafür lerne ich schon ein wenig Spanisch und hoffentlich werde ich genug sprechen können, um[8] mich verständlich zu machen. Es interessiert mich nicht,[12] Englisch im Ausland zu schreien, damit ich etwas bekommen kann.

Turn to page 155 for a translation of this passage.

Examiner's comments

Choosing a controlled writing assessment on holidays may well be to your advantage, since it gives you the chance to mix actual events and imagination. Remember, you can invent details in your writing or speaking controlled assessment, so do not be afraid to think up some colourful details that might not have happened.

This student has used a good number of the '40 points for improving your grade' from pages 8–9:

2	The past tense has been used
3	The future tense has been used
4	This student has displayed a good understanding of word order
5	'Weil' has been used
6	Several justified points of view
7	'Wo' is a good connecting word
8	'Um…zu' structures
9	Impressive vocabulary has been used
11	Just one of many examples of a 'haben' structure in this piece
12	A negative
19	An example of an adjective
26	A mix of perfect and imperfect tenses has been used
28	A personal pronoun has been used
35	Modal verbs have been used ('mögen', 'können')
39	The perfect tense has been used with 'sein'

Exam practice questions

Listening

1 🔘 **Track 19** You are at an airport departure lounge in Germany and the information screens are down. You hear the following announcement.

(a) Give the number, gate and time of the flight to Heathrow.

    (i) Number ....

    (ii) Gate ....

    (iii) Time .... **(3)**

(b) Which services are available on your plane? Tick **two** boxes.

    A An evening meal for an additional payment ☐
       for economy-class passengers

    B An upgrade to first class ☐

    C Recliner seats in business class ☐

    D A complimentary meal with champagne for ☐
       first-class passengers **(2)**

2 🔘 **Track 20** You are in Switzerland, queuing outside a theatre to buy tickets for a concert by the group *Die Prinzen*. You hear the following announcement.

(a) For which days are there still tickets? .... **(2)**

(b) At what prices are the tickets? .... **(2)**

(c) **(i)** What can you do if you come tomorrow afternoon?

       .... **(1)**

    (ii) What will you have the chance to do?

       .... **(1)**

3 🔘 **Track 21** A woman is answering questions about her holiday in Austria. Tick the correct box in each case.

(a)

    Favourable ☐

    Unfavourable ☐

(b)

    Favourable ☐

    Unfavourable ☐

Exam practice questions

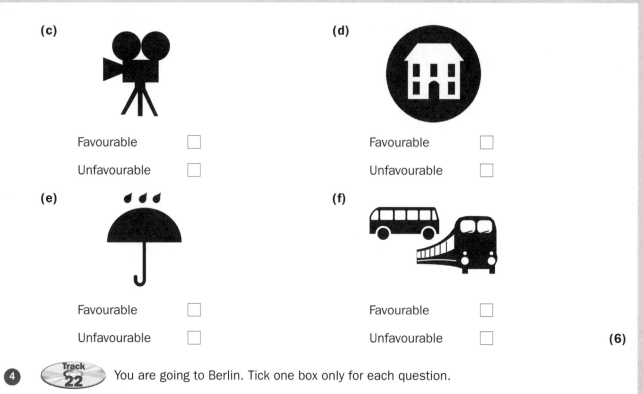

(c)

Favourable ☐

Unfavourable ☐

(d)

Favourable ☐

Unfavourable ☐

(e)

Favourable ☐

Unfavourable ☐

(f)

Favourable ☐

Unfavourable ☐

(6)

4 Track 22 You are going to Berlin. Tick one box only for each question.

(a) You ask what time your train will reach Berlin.

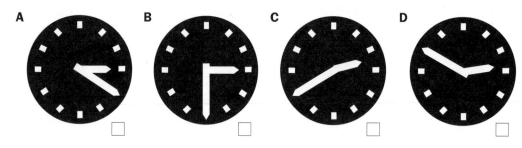

A ☐   B ☐   C ☐   D ☐

(b) You go to a hotel. How much is a room?

A €24 ☐   B €34 ☐   C €42 ☐   D €50 ☐

(c) What is your room like ?

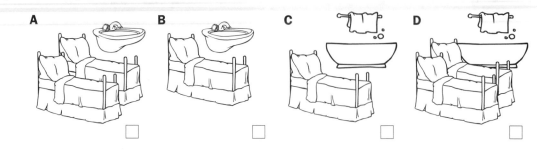

A ☐   B ☐   C ☐   D ☐

Exam practice questions

(d) How should you go to the town centre?

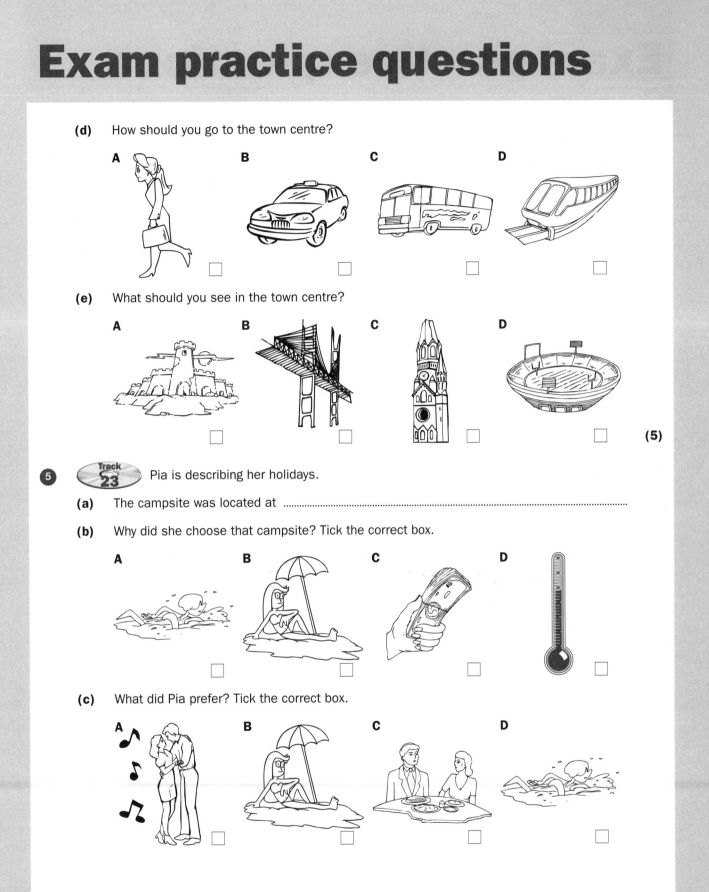

A   B   C   D

(e) What should you see in the town centre?

A   B   C   D

(5)

5 **Track 23** Pia is describing her holidays.

(a) The campsite was located at ....

(b) Why did she choose that campsite? Tick the correct box.

A   B   C   D

(c) What did Pia prefer? Tick the correct box.

A   B   C   D

Exam practice questions

(d) How did she get there? Tick the correct box.

A   B   C   D

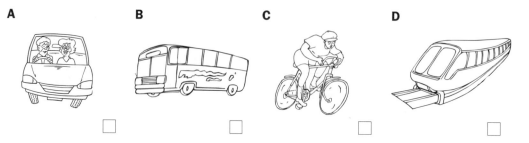

☐   ☐   ☐   ☐

(e) What was the weather like? Tick the correct box.

A   B   C   D

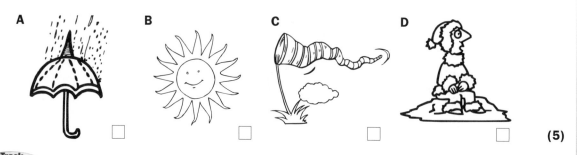

☐   ☐   ☐   ☐   **(5)**

6 **Track 24** A father and a mother are discussing the forthcoming trip of their twin children, Franki and Udi, to Switzerland. Tick the correct boxes to show which person is expressing each opinion.

		The mother	The father
(a)	Udi cannot organise himself.	☐	☐
(b)	Franki is not much better.	☐	☐
(c)	It is too far for Franki to drive.	☐	☐
(d)	Udi cannot read road maps.	☐	☐
(e)	It would be safer by plane.	☐	☐
(f)	They would see more by train.	☐	☐
(g)	Youth hostelling is not a good idea.	☐	☐
(h)	A hotel might be safer.	☐	☐
(i)	Bed and breakfast would be cheaper.	☐	☐
(j)	The twins are 18 and should decide for themselves.	☐	☐

(10)

Exam practice questions

7 **Track 25** Listen to this radio advertisement for the Europapaß and answer the following questions. Write the answers in English.

(a) What exactly is the Europapaß? .... **(1)**

(b) How much does it cost? .... **(1)**

(c) How much can the Europapaß save you? .... **(1)**

(d) Which towns can you visit with it? .... **(1)**

(e) What two facilities may be available for a supplement?

    (i) ....

    (ii) .... **(2)**

(f) When can you not travel? Give two time periods.

    (i) .... **(ii)** .... **(2)**

(g) To which age group does the Europapaß apply? .... **(1)**

(h) What two proofs of identity are required?

    (i) .... **(ii)** .... **(2)**

8 **Track 26** A group of German students is spending a few days in London, courtesy of Boreham Films. They are being tested for possible roles in an Anglo-German thriller, which is set in London. Listen to these short extracts from a series of interviews for German radio. Then, after each name, write the letter of the matching statement. The students speak in the order given.

(a) Jutta ....

(b) Karl ....

(c) Farida ....

(d) Michael ....

(e) Thea ....

A Totally impressed by the sights and very keen

B Keen, but doubts own ability

C Not right for the film, finds London boring

D Would do well, as (s)he likes Londoners

E A natural for the leading role

F The pollution has aggravated his or her asthma, so they must go home

Exam practice questions

9 🔲 **Track 27** Listen to these conversations about the summer holidays. Tick the correct boxes.

Conversation 1

(a) How will Sophie spend her summer holidays?

   A   At university in the United States   ☐

   B   At home, saving money for her studies   ☐

   C   Working at a *Spar* general store   ☐   **(1)**

(b) As far as The Bahamas are concerned, Heine is going to...

   A   forget those islands and go to Africa   ☐

   B   buy a black tent   ☐

   C   go camping   ☐   **(1)**

Conversation 2

(c) How does Willi answer Helga about the holidays?

   A   They cannot go, as his car has broken down   ☐

   B   They cannot go until the car is repaired   ☐

   C   He has to buy some new tyres first   ☐   **(1)**

(d) How does Willi reply to Helga's good idea?

   A   They need a new car   ☐

   B   He would like to go to Berlin in her car   ☐

   C   They can go in her car, but not to Berlin   ☐   **(1)**

Conversation 3

Hanna has had trouble getting her friends, Thea, Wolf and Peter, to make up their minds about the holidays. So, she has put together a short questionnaire for them. Listen to their conversation and tick the boxes to show where each of the four friends would like to go on holiday and how they would like to travel. Tick two boxes for each person.

	Fähre	Flugzeug	Zug	Schottland	Spanien	Amerika	
(e) Thea	☐	☐	☐	☐	☐	☐	**(2)**
(f) Wolf	☐	☐	☐	☐	☐	☐	**(2)**
(g) Peter	☐	☐	☐	☐	☐	☐	**(2)**
(h) Hanna	☐	☐	☐	☐	☐	☐	**(2)**

Exam practice questions

Reading

1 Read the e-mail message below.

> Ich danke Ihnen für Ihre E-Mail. Glücklicherweise haben wir einige Zimmer frei für die Periode,
> die Sie wünschen. Könnten Sie mir bitte am schnellsten mailen, da ich auch wissen sollte, was
> für Zimmer Sie brauchen. Raucher oder Nichtraucher? Einzelzimmer? Familienzimmer? usw.
> Das Hotel selbst liegt ganz in der Mitte der Stadt am Rande des Marktplatzes. Sie werden eine
> bessere Idee bekommen, wenn Sie unsere Website besuchen. Sie werden die Siteadresse
> unten finden.
> Mit besten Wünschen und aufs baldigste!
> Hans Haverkamp (Inhaber)

Choose the appropriate words from the box below to complete the sentences that follow.

brauchen	besuchen	schnell	langsam	Rande	Marktplatz
Webseite	frei	besetzt	Website	telefonieren	braucht

(a) Es gibt Zimmer, die .... sind.

(b) Man sollte Herrn Haverkamp eine E-Mail so .... wie möglich senden.

(c) Der Besitzer muss wissen, ob man Zimmer für Raucher oder Nichtraucher... .

(d) Das Hotel ist mehr oder minder im ....

(e) Es wäre eine gute Idee, die .... zu besuchen. **(5)**

2 You and your family are driving through Switzerland by car. Answer the following questions about signs you see.

Which sign would you be most likely to see if you had just…

(a) entered the outskirts of a village?

....

(b) entered a pay car park?

....

(c) entered a pedestrianised town centre?

....

(d) entered a car park reserved for disabled drivers?

....

(e) accidentally entered a police car park?

....

A
> Fußgängerzone
> Wagen strengst verboten!

B
> Parkplatz
> gebührenpflichtig
> zwischen 8h00–19h00

C
> Tempo 40 !
> Bitte, vergessen Sie
> nicht unsere Kinder!

D
> Keinen Eingang
> für unbefugte Personen

E
> Parkplatz
> gebührenfrei und nur
> für Behinderte

Exam practice questions

3 Read the e-mail message below, then answer the questions that follow in English.

> Sam
>
> Ich habe eine gute Nachricht für dich und für mich! Meine Tante Doro hat ein Restaurant in der Kieler Gegend und das Meer ist nur einige Kilometer entfernt. Tante Doro lädt uns ein, zwei bis drei Wochen bei ihr zu verbringen. Die Arbeit ist nicht so interessant: abspülen, Tische decken, Bier und Wein aus dem Keller bringen, aber Tante wird uns neun Euros pro Stunde zahlen! Kiel ist sehr lebendig und wir können mit meinem Onkel Udo segeln gehen. Auch sind die Niederlande und Polen nicht so weit entfernt und wir könnten sie besuchen. Was meinst du?
>
> Petra

(a) Why has Petra got in contact? .... **(1)**

(b) What do we learn about the Kiel area? Give two details.

    (i) ....

    (ii) .... **(2)**

(c) What has Aunt Doro invited them to do?

    .... **(2)**

(d) Give four details about the work.

    (i) ....

    (ii) ....

    (iii) ....

    (iv) .... **(4)**

(e) What do we learn about Kiel? Give two details.

    (i) ....

    (ii) .... **(2)**

(f) Which two other countries could they visit?

    (i) ....

    (ii) .... **(2)**

Exam practice questions

 4   Read these hotel advertisements.

A

Hotel Sylt

Willkommen in Ostfresien!

- Regionale Hauptgerichte
- Spielsaal
- Kegelbahn
- Englisch gesprochen

B

Hotel Barbarossa

echt Mittelalterliche Küche

Mittelalterliche Schlafzimmer

Personal historisch gekleidet

Historische Fernsehkanäle

Konferenzen über die deutsche Geschichte

C

MARTHAS ZWEITES ZUHAUSE

- Übernachtung mit Frühstuck oder längere Aufenthalte
- Englisches Fernsehen
- Häuslicher Komfort
- Häusliche Küche
- Offen das ganze Jahr

D

Das Hotel am Strand

Große Parkplatz

Im Meer im Nu!

38 Zimmer mit allem modernen Komfort

Bootausflüge

Meeresfrüchte im Fischrestaurant

Write the letter of the best hotel to stay at if you...

(a)   like home cooking.   ....

(b)   are very interested in history.   ....

(c)   speak no German.   ....

(d)   love seafood.   ....

(e)   like bowling.   ....

(f)   want to be right next to the sea.   ....

(g)   like the staff to be in fancy dress.   ....

(h)   want something that is probably less expensive.   ....

                                                                 (8)

5 Home, local area and environment

The following topics are covered in this chapter:

- Special occasions
- Home and local area
- The environment
- Grammar

5.1 Special occasions

LEARNING SUMMARY

After studying this section, you should be able to:

- describe different special occasions
- say how you celebrate special occasions

Special occasions

AQA	✓
OCR	✓
EDEXCEL	✓
WJEC	✓
CCEA	✓

You need to study the vocabulary and learn the German for special occasions like Christmas and Easter. These may well appear in your listening and reading exams. Special occasions prove to be a popular choice for the controlled writing or speaking assessments, since they allow you to write or speak enthusiastically about events with which you are very familiar.

Celebrations (Feiern)

Aid – Eid

Zum chinesischen Neuen Jahr – Chinese New Year

danken (+Dat) – to thank

Diwali – Diwali

der erste Weihnachtsfeiertag – Christmas Day

der Feiertag (-e) – bank holiday

Ein glückliches Neues Jahr! – Happy New Year!

Hannouka – Hanukkah

der Heiligabend – Christmas Eve

Herzlichen Glückwunsch
    zum Geburtstag! – Happy birthday!
    zum Jahrestag! – Happy anniversary!

die Hochzeit – wedding, marriage

der Jahrestag (-e) – anniversary

der Karfreitag – Good Friday

das Neujahr – New Year

der Neujahrsabend – New Year's Eve

der Neujahrstag – New Year's Day

das Osterei (-er) – Easter egg

(zu) Ostern – (at) Easter

der Ostersonntag – Easter Day

der Ramadan – Ramadan

schenken – to give (a present)

der/das Silvester – New Year's Eve

Frohe Weihnachten! – Happy Christmas!

das Weihnachtsgeschenk (-e) – Christmas present

der Weihnachtsmann – Father Christmas

der zweite Weihnachtsfeiertag – Boxing Day

Conversation starters

Zu Weihnachten	senden wir...	– we send...
Am Neujahrstag	schicken wir...	– we send...
Für Aid	singen wir...	– we sing...
Zu Diwali	tanzen wir...	– we dance...
Am Ende des Ramadans	essen wir...	– we eat...
zu Hannouka	trinken wir...	– we drink...
Zum chinesischen Neuen Jahr	beleuchten wir...	– we light...
	wünschen wir...	– we wish...
	feiern wir...	– we celebrate...
	fasten wir...	– we fast...
	versprechen wir...	– we promise...
	geben wir...	– we give...

Useful phrases

Wir kaufen Geschenke.

We buy presents.

Wir senden/schicken Karten.

We send cards.

Wir schmücken den Weihnachtsbaum.

We decorate the Christmas tree.

Wir essen (zu) viel.

We eat a lot (too much).

Man bekommt Karten und Geschenke.

We receive cards and presents.

Wir gehen zur Kirche, um das Christkind zu begrüßen.

We go to church, to welcome Baby Jesus.

Es gibt einen Umzug um die Kirche/Stadt.

There is a procession around the church/town.

> **KEY POINT**
>
> Notice how in most of the German sentences below, **man** is used to give the idea of the passive. It is probably easier for you to think of the translation as 'one arranges', 'one puts up', etc., even though this sounds rather formal in English.

Man veranstaltet einen Ball.

A ball is arranged.

Geschenke werden angeboten.

Presents are offered.

Man beleuchtet das Haus.

Lights are put up outside.

Man ißt Süßigkeiten.

Sweet things are eaten.

Man beleuchtet Kerzen.

Candles are lit.

Man spielt Spiele.

Games are played.

Man ißt Pfannkuchen und Berliner.

Pancakes and doughnuts are eaten.

Wir veranstalten eine Party.

We arrange a party.

Wir gehen sehr spät ins Bett.

We go to bed very late.

PROGRESS CHECK

Say or write the following in German:

1. There is a procession around the town.
2. We decorate the Christmas tree.
3. I went to bed very late.
4. We ate too much.
5. Presents are offered.
6. I bought no presents.

1. Es gibt einen Umzug um die Stadt.
2. Wir schmücken den Weihnachtsbaum.
3. Ich bin sehr spät ins Bett gegangen.
4. Wir haben zu viel gegessen.
5. Geschenke werden angeboten.
6. Ich habe keine Geschenke gekauft.

5.2 Home and local area

LEARNING SUMMARY

After studying this section, you should be able to:

- describe your home
- say what you do at home
- talk about your town, neighbourhood and region
- give and understand directions
- describe the weather and understand a weather forecast

Home

AQA	✓
OCR	✓
EDEXCEL	X
WJEC	✓
CCEA	✓

In your controlled speaking assessment, you may talk for a minute or two about your home, describing the rooms and the garden. You may talk in the perfect tense about what you did at home and in the future tense about what you will do there. A popular choice for the controlled writing or speaking assessment is to describe your ideal home. The following vocabulary will also help you in the listening and reading exams.

Around the home (Zu Hause)

die Badewanne (-n) – bathtub

das Badezimmer (-) – bathroom

mit Blick auf das Land – overlooking the countryside

der Briefkasten (-) – letterbox

das Büro – study

der Dachboden (ö) – attic, loft

die Diele (-n) – hall

das Doppelhaus – semi-detached house

die Dusche (-n) – shower

das Einfamilienhaus – detached house

das Esszimmer – dining room

die Garage (-n) – (home) garage

der Keller (-) – basement, cellar

das Kinderzimmer (-) – playroom

das Klo – toilet, loo

die Lampe (-n) – lamp

das Reihenhaus – terraced house

das Schlafzimmer (-) – bedroom

die Strasse (-n) – street

die Terrasse (-n) – patio, terrace

die Toilette (-n) – toilet

das Treppenhaus – staircase

der Wintergarten – conservatory

die Wohnung (-en) – flat, apartment

das Wohnzimmer (-) – lounge, living room

die Lampe

Adjectives

baufällig – dilapidated
bequem – comfortable
elektrisch – electric(al)
klar – clear, light
malerisch – picturesque
modern – modern

(nagel) neu – (brand) new
typisch (für) – typical (of)
ungeheuer – massive, gigantic
weit abgelegen – off the beaten track
winzig – tiny

Verbs

ab-spülen – to do the washing-up
ab-trocknen – to do the drying-up
auf-räumen – to tidy up
das Bett machen – to make the bed
faulenzen – to laze around
im Garten arbeiten – to do
 the gardening
die Hausarbeit machen – to do
 the housework
helfen (+Dat) – to help

den Hund spazieren führen – to walk
 the dog
die Pflanzen gießen – to water
 the plants
putzen – to polish
reinigen – to clean
schälen – to peel
staub-saugen – to hoover
den Tisch abräumen – to clear the table
den Tisch decken – to lay the table
den Wagen waschen – to wash the car

das Bett machen

den Hund spazieren führen

The living room (Das Wohnzimmer)

das Bild (-er) – picture
der Couchtisch (-e) – coffee table
der Fernseher (-) – TV set
die Gardine (-n) – net curtain
das Gemälde (-) – painting
der Kamin (-e) – fireplace
das Kissen (-) – cushion
der Schrank (¨e) – cupboard

der Sessel (-) – easy chair
das Sofa (-s) – sofa, settee
die Stereoanlage (-n) – stereo system
der Teppich (-e) – rug, carpet
der Teppichboden (¨) – fitted carpet
die Treppe – (flight of) stairs
der Vorhang (¨e) – curtain

The bedroom (Das Schlafzimmer)

das Bett (-en) – bed
der Föhn (-e) – hairdryer
der Kleiderschrank (¨e) – wardrobe
die Kommode (-n) – chest of drawers
das Kopfkissen (-) – pillow

die Lampe (-n) – lamp
der/die Poster (-) – poster
der Radiowecker (-) – radio alarm
der Schreibtisch (-e) – desk
der Stuhl (¨e) – chair

die Zahnbürste

The bathroom (Das Badezimmer)

das Badetuch (¨er) – bath towel
die Badewanne (-n) – bathtub
die Dusche (-n) – shower
das Duschgel – shower gel
die Haarbürste (-n) – hairbrush
die Schere (-n) – scissors
die Seife (-n) – soap

das Shampoo (-s) – shampoo
der Spiegel (-) – mirror
das Waschbecken (-) – wash basin
das Waschtuch (¨er) – flannel
die Zahnbürste (-n) – toothbrush
die Zahnpasta – toothpaste

The kitchen (Die Küche)

der Elektroherd (-e) – electric cooker
der Gasherd (-e) – gas cooker
kochen – to cook
der Kessel (-) – kettle
der Kühlschrank (¨e) – fridge
der Mikrowellenherd (-e) – microwave
   (oven)
der Schnellkochtopf (¨e) – pressure
   cooker

der Schrank (¨e) – cupboard
die Schublade (-n) – drawer
das Spülbecken (-) – sink
die Spülmaschine (-n) – dishwasher
die Tiefkühltruhe (-n) – freezer
der Toaster (-) – toaster
der Topf (¨e) – saucepan
die Waschmaschine (-n) – washing
   machine

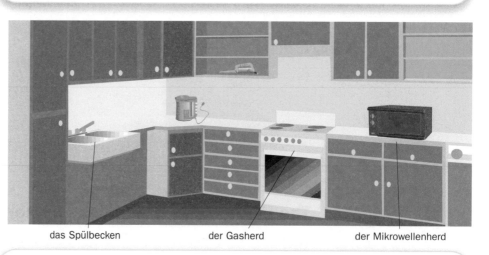

das Spülbecken   der Gasherd   der Mikrowellenherd

The garden (Der Garten)

die Bank (¨e) – bench
der Baum (¨e) – tree
die Blume (-n) – flower
das Blumenbeet – flower bed
die Gartenarbeit – gardening
das Gras (¨er) – grass
die Hängematte (-n) – hammock

die Hecke (-n) – hedge
mähen – to mow
die Pflanze (-n) – plant
der Rasen (-) – lawn
der Rasenmäher (-) – lawnmower
die Schaukel (-n) – swing
der Schubkarren (-) – wheelbarrow

der Baum   die Blume   der Rasenmäher

putzen

The housework (Die Hausarbeit)

auf-räumen – to tidy up

putzen – to dust

reinigen – to clean

das Seifenpulver – soap powder

der Staub – dust

der Staubsauger – vacuum cleaner

die Wäsche – washing

PROGRESS CHECK

Say or write the following in German:

1. I don't laze around at home
2. I like cooking, when I can.
3. Yesterday, I took the dog for a walk.
4. On Sunday, I shall mow the lawn.
5. I have tidied my room.
6. I always wash up!

1. Ich faulenze nicht zu Hause.
2. Ich koche gern, wenn (so oft) ich kann.
3. Gestern habe ich den Hund spazieren geführt.
4. Am Sonntag werde ich den Rasen mähen.
5. Ich habe mein Zimmer aufgeräumt.
6. Ich spüle immer ab!

Conversation: Grades G–D

AQA	✓
OCR	✓
EDEXCEL	✗
WJEC	✓
CCEA	✓

If you can answer these questions without thinking it will help you to do well in the controlled speaking assessment. The longer your answers are, the more marks you will get. If you give very short answers or answers without a verb, you will not get the marks you hope for.

🗩 **Wohnst du in einem Haus oder einer Wohnung?**

🗩 Ich wohne in einem Haus.

🗩 **Wie ist denn dein Haus?**

🗩 Sie ist angenehm und bequem.

🗩 **Wie weit von der Schule liegt dein Zuhause?**

🗩 Es ist ein Kilometer entfernt vom College.

🗩 **Wieviele Zimmer gibt es?**

🗩 Es gibt sieben.[1]

🗩 **Was siehst du aus dem Fenster in deinem Schlafzimmer?**

🗩 Ich sehe die Gebäude auf der Straße und ein bisschen weiter die Hügel.[2]

🗩 **Was gibt es im Garten?**

🗩 Es gibt Bäume und Blumen.

🗩 **Was hast du in deinem Schlafzimmer?**

🗩 Es gibt ein Bett, einen Tisch und einen Kleiderschrank.

1. You would get more marks if you named some or all of the rooms.

2. You could add details such as 'Häuser und Geschäfte', 'Wagen und Kraftwagen.... und die Autobahn in der Ferne'.

Conversation: Grades C–A*

AQA	✓
OCR	✓
EDEXCEL	✗
WJEC	✓
CCEA	✓

The conversation below is a very confident performance and the candidate has used a large amount of the vocabulary from this chapter. They have produced something lively that is not beyond your reach, so try to do the same.

Remember to…

- use long sentences
- give opinions
- justify your opinions
- use, past, present and future tenses
- ask the teacher a question!

🗣 **Beschreib dein Zuhause.**

🗣 **Mein Haus ist sehr schön und bequem. Es gibt drei Schlafzimmer, ein Wohnzimmer, ein Arbeitszimmer, eine Küche, eine Wäscherei und neulich haben wir einen Wintergarten gebaut.[1]**

🗣 **Und wie ist dein Zimmer?**

🗣 **Mein Schlafzimmer ist äußerst bequem. Ich habe die normalen Dingen da drinnen aber das Beste ist, die Fenster haben Blick auf das Land.[2] Ich verbringe viel Zeit in meinem Zimmer, weil es meine persönliche Insel ist.[3]**

🗣 **Was machst du in deinem Zimmer?**

🗣 **Letztes Wochenende hatte ich eine Party da, und wir haben viel Spaß gemacht aber das ist nicht normal.[4] Normalerweise, mache ich meine Hausaufgaben da, um ein wenig Stille zu haben. Wissen Sie wie es ist, wenn man jüngere Geschwister hat?[5]**

🗣 **Was hast du gestern abend zu Hause gemacht?**

🗣 **Zuerst habe ich meine Hausaufgaben fertiggemacht. Dann habe ich einen Eintopf für die Familie gekocht. Das ist meine Spezialität und sehr leicht zu machen! Später habe ich gelesen und ein wenig ferngesehen. Ach, tja, ich habe eine ganze Stunde am Telefon geplaudert. Vati war gar nicht zufrieden![6]**

🗣 **Und heute abend was wirst du zu Hause machen?**

🗣 **Kein Kochen, das ist sicher! Ich habe zu viele Hausaufgaben und was sein muss, muss sein![7] Also, ich werde drei Stunden arbeiten und dann werde ich joggen. Meine Freundin wird auch mitkommen.[8] Sie wohnt ganz nebenan.**

🗣 **Liebst du dein Zuhause?**

🗣 **Ohne weiteres![9] Es ist mein Lieblingsort, nicht nur weil ich meine Familie mag, aber weil wir auch einen schönen Garten haben und die Nachbarn sind sehr, sehr freundlich.[10]**

🗣 **Beschreib mir deinen Garten.**

🗣 **Wie gesagt, bin ich gern im Garten und ich mache viele Gartenarbeit. Dieses Wochenende, zum Beispiel, werde ich den Rasen mähen, da er ziemlich groß ist und zu anstrengend für meinen Vater![11] Wir haben, wie Sie wissen, einen hübschen Wintergarten mit vielen Pflanzen und eine winzige Bank nebenan, wo ich gern lese. Diesen Sommer werde ich mein ganzes Lesen für die GCSEs da machen, wenn wir schönes Wetter kriegen.**

1 The candidate gives a lot of detail and manages to work in a perfect tense. You can follow this example.

2 The candidate has managed to avoid the usual list, choosing to give some personal details instead.

3 A subordinate clause has been used to explain a personal idea/feeling.

4 The past tense has been used already. A major requirement is out of the way.

5 The candidate has asked a question with a touch of gentle humour!

6 Notice the liveliness of the answer and yet the candidate uses simple language to do it.

7 Use of a standard proverb.

8 Two confident uses of the future tense.

9 Several exclamations show that the candidate is confident and able to use humour and irony appropriately. Again, you can follow this example.

10 Two clearly expressed justifications, using subordinate clauses.

11 Enough future tenses have been used.

Town, neighbourhood and region

AQA ✓
OCR ✓
EDEXCEL ✓
WJEC ✓
CCEA ✓

In your controlled speaking assessment, you may find that you are asked to describe your town or region, or you may be asked questions about your local area. Weather is often examined in the listening and reading exams.

The environment (Die Umgebung/Die Umwelt)

der Berg (-e) – mountain
das Dorf (¨er) – village
der Fluss (¨e) – river
das Flussufer (-) – riverside
Förster (in) – forester, m/f
die Gegend (-en) – district, region
die Grosstadt (¨e) – city
der Hügel (-) – hill

hügelig – hilly
das Land (¨er) – country (countryside)
die See (-n) – lake
die Stadt (¨e) – town
der Wald (¨er) – wood, forest
der Weg (-e) – path, way

der Weg   der Berg   der Fluss

Animals (Tiere)

der Frosch (¨e) – frog
das Huhn (¨er) – chicken
das Insekt (-en) – insect, bug
die Kuh (-e) – cow

das Pferd (-e) – horse
das Schwein (-e) – pig
der Stier (-e) – bull
der Vogel (ö) – bird

das Pferd   der Vogel   das Schwein

Colours (Farben)

blau – blue
braun – brown
bunt – bright
dunkel – dark
gelb – yellow

grau – grey
grün – green
hell – pale
rosa – pink
rot – red

rötlichbraun – auburn
schwarz – black
türkis – turquoise
weiß – white

Compass points and directions (Himmelsrichtungen und andere Richtungen)

Nord – North
im Norden – in the North
Ost – East
im Osten – in the East
Süd – South
im Süden – in the South
West – West
im Westen – in the West

da – there
daher – from there
dahin – to there
dort – there
dorther – from there

dorthin – to there
entfernt von – far (away) from
gegenüber – opposite
geradeaus – straight on
hier – here
hierher – from here
links – (on/to the) left
neben (+Dat) – near
oben – above, upstairs
rechts – (on/to the) right
unten – below, downstairs
Wie komme ich am besten zu...? –
How do I get to...?

Adjectives

altmodisch – old fashioned
bequem – comfortable
ehemalig – former
futuristisch – futuristic
gesund – healthy
modern – modern

negativ – negative
(nagel) neu – (brand) new
positiv – positive
schädlich (für) – damaging (to)
(un)typisch (für) – (un)typical (of)

die Wolken

der Regen

das Gewitter

The weather (Das Wetter)

der Blitz (-e) – lightning, flash
of lightning
der Donner – thunder
das Eis – ice
gemischt – mixed
das Gewitter (-) – thunderstorm
(20) Grad – (20) degrees
der Himmel – sky, heavens
die Hitze – heat
das Klima – climate
kühl – cool
nass – wet
der Nebel (-) – fog, mist

der Regen – rain
der Schauer (-) – shower
der Schnee – snow
die Sonne – sun
ständig – unbroken
der Sturm (¨e) – storm
die Temperatur (-en) – temperature
warm – warm
der Wetterbericht (-e) – weather report
die Wettervorhersage (-n) – weather
forecast
der Wind (-e) – wind
die Wolke (-n) – cloud

Weather verbs

es friert – it is freezing
es ist kalt – it is cold
es ist nebelig – it is foggy
es nieselt – it is drizzling
es regnet – it is raining
es schneit – it is snowing

die Sonne scheint – the sun is shining
es ist sonnig – it is sunny
es taut – it is thawing
es ist warm – it is warm
es ist windig – it is windy
es ist wolkig – it is cloudy

In the street (Auf der Straße)

der Fußgängerüberweg

die Ampel (-n) – traffic lights
der Bürgersteig (-e) – pavement
die Ecke (-n) – corner
Fußgänger (in) – pedestrian, m/f
der Fußgängerüberweg – pedestrian crossing
die Kreuzung – crossroads
der Lärm – noise
lärmend – noisy (people)

laut – noisy (environment)
Passant (in) – passerby, m/f
die Schlange (-n) – queue
Schlange stehen – to queue
die Stadtmitte – town centre
das Stadtzentrum – town centre
der Stau (-s) – tail-back
die Straße (-n) – street, road
der Verkehr (-) – traffic

In town (In der Stadt)

der Springbrunnen

die Brücke (-n) – bridge
Einwohner (in) – inhabitant, m/f
das Hallenbad (¨er) – indoor swimming baths
die Industrie (-n) – industry
der Park (-s) – park
das Parkhaus – multi-storey car park
der Parkplatz (¨e) – car park
der Platz (¨e) – square

die Sackgasse (-n) – cul-de-sac
das Schwimmbad (¨er) – swimming baths
der Springbrunnen (-) – fountain
der Stadtplan (¨e) – street map
am Stadtrand – in the suburbs
der Turm (¨e) – tower
das Viertel (-) – town district
der Vorort (-e) – suburb

Buildings (Gebäude)

die Bibliothek (-en) – library
der Dom (¨e) – cathedral
das Einkaufszentrum (-ren) – shopping centre
das Fremdenverkehrsamt – tourist office
das Gebäude (-) – building
die Kirche (-n) – church
die Klinik (-en) – clinic, hospital
das Krankenhaus (¨er) – hospital

die Moschee (-n) – mosque
das Museum (-een) – museum
die Polizeiwache (-n) – police station
das Rathaus (¨er) – town hall
das Schloß (Schlösser) – castle
das Sportstadion (-ien) – sports stadium
die Synagoge (-n) – synagogue
der Wohnblock (¨e) – block of flats

Conversation: Grades G–D

AQA	✓
OCR	✓
EDEXCEL	✓
WJEC	✓
CCEA	✓

🔊 **Was für interessante Orte gibt es in der Gegend?**

🔊 Es gibt einen alten Dom, das Sportstadion, gute Geschäfte, das Museum, das Theater, das Rathaus, und drei Parks.

🔊 **In welcher Entfernung vom Gebirge befindet sich Ihr Zuhause?**

🔊 Mein Zuhause ist fünfzig Kilometer entfernt vom Gebirge.

🔊 **Wieviele Leute wohnen in Ihrer Stadt/Ihrem Dorf?**

🔊 Es gibt fünfundzwanzigtausend Einwohner.

🔊 **Was kann man für junge Leute finden?**

🔊 Es gibt zwei Kinos viele Sportklubs, einen Jugendklub und eine Kegelbahn.

> There are only two verbs used here, 'ist' and 'es gibt'. This is why the conversation cannot achieve above a grade D.

Conversation: Grades C–A*

AQA	✓
OCR	✓
EDEXCEL	✓
WJEC	✓
CCEA	✓

🔊 **Wie ist das Wetter?**

🔊 Heute hat man schönes Wetter. Die Sonne scheint.

🔊 **Und wie war das Wetter gestern?**

🔊 Es war nebelig und es hat geregnet.

🔊 **Wie wird das Wetter morgen sein?**

🔊 Laut dem Wetterbericht werden wir gemischtes Wetter haben. Bis Mittag wird es nass sein, dann am Nachmittag wird die Sonne wiederkommen.

🔊 **Beschreib deine Stadt/deine Gegend. Gefällt sie dir oder?**

🔊 Ich habe meine Gegend ziemlich gern aber es gibt Nachteile.[1] Das Positive wäre, die Gegend ist immer sehr ruhig gewesen, anders gesagt, die Stadt, selbst, ist schön und ordentlich ohne zu viel Verbrechen. Man kann Spaziergänge innerhalb und ausserhalb der Stadt machen und interessante Orte besuchen.

> 1 The candidate has justified their opinion.

🔊 **Deine Gegend, wo genau befindet sie sich?**

🔊 Sie befindet sich in Nordengland nicht so weit von Sheffield neben der Peak District, einer kleineren Fassung von der Lake District. Unheimlich schön.

🔊 **Hast du sie schon besucht?**

🔊 Hab' ich schon!

🔊 **In deiner Stadt, was sind die interessanten Gebäude?**

🔊 Das Stahlmuseum, das Rathaus und das Theater würden Sie interessieren aber ich würde den Kanal empfehlen. Er ist nicht ein Gebäude, aber da kann man so viel industrielle Geschichte sehen.

🔊 **Und wo bist du geboren? In dieser Gegend?[2]**

🔊 Leider, nein! Mein Geschwister, ja. Aber ich bin in Glasgow in Schottland geboren.

🔊 **Wo wirst du in der Zukunft wohnen?[3]**

🔊 Das wird von meiner Karriere abhängen. Ich werde da gehen, wo es Arbeit gibt.

> 2 An opportunity to use the perfect tense.
>
> 3 Here is a chance to use a future tense.

5.3 The environment

LEARNING SUMMARY

After studying this section, you should be able to:

- name different endangered species
- describe and give views about dangers to the environment
- talk about how you help the environment

Environmental issues

AQA	✓
OCR	✓
EDEXCEL	✗
WJEC	✓
CCEA	✓

Endangered animals
(Vom Aussterben bedrohte Tiere)

der **Affe (-n)** – ape
ausgestorben – extinct
der **Bär (-en)** – bear
bedroht – endangered
der **Dachs (-e)** – badger
der **Delphin (-e)** – dolphin
der **Eisbär (-en)** – polar bear
der **Elefant (-en)** – elephant
der **Fisch (-e)** – fish
die **Fledermaus (-̈e)** – bat

der **Gepard (-e)** – cheetah
der **Gorilla (-s)** – gorilla
der **Orang-Utan (-s)** – orangutan
der **Panda (-s)** – panda
das **Rhinozeros (-se)** – rhinoceros
die **Robbe (-n)** – seal
der **Tiger (-)** – tiger
verschwinden – to disappear
der **Wal (-e)** – whale

Dangers to the environment

Wir sollten bedrohte Spezies schützen.
We should protect threatened species.
Der Tiger ist vom Aussterben bedroht.
The tiger is in danger of extinction.
Gewisse Meere sterben an Verschmutzung.
Certain seas are dying from pollution.
Der Treibhauseffekt bedroht die ganze Welt.
The greenhouse effect threatens the whole world.
Wir tun so viel wir können aber es ist längst nicht genug.
We do as much as we can, but it is far from being enough.
Man muß weder überfischen, noch Fabrikschiffe erlauben.
We must neither over fish, nor allow factory ships.

> **KEY POINT**
>
> Think of **müssen** as a stronger form of **sollen**, i.e. 'must' instead of 'ought to'.

The local environment

Meine Stadt ist still/ruhig/laut/industriell.
My town is quiet/peaceful/noisy/industrial.

Die Luft ist schmutzig/verschmutzt/sauber.

The air is dirty/polluted/clean.

Es gibt zu viele Fabriken und Wagen.

There are too many factories and cars.

Die Leute lassen allerlei Abfälle zurück.

People leave all sorts of litter behind.

Die Luft und die Flüsse werden verschmutzt.

The air and the rivers become polluted.

Man braucht ein Recyclingzentrum.

We need a recycling centre.

Auspuffabgase verschmutzen die Luft.

Exhaust emissions pollute the air.

Die Asthmarate steigt immer dank der Verschmutzung.

The incidence of asthma is rising all the time thanks to pollution.

Verkehrsstaue verschlimmern ein schon wichtiges Problem.

Traffic jams make an already serious problem worse.

Wir sollten dazu verpflichtet werden, die öffentlichen Verkehrsmittel statt unserer PKWs zu gebrauchen.

We should be made to use public transport instead of our own cars.

Um diese Politik zu fördern, sollte die Regierung die öffentlichen Verkehrsmitteln verbessern.

In order to encourage this policy, the government should improve public transport.

Man hat Fußgängerzonen und Radwege geschaffen.

Pedestrian zones and cycle lanes have been created.

Überall in Europa sind Wagen und Fahrzeuge in den Stadtzentren verboten.

Everywhere in Europe, cars and lorries have been banned from the town centres.

Plastiktüten töten die Tier- und Pflanzenwelt und bedrohen die Ozonschicht.

Plastic bags are killing wildlife and threatening the ozone layer.

Jetzt hat die Umweltbewegung begonnen, Fortschritte zu machen.

Now the environmental movement has started to make progress.

Die neuen Plastiktüten sind biologisch abbaubar.

The new plastic bags are biodegradable.

Innerhalb der Europäischen Union bauen wir weniger Strassen, Autobahnen und Flughäfen.

Inside the European Union we are building fewer roads, motorways and airports.

What I do for the environment

Ich tue, was ich kann, um die Umwelt zu schützen/schonen.

I do what I can to protect the environment.

Vielleicht tue ich nicht genug.

Perhaps I don't do enough.

Ich gehe zu Fuß zur Schule.

I walk to school.

Ich gebrauche die öffentlichen Verkehrsmittel.

I use public transport.

Ich lasse keine Abfälle zurück.

I don't leave any litter.

Ich schalte die Lichter aus und drehe die Wasserhähne ab.

I turn off the lights and the taps.

Ich ermutige die Leute, ihre Wagen nicht zu gebrauchen.

I encourage people not to use their cars.

Adjectives

bedroht – threatened
gefährlich – dangerous
harmlos – harmless
laut – noisy
recycelbar – recyclable
ruhig – peaceful
sauber – clean
schädlich – damaging, harmful
schmutzig – dirty
schuldig – guilty

(un)sichtbar – (in)visible
still – calm
toxisch – toxic
überbevölkert – over-populated
umweltfreundlich – environmentally friendly
unterbevölkert – under-populated
verschmutzt – polluted
verschwenderisch – wasteful
weltweit – worldwide

Environmental issues (Umweltfragen)

der Sauerregen

der Abfall (¨e) – waste
die Abfallbeseitigung – waste disposal
die Atmosphäre (-n) – atmosphere
der Atommüll – nuclear waste
die Entwaldung – deforestation
die Erde – earth
der Globus – globe, world
die Grünen – the Greens, Green Party
die Kernkraft – nuclear power
die Kohle – coal
die Menschheit – humanity, humankind

der Missbrauch – abuse, misuse
die Ökologie – ecology
das Ökosystem – ecosystem
der Ozean (-e) – ocean
die Ozonschicht – ozone layer
der Planet (-en) – planet
das Recycling – recycling
das Recyclingwerk (-e) – recycling plant
der Sauerregen – acid rain
der Verbrauch – consumption
Wissenschaftler (in) – scientist, m/f

Verbs

beschädigen – to damage
beseitigen – to dispose of
bewohnen – to inhabit
demonstrieren – to demonstrate
ersetzen – to replace
heizen – to heat

missbrauchen – to abuse
produzieren – to produce
recyceln – to recycle
reduzieren – to reduce
reinigen – to clean (up)
retten – to save, to rescue
schonen – to protect
schützen – to protect

verbessern – to improve
vergeuden – to waste
vermindern – to reduce
vernachlässigen – to neglect
verschlimmern – to make worse
verschwenden – to waste

PROGRESS CHECK

Say or write the following in German:
1 Thanks to pollution.
2 I don't leave any litter.
3 I do what I can to protect the environment.
4 We should protect threatened species.
5 Now the environmental movement has started to make progress.

1. Dank der Verschmutzung. 2. Ich lasse keine Abfälle zurück. 3. Ich tue, was ich kann, um die Umwelt zu schützen/schonen. 4. Wir sollten bedrohte Spezies schützen. 5. Jetzt hat die Umweltbewegung begonnen, Fortschritte zu machen.

5.4 Grammar

Modal verbs

AQA	✓
OCR	✓
EDEXCEL	✓
WJEC	✓
CCEA	✓

KEY POINT

A modal verb is simply a helper (or auxiliary) verb, which is used to show that a particular action is necessary or possible.

The modal verbs are:

- **müssen** – to have to (must)
- **sollen** – to be expected to (should)
- **dürfen** – to be allowed to (may)
- **können** – to be able to (can)
- **mögen** – to like to (want to)
- **wollen** – to want to (will)

	Need		Possibility			
	müssen	sollen	dürfen	können	mögen	wollen
ich	muss	soll	darf	kann	mag	will
du	musst	sollst	darfst	kannst	magst	willst
er/sie/es/man	muss	soll	darf	kann	mag	will
wir	müssen	sollen	dürfen	können	mögen	wollen
ihr	müsst	sollt	dürft	könnt	mögt	wollt
Sie	müssen	sollen	dürfen	können	mögen	wollen
sie	müssen	sollen	dürfen	können	mögen	wollen
	I must, have to, etc.	I should, am expected to, etc.	I may, am allowed to etc.	I can, am able to, etc.	I want to, like to, etc.	I will, wish to, want to, etc.

Here are some examples of modal verbs being used in sentences:

Ich muss mein Bestes tun.

I must do my best.

Du sollst deinen Abfall recyceln.

You should recycle your rubbish.

Man darf solche Produkte gebrauchen.

We may (are allowed to) use such products.

Wir können unsere eigene Umgebung verbessern.

We can improve our own environment.

Sie mögen nicht helfen.

You do not want to help.

Sie wollen mitarbeiten.

They wish to co-operate.

Here are some important points to remember about modal verbs:

- Modal verbs are particularly useful for a controlled speaking or writing assessment on the environment. This is because they give the idea of actions that need to be taken, or the possibility of making our own choice of action.
- You will see from the examples above that modal verbs work in pairs with an infinitive, which goes at the end of the clause.
- The **ich** and the **er/sie/es/man** forms are always identical.

PROGRESS CHECK

Say or write the following in German:

1. You (**Sie**) should produce more bio-products.
2. We are not allowed to use coal.
3. They must recycle as much as possible.
4. She does not like to waste energy.
5. I cannot dispose of all my rubbish.
6. You (**du**) do not wish to improve the environment.

1. Sie sollten mehr Bioprodukte produzieren. 2. Wir dürfen nicht Kohle gebrauchen. 3. Sie müssen so viel wie möglich recyceln. 4. Sie mag nicht Energie verschwenden. 5. Ich kann nicht alle meine Abfälle beseitigen. 6. Du willst nicht die Umwelt verbessern.

Separable verbs

AQA	✓
OCR	✓
EDEXCEL	✓
WJEC	✓
CCEA	✓

A separable verb can be separated into two parts – a prefix and a main verb. The prefix is actually a preposition or 'place' word.

Looking at these compounds of the English verb 'get' will help you to understand what German separable verbs are: get at, get by, get down, get in, get low, get near, get out, get over, get past, get through, get to, get under, get wide, get with.

When each preposition in red is added to the basic verb, it changes its meaning. Because of the ability of the English language to use a base verb + a preposition in a variety of ways, the language has enormous flexibility.

German separable verbs work on a very similar principle because the preposition alters the meaning of the verb.

Look at these examples using **ab-fahren** (to leave) and **auf-schreiben** (to write down):

> For GCSE you may find it easier to just use separable verbs in a main clause.

Ich fahre nach Berlin ab.

I am leaving for Berlin.

Ich schreibe die Nachricht auf.

I am writing the message down.

In the infinitive, the preposition is attached to the front of the verb, for example:

Ich muss nach Berlin abfahren.

I must go off to Berlin.

Ich will die Nachricht aufschreiben.

I want to write down the message.

In a subordinate clause, the preposition also stays attached to the front of the verb, for example:

Ich komme jetzt, weil ich morgen nach Berlin abfahre.
I am coming now because I go off to Berlin tomorrow.
Ich vergesse nicht, wenn ich die Nachricht aufschreibe.
I don't forget when I write the message down.

The same happens with the past participle in the perfect tense, for example:

Wir sind abgefahren.
We drove off.
Wir haben die Nachricht aufgeschrieben.
We wrote down the message.

Just like with other verbs, the future tense of separable verbs is formed using **werden** + the infinitive of the verb, for example:

Ich werde abfahren
I will drive off/leave.
Wirst du die Nachricht aufschreiben?
Will you write down the message?

Here is a list of the separable verbs that you are most likely to come across at GCSE. To show that they are separable, dictionaries and grammar books tend to write the infinitive like this: **ab-fahren**, **auf-schreiben**, etc.

Separable verb	Meaning
ab-fahren	to leave
an-fangen	to start, to begin
an-kommen	to arrive
an-rufen	to telephone
an-ziehen	to put on, to dress
auf-hören	to stop
auf-machen	to open
auf-schreiben	to write down
auf-stehen	to get up
auf-wachen	to wake up
aus-gehen	to go out
aus-steigen	to get off, to get out
aus-ziehen	to take off, to undress
ein-laden	to invite
ein-schlafen	to fall asleep
fern-sehen	to watch TV
mit-gehen	to go with
statt-finden	to take place
teil-nehmen	to take part
um-steigen	to change (trains, etc.)
um-ziehen	to change (clothes)
weg-gehen	to go away
zu-hören	to listen (to)
zu-machen	to close
zurück-gehen	to go back
zurück-kommen	to come back

Sample controlled assessment

Speaking

1 Track 28 You are going to have a conversation with your teacher about environmental problems.

Teacher: Was für Umweltprobleme beunruhigen dich?

Student: Ich glaube,[1] wir mißhandeln[1] die Erde und das macht mir Sorgen. Vielleicht ist es[1] schon zu spät aber ich bin mir[28] nicht sicher, da einige Wissenschaftler ja sagen und andere nein. Ich weiss, dass wir gewisse Dinge tun um[8] die Umwelt zu schützen aber es ist längst nicht genug.

Teacher: Was machst du für die Umwelt in deiner persönlichen Umgebung und im Allgemeinen?

Student: Ich tue, was ich kann um[8] den Globus zu schonen. Vielleicht tue ich nicht genug aber gestern zum Beispiel, bin ich zu Fuß zur Schule gegangen.[39] Meine Mutter würde[25] mich immer mitnehmen aber das ist zweimal drei Kilometer mehr für sie. Sie ist gezwungen, mit dem Wagen zur Arbeit zu fahren aber ich habe meine Beine! Wenn wir schlechtes[19] Wetter haben, nehme ich das Angebot an, mit Mutti zu fahren. Gewitter und Schnee beiseite, das letzte Mal, wo[7] ich zur Schule gefahren bin,[39] war vor zwei Jahren!

Teacher: Imponierend! Und was machst du sonst für die Umwelt?

Student: Natürlich benutze ich öffentliche Verkehrsmittel, um[8] in die Stadt zu fahren. Meine Abfälle[9] nehme ich immer mit und ich gehe mit den leeren Flaschen und Dosen zum Recyclingzentrum. Ich wasche die Flaschen nicht im Voraus, weil[5] man[34] sie im Recyclingzentrum sowieso wäscht. Ich verschwende[9] kein wertvolles Wasser! Und ich tue genau dasselbe mit dem Strom. Ich schalte alles aus! Lichter, Fernsehen und Computer. Ich fülle den Wasserkessel nur mit dem Wasser, das ich benötige. Den mache ich nie voll, ausgenommen, wenn wir zu viert oder fünft sind!

Teacher: Ich bin beeindruckt! Jetzt kommen wir zu dem was dich beunruhigt. Was möchtest du mir dazu sagen?

Student: Zuerst möchte[35] ich sagen, daß ich vielleicht zu pessimistisch war,[4] als wir diese Unterhaltung begonnen haben.[2] Die Lage ist schlimm, aber nicht so[21] schlimm, daß wir nichts dafür tun können. Zum Beispiel bin ich mir sicher, dass wir eines Tages dazu verpflichtet werden, öffentliche Verkehrsmittel anstelle unserer Autos zu benutzen. Um diese Politik zu fördern, wird die Regierung die öffentlichen Verkehrsmittel verbessern müßen. Dadurch werden wir[3] weniger Abgase verursachen, die die Luft verschmutzen. Das wird[3] Leuten wie Asthmatikern helfen und die Asthma Rate herunterbringen. Es gibt bestimmte Probleme, die global sind. Beispielsweise das Aussterben von bedrohten[19] Spezien, das Austrocknen[9] der Meere und das Überfischen[9] durch Fabrikschiffe, den Gebrauch von Plastiktüten, die die Tier-und Pflanzenwelt töten, und die Ozonschicht[9] bedrohen. Aber es ist nicht wirklich zu spät! Wir müssen alle auf einer globalen Ebene zusammenarbeiten. Dann wird die nächste Generation eine schöne Welt haben![18]

Teacher: Ich danke dir für ein inspierendes Gespräch!

Turn to page 156 for a translation of this passage.

Examiner's comments

The environment topic gives students the opportunity to talk with feeling on something they care deeply about. This sets them on the road to a good mark because enthusiasm tends to bring confidence.

Take a look at how much of the vocabulary in this chapter has been used and adapted by the student to produce an impressive piece of work. Refer to the '40 points for improving your grade' on pages 8–9 to see why this is a high-quality piece of work:

1 Examples of the present tense

2 The past tense in use

3 The future tense has been used

4 A good understanding of word order has been shown

5 An example of the use of 'weil'

7 'Wo' is a good connecting word

8 'Um…zu' structures

9 Impressive vocabulary, e.g. 'Abfälle', 'verschwende', 'Austrocknen', 'Überfischen', 'Ozonschicht'

18 An exclamation

19 Examples of adjectives

21 A comparative

25 The conditional tense has been used

28 A personal pronoun has been used

34 An example of 'man' being used

35 A modal verb ('mögen')

39 Examples of the use of the perfect tense with 'sein'

Sample controlled assessment

Writing

1 Write about how you help the environment. You could…
- explain whether you have positive, negative or mixed feelings about the present state of the environment
- state what you and your family do to try to make a difference to the environment
- mention some global issues (global warming, species under threat, etc.)
- finish by explaining how you see the future of the world.

Meine Familie und ich tun, was wir können, um[8] die Umwelt zu schützen. Auch wenn es nicht genug ist,[4] werden wir kein schlechtes Gewissen darüber haben müssen. Einige Wissenschaftler[9] sind der Meinung, dass unsere Welt verloren ist. Ich bin nicht total damit einverstanden. Ich werde erklären[3] warum aber zuerst werde ich[3] die Dinge auflisten, die wir in meinem kleinen Zuhause kollektiv für die Umgebung und Umwelt tun.

Die Eltern benutzen den Wagen so selten[15] wie möglich und wir alle fahren normalerweise mit den öffentlichen Verkehrsmitteln oder dem Rad. Man[34] fährt mich[28] und meine Schwester nie[12] zur Schule ausgenommen bei schlechtem Wetter.

Einer meiner Aufträge[9] ist, mit den leeren Flaschen und Dosen zum Recyclingzentrum zu gehen, und ich meine gehen, auch wenn das Zentrum ziemlich entfernt ist. Ich mähe auch den Rasen und muss[35] das Gras auf den Komposthaufen[9] stecken. Wir haben[1] einen Gemüsegarten und wir gebrauchen den Kompost, um[8] die Erde auf der Höhe zu behalten! Wir kultivieren[1] genug Gemüse und Obst, um[8] uns das Ganze Jahr zu ernähren.

Natürlich geben wir Gemüse den Nachbarn und neulich haben drei oder vier mit ihren eigenen[19] Gemüse- und Schrebergärten angefangen. Bald werden wir[3] genug kultivieren, um Pakete von Gemüse den Alten in der Nachbarschaft zu geben. Ich habe schon drei Jahre in unserem Garten gearbeitet und ich kann[35] Ihnen nicht sagen, wie viel Spass das mir macht!

Auf der globalen[19] Ebene sind die Dinge natürlich etwas anders. Letzte Woche habe ich in einer deutschen Zeitung gelesen, wie der Tiger, der Wal und andere Spezies[9] vom Aussterben[9] bedroht[9] sind. Ich weiss schon, dass gewisse Meere an Verschmutzung sterben und, dass ein oder zwei kleinere Meere schon gestorben sind. Daraus können wir sehen, wie der Treibhauseffekt die ganze Welt bedroht.[6] "Eine kollektive Aktion!", das ist der Schlachtruf![18] Sonst sind wir in der schlimmsten Lage.

Ich bin ein positiver Mensch und werde[3] auf eine positive Seite enden. Die Umweltbewegung hat schon begonnen,[2] wirkliche Fortschritte zu machen. Dank ihren Kampagnen, sind die neuen Plastiktüten und Fastfoodverpackungen[9] biologisch abbaubar.[9] Innerhalb der Europäischen Union hat man angefangen, weniger[21] Strassen, Autobahnen und Flughäfen zu bauen und der amerikanische Präsident hat das Kyoto Abkommen befürwortet.[9] Wir haben[11] noch Zeit![18]

Turn to page 156 for a translation of this passage.

Examiner's comments

This student has improved his or her chances of a high grade by including a good number of the 40 points from pages 8–9:

1 Use of the present tense
2 The past tense has been used
3 Future tenses have been used
4 Good understanding of word order has been demonstrated
6 A justified point of view
8 'Um…zu' structures
9 Impressive vocabulary, e.g. 'Wissenschaftler', 'Aufträge', 'Komposthaufen', 'Spezies', 'Aussterben', 'bedroht', 'Fastfoodverpackungen', 'abbaubar', 'befürwortet'
11 One example of a 'haben' structure
12 A negative
15 'So' + an adverb
18 Exclamations have been used
19 Examples of an adjective before the noun
21 A comparative has been included
28 A personal pronoun
34 Use of 'man'
35 Modal verbs have been used ('müssen', 'können')

Exam practice questions

Listening

1 🔘 **Track 29** Where are these people going and which direction should they take? Tick the correct box in each case.

Section 1

(a) She is going:

A ☐ B ☐ C ☐

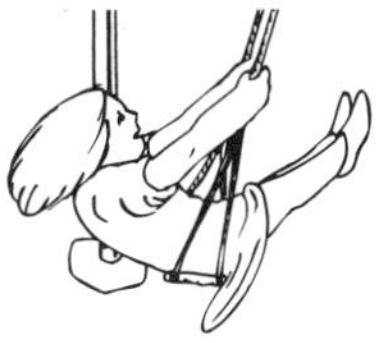

(b) She must:

A ☐ B ☐ C ☐

Section 2

(c) He is going:

A ☐ B ☐ C ☐

(d) He must:

A ☐ B ☐ C ☐

Section 3

(e) She is going:

A ☐ B ☐ C ☐

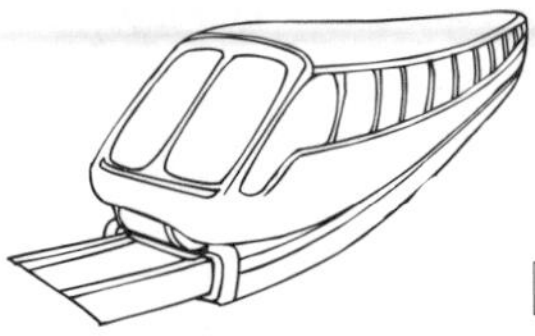

(f) She must:

A ☐ B ☐ C ☐

(6)

Exam practice questions

2 Track **30** Four young people are being asked about how they help at home. Write the correct two letters for each person in the spaces provided.

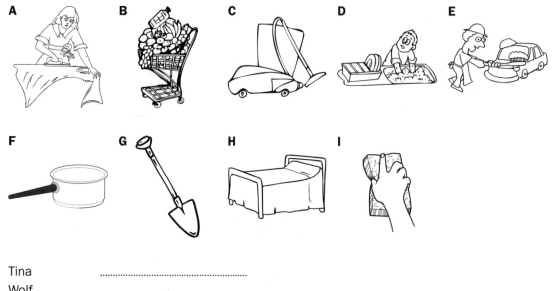

A   **B**   **C**   **D**   **E**

F   **G**   **H**   **I**

Tina   ....

Wolf   ....

Chrissi   ....

Reinhardt   ....

(8)

3 Track **31** Listen to the weather forecast. Write the correct letter in the boxes on the map of Germany.

A   Rain

B   Snow

C   Fog

D   Wind

E   Cold

F   Sun

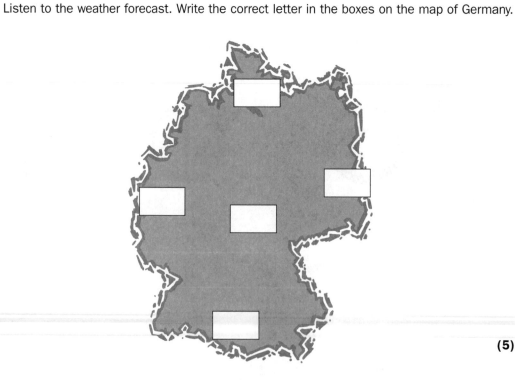

(5)

Exam practice questions

Reading

1   Read the e-mail message below and look at the plan that follows.

> Du wirst bald bei uns sein. Klick im Ordner und du wirst unseren Wohnungsplan finden. Das
> Wohnzimmer steht rechts neben dem Eingang. Die Küche ist links gegenüber dem
> Wohnzimmer. Auch links ist das Badezimmer. Neben dem Badezimmer steht Omas Zimmer
> und neben Omas am Ende des Flurs ist mein Schlafzimmer. Gegenüber steht Muttis und
> Vatis Zimmer. Hoffentlich ist alles klar.
>
> Bis bald! Maria.
>
>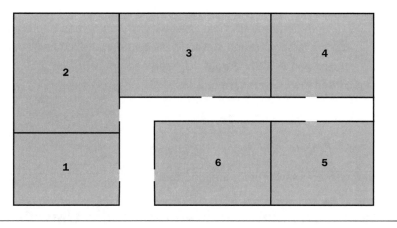

Using the information in the e-mail, match each room to the descriptions given below. Write a number
in each answer space.

(a)   Maria's bedroom   ....

(b)   Kitchen   ....

(c)   Bathroom   ....

(d)   Grandmother's bedroom   ....

(e)   Parents' bedroom   ....

(f)   Living room   ....   **(6)**

Exam practice questions

2 Read the text message below. Choose from the words given in the box to complete the sentences.

Treibhauseffekt	vergessen	Tier-	gelernt	verrückt	Meere	Menschen
	sprechen	klug	Schock	Umwelt		

Hallo Hansi!

Ich war heute bei einer Grünkonferenz für Schüler und Schülerinnen. Alles war imponierend und ich habe so viel **(a)** .... ! Ich bin so davon begeistert, dass ich gedacht habe, ich muss mit Hansi darüber **(b)** .... Ich glaube, ich werde der Junggrünpartei beitreten, um die **(c)** .... zu schützen. Wusstest du, dass in der **(d)** .... und Pflanzenwelt, viele Spezies vom Aussterben bedroht sind und, dass **(e)** .... an Verschmutzung sterben? Bis heute, hatte ich keine Ahnung, dass der **(f)** .... die ganze Welt bedroht. Ich stehe so unter **(g)** .... , dass ich deine Meinung hören muss! Bin ich **(h)** .... oder was?

*Mediwi! Babs.

(*Mediwi is text-speak for <u>me</u>lde <u>di</u>ch <u>wi</u>eder – get in touch)   **(8)**

3 Read the leaflet below, then answer the questions that follow.

10 Tipps Was wir zu Hause tun können, um die Umwelt zu schonen

- Lichter ausschalten, wenn wir ein Zimmer verlassen.
- Die Fernbedienung* für den Fernseher verbieten.
- Den Müll für die Abfalltonnen korrekt sortieren.
- In der eigenen Stadt, den Wagen zu Hause lassen.
- Mit den öffentlichen Verkehrsmitteln fahren.
- Lieber warme Kleidung tragen als 23 Grad am Thermostat haben.
- Nicht zu viel Wasser im Kessel kochen.
- Einen Wasserfass im Garten installieren.
- Einen Gemüsegarten pflanzen.
- Einen Komposthaufen aufbauen.

(*Die Fernbedienung – the remote)

(a) Who is the leaflet targeted at? .... **(1)**

What should we do…

(b) to save electricity? Give two details.

    (i) ....   **(ii)** .... **(2)**

(c) with household waste? .... **(1)**

(d) with the car? .... **(1)**

(e) when it is cold? .... **(1)**

(f) with the kettle? .... **(1)**

(g) in the garden? Give three details.

    (i) ....   **(ii)** ....   **(iii)** .... **(3)**

Exam practice questions

4 Read the following Internet account of a teenager's disastrous holiday and answer the questions that follow.

> Letzten August wollten meine drei Freunde und ich nach einem Campingplatz in Süddeutschland fahren und alles ging gut, als wir durch Belgien fuhren.
>
> Einmal in Deutschland hat unser Fahrer, Max, seine Brieftasche an der ersten Tankstelle auf der Autobahn gelassen und wir mussten wieder zur Tankstelle. Aber die Brieftasche war nicht mehr da. Dann auf halbem Wege zum Campingplatz hatten wir eine Reifenpanne. Leider hatte Max kein rotes Dreieck. Er erhielt eine Geldstrafe, die wir andere zahlen mussten.
>
> Wir sind also zu spät in den Campingplatz angekommen und unser Platz war nicht mehr frei! Wir mussten also ein Hotel aussuchen und endlich haben wir eines gefunden, das sehr alt und schmutzig war und keinen Feuermelder hatte.
>
> Bill, der Raucher in unserer Gruppe hat eine Zigarette im Bett geraucht und hat das Hotel in Brand gesteckt. Die Feuerwehr ist zu spät angekommen und Bill ist verhaftet worden. Nach dieser Liste von Katastrophen haben wir den Entschluss gemacht, in den Hügeln zu zelten.

(a) How long did the good luck last? .... **(1)**

(b) What happened to the wallet?

....

.... **(3)**

(c) What was the result of the breakdown?

....

.... **(3)**

(d) Why did the friends have to find a hotel?

.... **(2)**

(e) Why did the friends not like the hotel? Give three details.

    (i) ....   **(ii)** ....   **(iii)** .... **(3)**

(f) What did Bill do and what were the results?

.... **(3)**

6 Education and work

The following topics are covered in this chapter:

- School and college
- Pressures and problems at school
- Jobs
- Grammar

6.1 School and college

LEARNING SUMMARY

After studying this section, you should be able to:

- describe your school and school routine
- understand information about a school in a German-speaking country
- say what you like and dislike about school, giving reasons

School and college

AQA	✓
OCR	✓
EDEXCEL	✓
WJEC	✓
CCEA	✓

The following vocabulary will help you in the listening and reading exams. Your teacher could ask you to describe your school in the controlled speaking assessment. You should learn answers to all the obvious questions: questions about your subjects, the school building itself, the teachers and your plans for after school. You should realise that you may be tested on your tenses by questions about what you did yesterday at school and what you will do tomorrow. You may also be asked an opinion about your school.

Back to school (Wieder zur Schule)

die Prüfung

Das Abi(tur) – an exam that is the equivalent of A-level

der (Schul)Austausch – (school) exchange

das (Lieblings)Fach ("er) – (favourite) subject

der Fehler (-) – mistake, error

die Hausaufgaben – homework

die Klasse (-n) – class

die Mittagspause (-n) – lunchtime

die mittlere Reife – an exam that is the equivalent of GCSE

nach-sitzen – to be in detention

die Pause (-n) – break time

die Prüfung (-en) – exam

die Schwäche (-n) – weak point

die Sommerferien – summer holidays

die Stärke (-n) – strong point

die Stunde (-n) – lesson

der Stundenplan ("e) – timetable

der Test (-e) – test

School subjects (Schulfächer)

Sport

Betriebswirtschaft – business studies
Biologie – biology
Chemie – chemistry
Deutsch – German
Drama – expressive arts
Englisch – English
Erdkunde – geography
Französisch – French
die Fremdsprache (-n) – foreign language
Geisteswissenschaften – humanities

Geschichte – history
Informatik – information technology, computer studies, CDT
Kochen – food technology
Kunst – art
Latein – Latin
*LER – PSE and RE combined
Mathe – maths
Medienwissenschaft – media studies
Musik – music

Physik – physics
Religion – religious studies
Spanisch – Spanish
Sport – sport, PE
Technologie – technology
Theater – drama
Turnen – gymnastics
Wissenschaft – science
Zeichnen – drawing
*(LER = Lebensgestaltung, Ethik, Religion)

der Stundenplan

	Montag	Dienstag	Mittwoch	Donnerstag	Freitag
08:30	Chemie	Deutsch	LER	Mathe	Erdkunde / Geschichte
09:30	Französisch	Deutsch	Englisch	Deutsch	Technologie
10:30	Pause	Pause	Pause	Pause	Pause
10:50	Französisch	Mathe	Erdkunde / Geschichte	Französisch	Kunst
11:50	Mathe	Informatik	Biologie	Physik	Kunst
12:50	Mittagspause	Mittagspause	Mittagspause	Mittagspause	Mittagspause
13:45	Deutsch	Physik	Chemie	Mathe	Sport
14:45	Technologie	Englisch	Informatik	Englisch	Sport

Adjectives

abwesend – absent
anwesend – present
durchschnittlich – average
falsch – wrong
fantastisch – fantastic
fortgeschritten – advanced
gemischt – mixed

Grundschule – primary school
kompliziert – complicated
leicht – easy
privat – private
rechnergesteuert – computer-controlled

richtig – right, correct
schrecklich – terrible, awful
schwierig – difficult
wunderbar – wonderful

At school (In der Schule)

die Bibliothek

die Aula (Aulen) – school hall(s)
die Bibliothek (-en) – library
das Büro (-s) – office
das College – college
der Gang (¨e) – corridor
die Gesamtschule (-n) – comprehensive school
das Gymnasium (-ien) – grammar school

die Hauptschule (-n) – secondary modern school
die Kantine (-n) – canteen
das Klassenzimmer (-) – classroom
das Lehrerzimmer (-) – staff room

die Realschule (-n) – secondary modern school
der Schulhof (¨e) – playground
das Schwimmbad (¨er) – swimming pool
die Toiletten (f, pl) – toilets
die Turnhalle (-n) – gym

das Lehrbuch

Equipment (Die Ausrüstung)

der Bleistift (-e) – pencil
das Heft (-e) – exercise book
der Kugelschreiber (-) – ball-point pen
der Kuli (-s) – pen
das Lehrbuch (¨er) – text book

das Lineal (-e) – ruler
der (Schul)Ranzen (-) – school bag
der Radiergummi (-s) – eraser
der Rechner (-) – calculator
der Stift (-e) – pen

People (Die Leute)

Abiturient (in) – A-level student, m/f
Direktor (in) – head teacher, m/f
Hausmeister (in) – caretaker, m/f
Lehrer (in) – teacher, m/f

Raumpfleger (in) – cleaner, m/f
Schüler (in) – pupil, m/f
Sekretär (in) – secretary, m/f
Student (in) – student, m/f

Verbs

läuten

ab-haken – to tick (off) (e.g. the register)
die Anwesenheit fest-stellen – to call the register
beenden – to finish
beschreiben – to describe
bestrafen – to punish

demonstrieren – to demonstrate
erklären – to explain
fertig machen – to finish
korrigieren – to correct
sich langweilen – to get bored
läuten – to ring

lernen – to learn
plaudern – to chat
schreiben – to write
studieren – to study
übersetzen – to translate
wissen – to know
zu-hören – to listen (to)
zusammen-fassen – to summarise

PROGRESS CHECK

Say or write the following in German:
1. I don't like technology.
2. My favourite subject is physics.
3. I am learning two foreign languages.
4. Yesterday evening I did three hours of homework.
5. Next year I will be an A-level student.

1. Ich mag nicht Technologie.
2. Mein Lieblingsfach ist Physik.
3. Ich lerne zwei Fremdsprachen.
4. Gestern abend habe ich drei Stunden Hausaufgaben gemacht.
5. Nächstes Jahr werde ich Abiturient(in) sein.

Conversation: Grades G–D

AQA	✓
OCR	✓
EDEXCEL	✓
WJEC	✓
CCEA	✓

Make sure you can answer these questions without thinking. Get someone to ask you them, so you can practise answering them without using the book.

🗣 **Was ist dein Lieblingsfach?**
💬 **Ich studiere am liebsten Deutsch.**
🗣 **Warum?**
💬 **Mein(e) Austauschpartner(in) und ich verstehen uns gut.**
🗣 **Gibt es ein Fach, das du nicht gern hast?**
💬 **Ich mag nicht LER.**
🗣 **Treibst du Sport in der Schule?**
💬 **Ich spiele Hockey und Tennis.**

1 The student has used a perfect tense here. A little more of this plus the use of a future tense would have pushed him/her towards a C grade.

2 You can also say 'um dreiviertel neun/acht Uhr fünfundvierzig'. Use whichever you find easiest but if you have to repeat it, try one of the other ways. You get credit for varying the way you say things.

3 The more information you give, the more marks you get.

🗨 Wie kommst du in die Schule?

🗨 Ich komme zu Fuss/mit dem Bus/mit dem Wagen.

🗨 Und wie bist du heute morgen gekommen?

🗨 Ich bin zu Fuss gekommen.[1]

🗨 Um wieviel Uhr kommst du an?

🗨 Um halb neun.

🗨 Um wieviel Uhr fangen die Stunden an?

🗨 Die Stunden beginnen um Viertel vor neun.[2]

🗨 Du hast wie viele Stunden pro Tag?

🗨 Ich habe sechs Stunden.

🗨 Wie lange dauert jede Stunde?

🗨 Jede Stunde dauert fünfzig Minuten.

🗨 Um wie viel Uhr macht man eine Pause?

🗨 Wir haben eine Pause um zehn Uhr fünfundzwanzig.

🗨 Und wie lange dauert diese Pause?

🗨 Die Pause dauert eine Viertelstunde.

🗨 Was machst du während der Pause?

🗨 Ich esse oder trinke etwas und spreche mit meinen Freunden.[3]

Conversation: Grades C–A*

AQA	✓
OCR	✓
EDEXCEL	✓
WJEC	✓
CCEA	✓

Make sure you can answer these questions without thinking. Get someone to ask you them, so you can practise answering them without using the book.

In this conversation, it is evident that the student has researched and used more complex language. Try noting down all the underlined words and expressions and use as many of them as you can in your own work to impress the examiner.

🗨 Morgens was für Vorbereitungen machst du für die Schule?

🗨 Ich wache um Viertel nach sieben auf, ich stehe <u>fünf oder zehn Minuten später</u> auf, ich nehme eine Dusche oder wasche mich, wenn meine Schwester <u>da drinnen steckt</u>, ich ziehe mich an, ich nehme mein Frühstück, ich packe meine Bücher ein und ich verlasse das Haus.

🗨 Beschreib mir einen Tag zur Schule.

🗨 Ich komme um halb neun an, meine Klassenlehrerin stellt die Anwesenheit fest und wir haben eine Viertelstunde mit ihr. Die erste Stunde fängt um acht Uhr fünfundfünfzig an. Sie dauert <u>knapp</u> eine Stunde. Wir haben zwei Stunden, dann kommt die Pause.

🗨 Und was machst du während dieser Pause?

🗨 <u>Es kommt darauf an</u>. Manchmal esse ich oder trinke ich etwas, oder ich plaudere mit meinen Kameraden oder ich spiele ein bißchen Fußball im <u>Schulhof</u>. Aber von Zeit zu Zeit muss die Klasse <u>nachsitzen</u>. Das habe ich nicht so gern.

🗨 Und nachher?

🗨 Nachher haben wir noch zwei Stunden bis zur Mittagspause, die um ein Uhr zehn <u>stattfindet</u>! Ich kann nicht nach Hause für mein Essen gehen, weil mein Zuhause zu weit entfernt ist. <u>Deshalb</u> esse ich in der Kantine, was <u>gar nicht</u> so schlecht ist. Dann, um zwei Uhr zehn haben wir unsere letzte Stunde und ich gehe um drei Uhr zwanzig <u>so ungefähr</u> nach Hause. Dann ist es <u>Hausaufgabenzeit</u>. Das dauert zwei bis zweieinhalb Stunden, dann <u>habe ich frei</u>!

🗨 Beschreib mir deine Schule.

🗨 Sie ist ganz ordentlich, <u>nicht so alt</u>, <u>nicht so neu</u>. Wir haben viele Labors und Sportplätze <u>zur Verfügung</u> und eine <u>nagelneue</u> Bibliothek. Sie gefällt mir gut. Es gibt sehr schöne Bilder an den Wänden und wir können Computerspiele und DVDs <u>borgen</u>. Das ist <u>einmalig</u>! Auch ist die Schule total <u>rechnergesteuert</u>. Einige Schüler und Lehrer sind <u>wandelnde Computerschirme</u>! Ich nicht.

- Und deine Schulfächer?
- Ich studiere neun Fächer <u>insgesamt</u> Deutsch, Englisch, Französisch, Mathe, Physik, Englische Literatur, Technologie und Geschichte.
- Seit wann studierst du Deutsch?
- <u>Seit der Sintflut, scheint es mir!</u> Seit schon fünf Jahren aber es scheint länger, nicht weil ich Deutsch nicht gern habe, sondern, weil ich schon dreimal in Deutschland war und es gefällt mir Deutsch zu sprechen.
- Wirst du Deutsch in der Unterstufe weiter studieren?
- <u>Sicher</u>, weil ich europäische Juristik an der Uni studieren möchte.
- Imponierend. Was hast du gestern in der Schule gemacht?
- Ich habe die normalen Klassen gehabt, <u>insbesondere</u> Deutsch, Mathe, Geschichte und Sport, die meine Lieblingsfächer sind. Sport war die letzte Stunde und ich bin abgereist, um Rugby für die Schule zu spielen.
- Ein rugbyspielender Jurist, unglaublich! Was wirst du heute abend machen?
- Weil heute Freitag ist, werde ich <u>ohne weiteres</u> mit meiner Freundin ins Kino gehen. Wir werden den neuen Film mit Brad Pitt und Nicole Kidman sehen. Dann werden wir bei Pizza Shack essen. Sehr <u>romantisch</u>!
- Deine Schule gefällt dir?
- <u>Wie gesagt</u>, ich habe sehr gute Lehrer <u>beziehungsweise</u> Lehrerinnen gehabt und der Ort ist ganz still und ruhig. Ich bin <u>wie zu Hause</u> hier.
- Und machst du auch deine Hausaufgaben gern?
- <u>Man macht, was man muss.</u> Wenn ich hart arbeite, werde ich eine gute Stelle erhalten.

6.2 Pressures and problems at school

LEARNING SUMMARY

After studying this section, you should be able to:

- describe the pressures and problems of school life
- explain what you must do and should not do at school

Pressures and problems at school

AQA	✓
OCR	✓
EDEXCEL	✓
WJEC	✓
CCEA	✓

The following words and phrases will help you in the listening and reading exams, and in the controlled assessment.

Pressures (Belastungen)

begeistern – to fill with enthusiasm

deprimieren – to depress

die Ergebnisse (n, pl) – results

die Leistung (-en) – performance

die Note – grade

die Noten – marks

der Stress – stress

stressen – to stress (out)

stressig – stressful

die Zensur (-en) – grade

das Zeugnis (-se) – school report

What is not allowed in school

Es ist uns verboten… Es ist uns nicht gestattet… Es ist uns nicht erlaubt… Es ist uns unbefugt…	We are not allowed…
zu wählen, was wir tragen	to choose what we wear
Schminke oder Schmuck zu tragen	to wear make-up or jewellery
zu sprechen, wenn der Lehrer spricht	to talk when the teacher is talking
unsere Meinungen zu geben	to give our opinions
frech zu sein	to be cheeky/insolent
im Klassenzimmer zu rauchen/essen/trinken	to smoke/eat/drink in class
zu spät anzukommen	to arrive late
die Schule zu verlassen	to leave school

What we have to do in school

Man muss… Man sollte…	We have to… We should…
unsere Lehrer respektieren	respect our teachers
den Lehrern zuhören	listen to the teachers
immer aufpassen	pay attention all the time
artig sein	be good
nie wiedersprechen	never contradict
hart arbeiten	work hard
zu viel schreiben	write too much
eine scheußliche Uniform tragen	wear a dreadful uniform

Sources of stress

Ich stehe nie an erster Stelle bei einem.
I am never anyone's first priority.
Die Schulregeln sind altmodisch und unfair.
School rules are old-fashioned and unfair.
Die Schule ist mir auf die Nerven gegangen!
School (has) got on my nerves!
Ich habe die Schule satt.
I have had enough of school.
Einige Lehrer können nicht loben.
Some teachers don't know how to praise.
Aber sie kritisieren gern.
But, they like to criticise.
Ich bin ein reiner Versager/eine reine Versagerin.
I am a real failure.
Ich mache keine Fortschritte, auch wenn ich hart versuche.
I make no progress, even when I try hard.
Meine Ergebnisse waren katastrophal!
My results were catastrophic!
Einige Lehrer sind tyrannisch.
Some teachers are like tyrants.
Wenn Lehrer keine Authorität haben, kann die Stunde chaotisch sein.
If teachers have no authority, the lesson can be chaotic.

Ich bin nur ein Name auf einer Liste.

I am only a name on a list.

Der Schultag scheint mir sehr stressig zu sein.

The school day seems to me to be very stressful.

Eltern und Lehrer können uns stressen.

Parents and teachers can stress us out.

Wenn ein Lehrer einen nicht mag, kann das deprimierend sein.

If a teacher doesn't like someone, that can be depressing.

Es existiert viel Schikanieren besonders im Schulhof und in den Toiletten.

There is a lot of bullying, especially in the schoolyard and toilets.

Wenn man nicht Mitglied einer bestimmten Clique ist, kann man Schwierigkeiten haben.

If you are not a member of a particular gang, you can have problems.

Manchmal werden wir zusammengeschlagen.

Sometimes we get beaten up.

Ziemich oft wird eine(r) geschnitten werden.

Quite often someone gets ignored.

Beschimpfungen können weh tun.

Name-calling can hurt.

Wir können nicht mit unseren Lehrern oder Eltern darüber sprechen.

We cannot talk with our teachers or parents about it.

Es gibt auch Drogen zur Verfügung.

There are also drugs available.

Ich bin gar nicht so dumm!

I am not stupid enough for that!

Es gibt Gewalt und Graffiti. Ich fühle mich (wie) bedroht.

There are violence and graffiti. I feel threatened.

Wenn man intelligent oder fleißig ist, muss man anonym bleiben.

If you are intelligent or hard-working, you have to keep your head down.

Wenn eine Klasse unartig für einen netten Lehrer ist, ärgert das mich.

If a class is badly behaved for a nice teacher, it makes me angry.

Wenn der Lehrer die Klasse nicht kontrollieren kann, bringt das Probleme für artige Schüler.

If the teacher cannot control the class, that creates problems for well-behaved pupils.

Unsere Uniform ist scheußlich. Sie kann vielleicht mit der Diziplin helfen aber sie ist hässlich und nicht sehr elegant. Wir verlieren auch unsere Individualität.

Our uniform is awful. Perhaps it can help with discipline, but it is ugly and not very elegant. We also lose our individuality.

PROGRESS CHECK

Say or write the following in German:

1. The school day seems to me to be very stressful.
2. School rules are old-fashioned and unfair.
3. We should respect our teachers.
4. I feel threatened.
5. My results were catastrophic!
6. School (has) got on my nerves!

1. Der Schultag scheint mir sehr stressig zu sein. 2. Die Schulregeln sind altmodisch und unfair. 3. Man sollte unsere Lehrer respektieren. 4. Ich fühle mich (wie) bedroht. 5. Meine Ergebnisse waren katastrophal! 6. Die Schule ist mir auf die Nerven gegangen!

6.3 Jobs

LEARNING SUMMARY

After studying this section, you should be able to:

- talk about current and future jobs
- outline your future plans
- describe the advantages and disadvantages of different jobs

Current and future jobs

AQA	✓
OCR	✓
EDEXCEL	✓
WJEC	✓
CCEA	✓

You may wish to talk about jobs and other future plans in your controlled speaking and writing assessments. There will be plenty of opportunities for you to use the future tense. You should be ready to talk and write about your work experience. The vocabulary that goes with this section often comes up in the listening and reading exams, so make sure you learn it!

The world of work (Die Arbeitswelt)

der Betrieb

der akademische Grad – degree (university)
Angestellte (-n) – employee
die Anzeige (-n) – advert
die Arbeit – work
Arbeitgeber (in) – employer, m/f
die Beförderung (-en) – promotion
der Beruf (-e) – profession
der Betrieb (-e) – factory
die Bildung – training
das Büro (-s) – office
Chef (in) – boss, m/f
die Fabrik (-en) – factory
die Gesellschaft (-en) – company

die Industrie (-n) – industry
das Interview (-s) – interview
der Job (-s) – job
die Karriere (-n) – career
der Kurs – course (of study)
der Lehrgang (¨e) – course
der Lohn (¨e) – salary
das Potenzial – potential
das Praktikum – practical training, induction
die Stelle (-n) – job, post
die Stellung (-en) – job, post
die Universität (-en) – university

Jobs (Stellen)

eine Friseuse

Arbeiter (in) – worker, m/f
Architekt (in) – architect, m/f
Arzt/Ärztin – doctor, m/f
Bauer/Bäuerin – farmer, m/f
Beamter/Beamtin – civil servant, m/f
Chirurg (in) – surgeon, m/f
Frisör/Friseuse – hairdresser, m/f
Geschäftsfrau – businesswoman
Geschäftsmann – trader, businessman
die Hausfrau (-en) – housewife
der Hausmann (¨er) – house husband
Informatiker (in) – IT specialist, m/f
Ingenieur (in) – engineer, m/f

Journalist (in) – journalist, m/f
Kassierer (in) – cashier, m/f
Maler (in) – artist, painter, m/f
Mechaniker (in) – mechanic, m/f
Moderator (in) – TV presenter, m/f
Musiker (in) – musician, m/f
Physiotherapeut (in) – physiotherapist, m/f
Pilot (in) – pilot, m/f
Politiker (in) – politician, m/f
Polizist (in) – police officer, m/f
Programmierer (in) – programmer, m/f
Rechtsanwalt (¨in) – lawyer, m/f

Schulleiter (in) – head teacher, m/f	**Taxifahrer (in)** – taxi driver, m/f
Sekretär (in) – secretary, m/f	**Tierarzt (¨in)** – vet, m/f
Soldat (in) – soldier, m/f	**Verkäufer (in)** – shop assistant, m/f
Sozialarbeiter (in) – social worker, m/f	**Wissenschaftler (in)** – scientist, m/f
Steuerberater (in) – accountant, m/f	**Zahnarzt (¨in)** – dentist, m/f
Steward (ess) – steward(ess)	

an-stellen

Verbs and phrases

an-stellen – to employ, to hire

arbeiten – to work

den Arbeitsplatz verlieren – to lose one's job

befördern – to promote

sich bewerben um – to apply for

degradieren – to demote

entlassen – to dismiss, to make redundant

fahren – to drive

gut bezahlt – well paid

krank werden – to fall ill

einen Kurs machen – to go on a course

schlecht bezahlt – badly paid

seine Stelle kündigen – to leave one's job

Conversation

AQA ✓
OCR ✓
EDEXCEL ✓
WJEC ✓
CCEA ✓

Was für Arbeit hast du gemacht?

Während meines Praktikums habe ich in einem grossen Geschäft gearbeitet.

Was genau hast du gemacht?

Ich habe allerlei Dinge gemacht, interessante und langweilige Dinge.

Fangen wir mit den langweiligen Sachen an. Dann können wir später positiver sein!

Alles klar! Ich musste die Ablage in den Aktenschränken besorgen und ich bin fast vor Langeweile gestorben! Ich war bei einer Maschinenbaufirma und alles war so technisch, dass ich nichts dabei verstehen konnte. Ich musste alles nach Namen, Adresse und Datum klassifizieren und es gab Hunderte von Akten.

Und was waren die Dinge, die dich mehr interessierten?

Ich antwortete gern, wenn Kunden mit uns telefonierten. Natürlich waren einige ungeduldig oder unhöflich aber die Mehrheit waren ganz nett und von Zeit zu Zeit habe ich mit ihnen gut geplaudert.

Gut und was sonst?

Gegen Ende meines Praktikums habe ich mich am Empfang befunden. Ich war "eine Empfangsdame" um so zu sagen und das hat mir äußerst gut gefallen. Ich helfe gern Leuten mit Fragen und Problemen und ich habe das Gefühl gehabt, dass ich nützlich war.

Und was für Probleme hatten die Kunden?

Es waren nicht nur die Kunden, sondern auch Besucher und leitende Angestellte aus anderen Filialen der Firma. Meistens wollten Sie wissen, wo sie eine bestimmte Person finden könnten oder sie brauchten einen Pass für ihren Wagen. Zwei- oder dreimal musste ich mit der Frau oder dem Mann des Besuchers telefonieren, um zu erklären, dass der Partner oder die Partnerin verspätet bei der Rückkehr sein würde. Das Beste habe ich fürs Ende gelassen.

- 🔵 **Und was war denn das?**
- 🔵 Sie haben mich eingeladen ständig für die Firma nach dem Sommer zu arbeiten, weil sie ganz zufrieden mit mir waren!
- 🔵 **Und was war deine Antwort?**
- 🔵 Ich habe ohne weiteres ja gesagt. Ich bin ganz froh, eine Stelle zu haben!
- 🔵 **Das kann ich leicht verstehen!**

Future plans/advantages and disadvantages of jobs

AQA	✓
OCR	✓
EDEXCEL	✓
WJEC	✓
CCEA	✓

The table below provides some good structures to help you express your views about different jobs.

	Pilot (in) Politiker (in) Polizist (in) Ingenieur (in) Journalist (in) Kassierer (in) usw.	sein, werden,	weil da	der Job die Stelle die Stellung die Arbeit	angenehm gut bezahlt (nicht) leicht hart schwierig monoton	ist scheint
Ich möchte Ich möchte nicht Ich will Ich will nicht Ich würde gern Ich würde nicht		draussen drinnen im Freien				
	in einem/ einer	Büro Geschäft Krankenhaus Bürogebäude Großstadt Klinik Fabrik Bank	mit	Kollegen Kindern Erwachsenen Freunden Unbekannten Tieren Computer Maschinen Stress	arbeiten sein	

langweilig

Describing places of work
(Um Arbeitsplätze zu beschreiben)

beengend – claustrophobic

befriedigend – satisfying

deprimierend – depressing

draussen – outside

drinnen – inside

erfrischend – refreshing

ermüdend – tiring

ermunternd – encouraging

ich finde… – I find…

im Freien – in the open air

das Geschäft (-e) – business(es)

geschäftlich – on business

hart – hard

langweilig – boring

leicht – easy

luftig – airy

monoton – monotonous

schwierig – difficult

stressig – stressful

vielseitig – varied

What I want to do/what I want to be

Vielleicht könnte ich Frisör/Friseuse sein, weil ich sehr praktisch bin und ich mich gut mit Leuten verstehe.

Perhaps I could be a hairdresser because I am very practical and get on well with people.

Ich möchte Arzt/Ärztin werden, um den Leuten zu helfen.

I would like to be a doctor (in order) to help people.

Ich möchte gern Journalist(in) werden, weil die Arbeit so vielseitig ist und man die Welt sehen kann.

I would really like to be a journalist because the work is so varied and you can see the world.

Ich habe den Entschluss gemacht, im Freien zu arbeiten, da ich mich immer besser draussen fühle.

I have made the decision to work in the open air as I always feel better outside.

Eines ist sicher, ich würde nie Lehrer werden!

One thing is certain, I would never become a teacher!

Es ist mein traum, Polizist(in) zu werden.

It is my dream to be in the police.

Ich werde weiter studieren.

I am going to continue with my studies.

Mit ein wenig Glück, werde ich auf die Uni(versität) gehen.

With a bit of luck, I will go to university.

Die Idee, weiter zu studieren ist scheußlich!

The idea of carrying on studying is terrible!

Ich habe keine Ahnung, was ich tun werde. Alles wird von meinen Ergebnissen abängen.

I have no idea what I shall do. Everything will depend on my results.

Meine Lehrer waren nicht sehr optimistisch. Deshalb würde ich lieber warten, bis die Ergebnisse kommen.

My teachers were not very optimistic. And so I'd rather wait until the results come.

bedienen

Part-time jobs (Teilzeitjobs)

an-fangen – to start

arbeiten – to work

babysitten – to babysit

bedienen – to serve

beenden – to finish

bekommen – to receive, to earn

sein Bestes tun – to do one's best

fertig machen – to finish

Geld verdienen – to earn money

helfen – to help

Schichtarbeit machen – to work shifts

Zeitungen austragen – to do a paper round

Part-time work

Ich habe keinen Job aber meine Eltern geben mir ziemlich viel Taschengeld, weil ich Aufgaben zu Hause erfülle.
I don't have a job but my parents give me quite a lot of pocket money because I do jobs at home.

Zum Beispiel, ich wasche die Wagen und mache die Gartenarbeit.
For example, I wash the cars and do work in the garden.

Ich habe einen Teilzeitjob.
I have a part-time job.

Ich suche seit sechs Monaten Arbeit.
I have been looking for work for six months.

> **KEY POINT**
>
> Notice the use of **seit** + the present tense in the sentence above to give the idea of 'I have been … for' + time.

Ich hatte einen Teilzeitjob aber die Firma existiert nicht mehr.
I had a part-time job but the firm no longer exists.

Ich arbeite einen Abend und den ganzen Samstag.
I work one evening and all (of) Saturday.

Am Wochenende arbeite ich in einem Supermarkt, wo ich Kassierer(in) bin.
At the weekend, I work in a supermarket where I am a cashier on the tills.

Ich beginne um … Uhr und mache um … Uhr Schluss.
I start at … o'clock and finish at … o'clock.

Ich verdiene sechs Euro pro Stunde und ich versuche Geld für meine Ferien zu sparen.
I earn six euros an hour and I try to save money for my holidays.

Ich brauche Geld, um mein Schulzeug zu kaufen.
I need money to buy my school things.

Ich habe Geld nötig, um meinen Eltern zu helfen.
I need money to help my parents.

Ich muss Geld verdienen, um Klamotten, CDs und DVDs zu kaufen.
I need to earn money to buy clothes, CDs and DVDs.

> **KEY POINT**
>
> Notice the three different ways of saying 'need' in the three sentences above. When you use **müssen** it works in combination with a second verb.

Normalerweise babysitte ich für meinen Bruder und seine Frau.
I normally babysit for my brother and his wife.

Ich trage Zeitungen aus, wofür ich sehr früh aufstehe!
I do a paper round, for which I get up very early!

Work experience

Letzten Juni habe ich ein unbezahltes Arbeitspraktikum gemacht.
Last June, I did unpaid work experience.

Dafür musste ich mich gut organisieren.
I had to get myself well organised for it.

Erstens musste ich sehr früh aufstehen.
First of all, I had to get up very early.

Der Arbeitstag begann um acht Uhr fünfzehn.

The working day began at 8.15.

Wir machten Schluss um fünf Uhr und hatten eine Mittagspause von halb eins bis halb zwei.

We finished at five o'clock and had a mid-day break from half past twelve to half past one.

Ich habe den Bus/den Zug/die S-bahn/die U-bahn genommen um zur Arbeit zu kommen.

I took the bus/train/tram/underground to get to work.

Ich habe in einem Büro/Laden/Salon/einer Werkstatt/einer Fabrik mit dem Bäcker/mit dem Klempner gearbeitet.

I worked in an office/shop/salon/workshop/factory with the baker/plumber.

Ich habe dem Leiter/der Leiterin geholfen.

I helped the boss.

Ich habe Dokumente fotokopiert.

I photocopied documents.

Ich habe die Telefonanrufe beantwortet.

I answered the telephone (calls).

Ich habe das Werkzeug getragen.

I carried the tools.

Ich war das Mädchen/der Junge für alles im Buro.

I was the general dogsbody in the office.

Ich habe den Tee und den Kaffee gemacht.

I made the tea and coffee.

Ich bin Expert (in) beim Abspülen geworden.

I became an expert at washing-up.

Ich habe die ganze Zeit gearbeitet.

I worked the whole time.

Ich hatte nicht genug zu tun.

I didn't have enough to do.

Es war ein sehr praktisches und nützliches Erlebnis.

It was a very practical and useful experience.

Ich habe viel gelernt.

I have learned a lot.

KEY POINT

If your work experience was rather negative, look for the good points and do not dwell on the bad things.

PROGRESS CHECK

Say or write the following in German:

1. I have been looking for work for six months.
2. I will go to university with a bit of luck.
3. I did work experience.
4. I had to get up very early.
5. I took the bus to get to work.

1. Ich suche seit sechs Monaten Arbeit.   2. Ich werde mit ein bisschen Glück auf die Uni(versität) gehen.   3. Ich habe ein Arbeitspraktikum gemacht.   4. Ich musste sehr früh aufstehen.   5. Ich habe den Bus genommen um zur Arbeit zu kommen

6.4 Grammar

LEARNING SUMMARY	**After studying this section, you should be able to understand:** ● the conditional tense ● the pluperfect tense ● the accusative and dative cases

The conditional tense

AQA	✓
OCR	✓
EDEXCEL	✓
WJEC	✓
CCEA	✓

The conditional tense is used to say that you would do something, e.g. I would go, I would come. If you think of the English word 'would' it will help you to remember how to form the conditional tense in German because it sounds very similar, e.g. **ich würde gehen**, **ich würde kommen**.

> **KEY POINT**
>
> You will get extra marks if you use the conditional tense in your controlled speaking and writing assessments. It will expand the scope of your work and, in the reading and listening exams, it will help you to understand the relationship between particular actions.

The conditional tense is formed in a very similar way to the future tense. Just think of any verb in the future tense and convert the **werden** part to **würden**, e.g.:

ich werde sagen (I will say) → **ich würde sagen** (I would say)
wir werden stehen (we will stand) → **wir würden stehen** (we would stand)

The conditional tense is often called the 'future in the past' as it follows the same pattern as the future tense, but the **werden** auxiliary verb is changed into a past tense.

Look at the examples below:

ich würde gehen (I would go) **du würdest gehen** **er/sie/es/man würde gehen** **wir würden gehen** **ihr würdet gehen** **Sie würden gehen** **sie würden gehen**	**ich würde kommen** (I would come) **du würdest kommen** **er/sie/es/man würde kommen** **wir würden kommen** **ihr würdet kommen** **Sie würden kommen** **sie würden kommen**
ich würde sagen (I would say) **du würdest sagen** **er/sie/es/man würde sagen** **wir würden sagen** **ihr würdet sagen** **Sie würden sagen** **sie würden sagen**	**ich würde stehen** (I would stand) **du würdest stehen** **er/sie/es/man würde stehen** **wir würden stehen** **ihr würdet stehen** **Sie würden stehen** **sie würden stehen**

Say or write the following in German:

1. She would do her best.
2. We would not earn a lot of money.
3. I would do a paper round.
4. The work would not be well paid.
5. He would not finish the work.
6. Would you (**du**) do shift work?
7. He would not work with us.
8. Would you (**ihr**) help in the factory?
9. We (**man**) would start in this workshop.
10. They would not go with me.

1. Sie würde ihr Bestes tun. 2. Wir würden nicht viel Geld verdienen. 3. Ich würde Zeitungen austragen. 4. Die Arbeit würde nicht gut bezahlt sein. 5. Er würde die Arbeit nicht fertig machen/beenden. 6. Würdest du Schichtarbeit machen? 7. Er würde nicht mit uns arbeiten. 8. Würdet ihr in der Fabrik helfen? 9. Man würde in diesem Arbeitsraum anfangen. 10. Sie würden nicht mit mir gehen.

The pluperfect tense

AQA	✓
OCR	✓
EDEXCEL	✓
WJEC	✓
CCEA	✓

Pluperfect literally means 'more than perfect', i.e. 'more past than the perfect tense'. The pluperfect tense is used to deal with events that are a stage further back in the past than the perfect tense. In English, this is done quite simply by changing 'have' or 'has' to 'had', e.g.:

Perfect tense			Pluperfect tense		
I	have	done	I	had	done
you	have	tried	you	had	tried
he	has	worked	he	had	worked
she	has	spoken	she	had	spoken
it	has	started	it	had	started
one	has	reserved	one	had	reserved
we	have	earned	we	had	earned
you	have	drunk	you	had	drunk
you	have	gone	you	had	gone
they	have	come	they	had	come

German does almost exactly the same as English. Look at the German equivalent of the two tenses in the table below.

Perfect tense			Pluperfect tense		
ich	habe	**gemacht**	**ich**	hatte	**gemacht**
du	hast	**versucht**	**du**	hattest	**versucht**
er	hat	**gearbeitet**	**er**	hatte	**gearbeitet**
sie	hat	**gesprochen**	**sie**	hatte	**gesprochen**
es	hat	**angefangen**	**es**	hatte	**angefangen**
man	hat	**reserviert**	**man**	hatte	**reserviert**
wir	haben	**verdient**	**wir**	hatten	**verdient**
ihr	habt	**getrunken**	**ihr**	hattet	**getrunken**
Sie	sind	**gegangen**	**Sie**	waren	**gegangen**
sie	sind	**gekommen**	**sie**	waren	**gekommen**

KEY POINT

Notice that the bottom two verbs in the table on page 142 use **sein** in the perfect tense. The verbs that take **sein** in the perfect do the same in the pluperfect, changing **bin** to **war**, etc. (See page 73 for a list of verbs that use **sein** in the perfect tense.)

Now, look at the pluperfect of the verbs **gehen** and **kommen** in full:

ich war **gegangen** (I had gone)	**ich** war **gekommen** (I had come)
du warst **gegangen**	**du** warst **gekommen**
er war **gegangen**	**er** war **gekommen**
sie war **gegangen**	**sie** war **gekommen**
es war **gegangen**	**es** war **gekommen**
man war **gegangen**	**man** war **gekommen**
wir waren **gegangen**	**wir** waren **gekommen**
ihr wart **gegangen**	**ihr** wart **gekommen**
Sie waren **gegangen**	**Sie** waren **gekommen**
sie waren **gegangen**	**sie** waren **gekommen**

PROGRESS CHECK

Put the present tense verbs in the following sentences into the perfect and pluperfect tenses:

e.g. **ich** bin **sehr praktisch** ➡ **ich** bin **sehr praktisch** gewesen; **ich** war **sehr praktisch** gewesen.

1. **Es ist mein Traum.**
2. **Man sieht die Welt.**
3. **Ich verstehe mich gut mit Leuten.**
4. **Die Arbeit ist nicht so vielseitig.**

1. Es ist mein Traum gewesen; Es war mein Traum gewesen. 2. Man hat die Welt gesehen; Man hatte die Welt gesehen. 3. Ich habe mich gut mit Leuten verstanden; Ich hatte mich gut mit Leuten verstanden. 4. Die Arbeit ist nicht so vielseitig gewesen; Die Arbeit war nicht so vielseitig gewesen.

The accusative and dative cases

AQA	✓
OCR	✓
EDEXCEL	✓
WJEC	✓
CCEA	✓

The accusative case

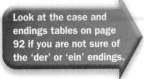
Look at the case and endings tables on page 92 if you are not sure of the 'der' or 'ein' endings.

- The accusative case is used after most verbs and is called the 'direct object'. It shows who or what receives the action, for example:

Ich bekomme einen Lohn.	I get a salary.
Warum hast du die Arbeit **so schnell gemacht?**	Why did you do the work so quickly?
Ich sehe die Eltern **sehr oft.**	I see the parents very often .
Er hat das Auto **versehentlich beschädigt.**	He accidentally damaged the car.

- The accusative case is also used after these prepositions:

bis	until	**gegen**	against, towards
durch	through	**ohne**	without
entlang	along	**um**	around, about
für	for	**wider**	against (contrary to)

For example:

Sie bleibt bis nächste Woche.

She is staying until next week.

Der Zug fährt jetzt durch den Tunnel.

The train is going through the tunnel now.

Der Dieb ging die Strasse entlang.

The thief was walking along the street.

Sie tut es für die Mannschaft.

She is doing it for the team.

Er ist nicht freundlich zu meinen Eltern.

He is not pleasant towards my parents.

Ohne dieses Geld, könnte ich nichts machen!

Without this money, I couldn't do anything!

Ich treffe dich um die normale Uhrzeit.

I will meet you at the normal time.

Der Leiter hat es gegen meinen Willen gemacht.

The boss did it against my will.

> Note the position of 'entlang'.

- An expression of definite time goes into the accusative, for example:

jeden Tag, letztes Jahr, nächstes Jahr, gute Nacht!

every day, last year, next year, good night!

Note that expressions of indefinite time go into the genitive, for example:

eines Tages, eines Nachmittags, eines Abends, einer Nacht.

one day, one afternoon, one evening, one night.

PROGRESS CHECK

Say or write the following in German:
1. He is travelling (**reisen**) without the passport.
2. I have photocopied the document.
3. I take the bus and the underground.
4. He walks along the beach.

4. Er geht den Strand entlang.
3. Ich nehme den Bus und die U-bahn.
2. Ich habe das Dokument fotokopiert.
1. Er reist ohne den Pass.

The dative case

- The dative case is used after certain verbs and is called the 'indirect object'. It shows that the action is done to or for someone or something, for example:

Die Chefin hat der Pratikantin einen Bonus angeboten.

The boss has offered the trainee a bonus.

Könntest du ihm einen Gefallen tun?

Could you do him a favour?

Meine Eltern geben mir ziemlich viel Taschengeld.

My parents give me quite a lot of pocket money.

> Although it would sound a little awkward in English, you could put 'to' or 'for' in front of each of the indirect objects in red and the sentences would still make sense. This is your test as to whether the object is in the dative case or not.

- The dative case is also used after these prepositions:

aus	out of, from	**nach**	after, to, according to
ausser	except (for)	**seit**	since
bei	at, at the house of, with	**von**	from, of, by, on
gegenüber	opposite	**zu**	to (a building), at
mit	with, by (transport)		

For example:

Fangen wir mit den langweiligen Sachen an.

Let's start with the boring things.

Ich war bei einer Maschinenbaufirma.

I was with an engineering firm.

Ich musste alles nach Namen, Adresse und Datum klassifizieren.

I had to classify everything according to the names, addresses and dates.

Angestellte aus anderen Filialen der Firma waren da.

Employees from other branches of the firm were there.

Ich habe mit ihnen gut geplaudert.

I had a good chat with them.

Accusative and dative prepositions

Some prepositions can be followed by the accusative case or the dative case. If there is movement into a place, the preposition takes the accusative. If there is no such movement, the preposition takes the dative. These prepositions are:

an	at, on	**über**	over, about
auf	on (top of)	**unter**	under, between
hinter	behind	**vor**	in front of, from
in	in, into	**zwischen**	(in) between
neben	near, next to		

Note that when many of these prepositions are placed with 'the', you can use a shortened form or the full form. Below are the three prepositions that are shortened the most often:

Accusative		Dative	
Full form	**Shortened form**	**Full form**	**Shortened form**
an das	**ans**	**an dem**	**am**
auf das	**aufs**	**–**	**–**
in das	**ins**	**in dem**	**im**

Here are some examples of accusative/dative prepositions in action:

Accusative	Dative
Ich gehe auf die Uni(versität).	**Sie war drei Jahre an der Uni.**
I am going to uni(versity).	She was three years at uni.
Sie sind in den Supermarkt gegangen.	**Ich arbeitete in dem Supermarkt.**
They went into the supermarket.	I used to work in the supermarket.
Sie fuhr schnell über die Brücke.	**Nebel hing über der Brücke.**
She drove quickly over the bridge.	Fog hung over the bridge.

Sie fuhr schnell über die Brücke.

Sample controlled assessment

Speaking

1 **Track 32** You are going to have a conversation with your teacher about your plans for the future. You could discuss the following:

- What work experience you have done
- What you plan to do after your GCSEs
- What studies you will continue after leaving school
- Which job or promotions these studies will qualify you for
- What work-related dreams you have for the future.

Teacher: Was hast du denn für Zukunftspläne?

Student: Es hat alles mit meinem Arbeitspraktikum angefangen.[2] Ich habe gute und schlechte Dinge dabei[17] gelernt, sowie meine Schwächen und Stärken entdeckt. Es war[26] ein äußerst interessantes[19] Erlebnis, spannend und von Zeit zu Zeit auch langweilig.

Teacher: Und wo fand dein Praktikum statt?

Student: Ich habe letztes Jahr im Juni in einer Maschinenbaufabrik in Glasgow gearbeitet.[2] Ich mußte[35] dafür sehr diszipliniert sein. Erstens mußte ich sehr früh aufstehen, da[5] der Arbeitstag um 8Uhr15 begann. Vielleicht scheint es nicht so bedeutend aber wenn man nicht lernt, diszipliniert zu sein, kann[35] es einem schwer fallen, einen Arbeitsplatz zu behalten. Die erste Lehre war, kein Fernsehen nach 10Uhr und früh ins Bett wie meine Eltern zu gehen.

Teacher: Sehr gut! Und was war die zweite Lehre?

Student: Ich habe den Bus, den Zug und die S-bahn genommen,[2] um[8] zur Arbeit zu kommen. Was die öffentlichen Verkehrsmittel betrifft,[4] hatte[11] ich vorher keine Ahnung wie abhängig man von diesen Mitteln ist, wenn man in der Großstadt arbeitet! Jetzt weiß ich es. Aber die bedeutendste[22] Lehre war, daß, obwohl ich das Mädchen für alles im Büro war,[4] mußte[35] ich lernen, daß wir alle Teile eines Teams sind, fast genau wie beim[23] Sport. Ich habe der Leiterin geholfen,[26] Dokumente fotokopiert,[9] Telefonanrufe[9] beantwortet usw. Ich habe auch ein- oder zweimal das Werkzeug für die Arbeiter getragen.[2] Was ich dabei[17] gelernt habe, ist, daß man sich mit seinen Mitarbeitern gut verstehen und so hilfsbereit[15] wie möglich sein sollte.[35] Man muss hart arbeiten wenn man erfolgreich sein will. Deshalb arbeite ich[1] sehr hart hier und zu Hause. Ich möchte[25] in die Unterstufe gehen, wenn[7] ich gute Ergebnisse bei den GCSEs bekomme. Ich werde auf die Ergebnisse warten, bevor ich einen Entschluß treffe.[9]

Teacher: Und was wirst du in der Unter- und Oberstufe studieren?

Student: Nächstes Jahr, würde ich[25] am liebsten Mathe, Physik, Biologie und Deutsch weiter machen. Deutsch, weil[5] ich hoffe, eines Tages in Deutschland zu arbeiten.[6]

Teacher: Was wirst du vorher machen?

Student: Es ist mein Traum, Ingenieurin zu werden. Mit ein wenig Glück werde ich[3] am Imperial College studieren. Imperial ist für Wissenschaft sehr berühmt, ganz wie Massachussetts Institute of Technology. Vielleicht könnte ich eines Tages auch dort studieren![18]

Teacher: Das hoffe ich auch für dich! Ich wünsche dir viel Glück dabei!

Turn to page 156 for a translation of this passage.

Examiner's comments

Try to use the same structure as in the other model answers, starting with past experience, moving to present studies and finishing with the future training and education you hope to have and the type of career you want for yourself.

Refer to pages 8–9 to see why this student has improved his or her chances of a high grade:

1 An example of the present tense
2 The past tense has been used
3 The future tense has been used
4 A good understanding of word order has been shown
5 Examples of the use of 'weil' and 'da'
6 A justified point of view
7 'Wenn' is a good connecting word
8 An 'um...zu' structure
9 Impressive vocabulary, e.g. 'fotokopiert', 'Telefonanrufe', 'treffe'
11 One example of a 'haben' structure
15 'So' + adjective
17 'Dabei' structures
18 An exclamation
19 An example of an adjective
22 An example of a superlative
23 'Bei' + a noun
25 Examples of conditionals
26 A mix of perfect and imperfect tenses has been used
35 Modal verbs have been used ('müssen', 'können', 'sollen')

Sample controlled assessment

Writing

1 Write about the pressures of school life. You could…
- list the kinds of stresses that occur at school
- explain the pressures caused by the need to produce good exam results
- explain how the school routine (uniform, classroom behaviour, etc.) causes extra problems
- comment on bullying either at your school or nationally.

`Stress in den Schulen´ ist ein heisses Eisen[37] und ich verstehe[1] nur zu gut warum. Für mich ist[1] dieser Stress eine Mischung von drei Dingen. Erstens, haben wir[1] den Drang, unsere Ergebnisse zu maximisieren, auch, wenn wir gar nicht so intelligent sind.[4] Zweitens haben wir die altmodischen[19] Regeln der Schulroutine und drittens haben wir das Schikanieren. Tyrannische und brutale junge Leute können[35] das Schulleben ruinieren.

Fangen wir mit dem Drangan, die besten[19] Ergebnisse zu bekommen. Letztes Jahr waren[26] meine Ergebnisse katastrophal und ich habe mich wie eine reine Versagerin gefühlt![2/26] Ich war überzeugt, dass ich keine Fortschritte machte, auch wenn ich sehr hart arbeitete. Das Problem war von einigen Lehrern verschlimmert,[9] die nicht loben[9] können,[35] doch immer gern kritisiert haben,[2] ein wenig wie meine Eltern. Sie sind sicher, dass ich Arzt sein werde,[3] während ich weiss, dass ich nur etwas mittelmäßiges finden werde.[3/4]

Dann kommt die Schulroutine, die[7] allerlei unnötige Belastungen schafft. Warum ist es[36] uns nicht erlaubt, zu wählen, was wir tragen? Auch kann[35] ich nicht verstehen, warum es verboten ist,[4] unsere Meinungen zu sagen. Ich verstehe, dass wir unsere Lehrer respektieren sollen, aber solche Regeln wie die erwähnten treiben es meiner Meinung nach, zu weit![18] Ach, es tut mir Leid, ich habe eine Meinung geäußert![18]

In unserer Schule wie überall ist der schlimmste[22] Stress das Schikanieren, das vielleicht aus der Tatsache stammt,[9] dass die Schulregeln so altmodisch und unfair sind. Es existiert[36] so viel Schikanieren besonders im Schulhof und in den Toiletten, das wenn man[34] nicht[12] Mitglied einer bestimmten Clique ist,[4] man[34] Schwierigkeiten haben kann. Es beginnt meistens mit Beschimpfungen[9] aber diese können weh tun. Ziemlich oft wird eine(r) geschnitten werden und manchmal werden wir zusammengeschlagen. Das Schwierigste[22] ist, dass wir nicht mit unseren Lehrern oder Eltern darüber sprechen können.[35] Ich würde[25] meine Schule wechseln, wenn das nur möglich wäre![40]

Turn to page 156 for a translation of this passage.

Examiner's comments

This student's performance has been enhanced by including a good number of the 40 points from pages 8–9:

1. The present tense has been used
2. The past tense has been used
3. The future tense
4. A good understanding of word order has been demonstrated
7. 'Die' is a good connective
9. Impressive vocabulary, e.g. 'verschlimmert', 'loben', 'stammt', 'Beschimpfungen'
12. A negative
18. Exclamations
19. Examples of adjectives
22. Superlatives have been used
25. An example of the conditional tense
26. A mix of perfect and imperfect tenses has been used
34. Use of 'man'
35. A modal verb has been used several times ('können')
36. Impersonal verbs have been included
37. A saying
40. A subjunctive. Very impressive!

Exam practice questions

Listening

1 🔘 **Track 33** Stephan and Ulrike are discussing a new teacher.

(a) What is Ulrike's attitude to the teacher? ....

Give four reasons to justify your answer.

(i) ....

(ii) ....

(iii) ....

(iv) .... **(5)**

(b) What is Stephan's attitude to the teacher? ....

Give four reasons to justify your answer.

(i) ....

(ii) ....

(iii) ....

(iv) .... **(5)**

(c) According to Ulrike, how was the teacher that morning?

.... **(1)**

(d) According to Stephan, how was the teacher during the lesson?

.... **(2)**

(e) What does Stephan say happened at the back of the classroom?

.... **(1)**

2 🔘 **Track 34** You are in Switzerland on holiday. You tune into a local radio station and hear a student called Dieter talking about school life.

(a) Why did Dieter stop going to school?

....

(b) What does Dieter do to earn money?

....

(c) What does he hope to do with this money?

....

(d) Why do so few children go to school?

.... **(4)**

Exam practice questions

3 **Track 35** Listen to this conversation between Sam and his teacher and then answer the questions that follow.

(a) What did the teacher think of Sam's work experience report?

.... **(1)**

(b) How often was Sam late for work?

.... **(1)**

(c) How did Sam explain his lateness?

.... **(1)**

(d) Which of Sam's habits could be dangerous in a factory?

.... **(1)**

(e) According to Sam, what caused him to do this dangerous thing?

.... **(1)**

(f) What did Sam say about his fellow workers? Give two details.

(i) ....

(ii) .... **(2)**

(g) Of what did Sam accuse the computer specialist?

.... **(1)**

(h) Why did Sam think the computer specialist did it?

.... **(1)**

(i) According to the teacher, what is Sam's reaction to being blamed?

.... **(1)**

(j) How does the teacher finally guess the truth of the report?

.... **(1)**

Exam practice questions

Reading

1   Read this e-mail, then answer the questions that follow.

Sam,

Ich mache mein Arbeitspraktikum fertig, während du deine erste Woche bei uns verbringst. Wie du weisst, man kann nicht so ein Praxis stoppen und ich habe eine geniale Idee gehabt! Du kennst mich und meine geniale Ideen, nicht wahr! Ich habe mit meiner Büroleiterin gesprochen und habe die Frage gestellt: kann Sam mit zur Arbeit kommen? Weisst du was, die Leiterin war ganz begeistert und hat folgende Dinge vorgeschlagen: die Firma hat viele britische Kunden, die immer auf Englisch schreiben und telefonisch mit ihnen sprechen. Du könntest im Büro arbeiten und die Briefe, E-Mails und Faxe beantworten. Auch mit englischsprachigen Kunden am Telefon sprechen, wenn das nicht zu kompliziert ist. Und das Beste daran? Du wirst gut bezahlt sein, während ich unbezahlt arbeite! Nicht schlecht, oder? Ich weiss, dass du total überrascht sein wirst aber was für ein Glück ist das?

Lass mich sofort Bescheid.
Deine
Susi.

(a)   How have the plans for Sam's visit to see Susi got complicated?

.... **(2)**

(b)   **(i)**   What was Susi's clever idea?

.... **(1)**

       (ii)   What was her manager's reaction?

.... **(1)**

(c)   Why did her manager react like that?

....

.... **(3)**

(d)   How could Sam be helpful? Give three details.

       (i)   ....

       (ii)   ....

       (iii)   .... **(3)**

(e)   Why is Sam going to be so lucky?

.... **(2)**

(f)   What must Sam now do?

.... **(1)**

Exam practice answers

NB: *In some of the questions where more than one mark is available, a forward slash has been used in the answers to indicate the breakdown of marks. This will help you to mark your own work.*

CHAPTER 1
Listening task 1
(a) A: 2 and 7; B: 4 and 6 **(b)** C: 3 and 5; D: 1 and 5
(c) E: 2 and 6; F: 2 and 7
Listening task 2
(a) A; **(b)** C; **(c)** B; **(d)** C; **(e)** C; **(f)** B; **(g)** A; **(h)** B
Listening task 3
(a) A; **(b)** C; **(c)** B; **(d)** C; **(e)** B
Reading task 1
(a) Ilse; **(b)** Antje; **(c)** Julia; **(d)** Konrad and Julia;
(e) Gisela; **(f)** Claudia; **(g)** Bert; **(h)** Siggi; **(i)** Blank answer; **(j)** Werner; **(k)** Sylvia; **(l)** Knud
Reading task 2
(a) Tina; **(b)** Boris; **(c)** Brigitte; **(d)** Brigitte; **(e)** Aldo; **(f)** Boris; **(g)** Brigitte; **(h)** Boris; **(i)** Aldo; **(j)** Tina
Reading task 3
(a) C; **(b)** A; **(c)** C; **(d)** A; **(e)** A; **(f)** A; **(g)** B; **(h)** B; **(i)** B; **(j)** C
Reading task 4
(a) He has had a car breakdown.
(b) Puncture and no petrol
(c) Because he always moans when she does something like this
(d) Ask the mechanic to collect him
(e) 10km away on the road to Bern
(f) In a parking bay/it is too dangerous to stay in the car
Reading task 5
(a) To report her daughter's absence from school
(b) She has stomach ache and fever.
(c) That she has cholera
(d) She works day and night.
(e) That she got the infection from her mother
(f) She could also be infected.
(g) (i)–(iii) In any order: organs turn to water; bleeding from the ears; nose bleeds
(h) (i)–(iii) In any order: a really high temperature; bad dreams; incurable
(i) In four or five days
(j) So as not to infect people at the school
(k) The daughter (Irene)

Reading task 6
(a) befinden; **(b)** geben; **(c)** Papiertaschentuch;
(d) nächsten; **(e)** Besteck; **(f)** fühlen; **(g)** Arztpraxis;
(h) Bett; **(i)** gegen; **(j)** holen; **(k)** informieren
CHAPTER 2
Listening task 1
(a) father; Konrad **(b)** quarrel; well **(c)** restaurant
(d) computer game **(e)** sixteen; a (one) month; adventure park
Listening task 2
(a) unhappy; Berlin; stepmother; hit
(b) left (run away from); bar; film director; role (part)
(c) (new) mother; forget; three years; tragic
Listening task 3
(a) A; **(b)** B; **(c)** B; **(d)** C; **(e)** C; **(f)** B; **(g)** A; **(h)** C
Reading task 1
(a) His parents are teachers.
(b) It is more important than his friends.
(c) That young people have a life outside of exams.
(d) Her parents are very understanding.
(e) (i)–(ii) In any order: drink no alcohol; be home by eleven
(f) Her boyfriend must go with her/otherwise she cannot go.
(g) She cannot go out at all/all outings are banned/ and boys are not allowed to phone
(h) Leaving home
(i) Partly good, partly bad
(j) During the working week
(k) Make sure she has done her homework
(l) (i)–(ii) In any order: the boyfriend does not take drugs; not to come home drunk
Reading task 2
(a) mehr; **(b)** Krebs; **(c)** fünfzig; **(d)** stinkt; **(e)** schlank
Reading task 3
(a) B; **(b)** A; **(c)** A; **(d)** C; **(e)** B; **(f)** C; **(g)** A and B; **(h)** C and D
Reading task 4
(a) (i)–(ii) In any order: her charity work; that Brad Pitt is her husband
(b) A happy life/she has a very handsome husband
(c) It has had its black side.
(d) Her obsession with a healthy life/and diet.
(e) French and German
(f) Her parents' break-up (divorce)
(g) It is said to be much better

(h) From cancer/Angelina was badly affected

CHAPTER 3

Listening task 1

Konzert; ausverkauft; gekauft; kommen; treffen; halbe; Aufführung; Schlag

Listening task 2

(a) 3; **(b)** 1; **(c)** 2; **(d)** 4; **(e)** Wait

Listening task 3

(a) Musicians on tour

(b) Bad weather casualties

(c) A sporting victory

(d) Interview with important politician

(e) Tail-back on major motorway

(f) German leader flies abroad

Listening task 4

Manni: D, F and G; Doro: A, B and F

Listening task 5

(a) >>Ich mache gern<<

(b) Last year

(c) The Oscar for Best Foreign Language Film

(d) Austrian

(e) 10 euros a month

(f) 060424957

Listening task 6

(a) D; **(b)** A; **(c)** B

Listening task 7

6.30 – G; 7.00 – D; 8.00 – H; 10.00 – C; 11.00 – F; 12.00 – B; 13.00 – E; 13.30 – I; 14.30 – J; 16.30 – A

Reading task 1

A, B, F, G, I and J

Reading task 2

(a) She sang

(b) **(i)–(iii) In any order:** beautiful; slim; blonde

(c) In the 1920s to 40s.

(d) Femme fatale/ruined them

(e) Giving (creating) her a false personality

(f) **(i)–(iii) In any order:** she was quite cold; she was reserved; she didn't seek stardom

(g) It was top of the hit-parade in Germany and English-speaking countries during the Second World War.

(h) She lived alone in a small flat in Paris.

Reading task 3

(a) 20.30; **(b)** 23.00; **(c)** 20.00; **(d)** 22.30; **(e)** 19.20

Reading task 4

(a) Gabriela; **(b)** Rita; **(c)** Antonia; **(d)** Siggi; **(e)** Ricki; **(f)** Peter; **(g)** Uschi

Reading task 5

(a) Uli's parents are PE teachers/they have access to lots of sporting opportunities.

(b) In the sports centre

(c) **(i)–(ii) In any order:** in the forest; in the beach area

(d) Swim every day/have a non-alcoholic beer/at the beach café.

(e) Younger brother and sister are slaves to computer games and the TV/seem to argue all day

(f) Bowling

(g) Joanna should let him know what she finds the most interesting/they will program them in.

(h) Next week/Uli cannot wait

Reading task 6

(a) Come off the A5 (E35), exit 60 (both parts needed)

(b) He has had a good idea/which is not usual.

(c) The Europa-Park is very close by/since Al's parents are staying the next day/the two families could go together.

(d) **(i)–(v) Any five from:** it's very modern; you can have a lot of fun; the rides are frightening; there are gentle rides for the parents; there are many good restaurants and snack bars; you can eat and drink well.

(e) Let Corinne know as quickly as possible/if his parents would like to go to the Europa-Park.

(f) Reserve tickets

(g) The park is on the way to where Al's parents are going.

CHAPTER 4

Listening task 1

(a) **(i)** 0479 **(ii)** 14 **(iii)** 12.30pm; **(b)** A and D

Listening task 2

(a) Wednesday and Thursday

(b) 30 and 50 euros

(c) **(i)** Go to a chat show with *Die Prinzen* **(ii)** Ask personal questions

Listening task 3

(a) Unfavourable; **(b)** Favourable; **(c)** Favourable;

(d) Unfavourable; **(e)** Unfavourable; **(f)** Favourable

Listening task 4

(a) D; **(b)** C; **(c)** D; **(d)** D; **(e)** C

Listening task 5

(a) the beach; **(b)** B; **(c)** A; **(d)** C; **(e)** B

Listening task 6

(a) The father; **(b)** The father; **(c)** The mother;

(d) The mother; **(e)** The father; **(f)** The father;

(g) The mother; **(h)** The mother; **(i)** The father;

(j) The mother

Listening task 7

(a) A discount rail card

(b) 20 euros

(c) 50%

(d) Any town in Germany with a mainline train station.

(e) **(i)–(ii) In any order:** eat in the restaurant carriage for 25 euros; use the sleeping carriage at 60% discount on the standard rates.

(f) **(i)–(ii) In any order:** before 9am; between 4.30pm and 7.30pm

(g) People between 18 and 59

(h) **(i)–(ii) In any order:** passport; identity card

Listening task 8

(a) C; **(b)** D; **(c)** F; **(d)** A; **(e)** B

Listening task 9

(a) B

(b) C

(c) A

(d) C

(e) Fähre; Schottland

(f) Zug; Spanien

(g) Flugzeug; Schottland

(h) Flugzeug; Amerika

Reading task 1

(a) frei; **(b)** schnell; **(c)** braucht; **(d)** Marktplatz;

(e) Website

Reading task 2

(a) C; **(b)** B; **(c)** A; **(d)** E; **(e)** D

Reading task 3

(a) She has good news.

(b) (i)–(ii) In any order: Aunt Doro has a restaurant; the sea is nearby.

(c) Come for 2–3 weeks/and work in her restaurant.

(d) (i)–(iv) Any four from: it is not very interesting; washing up; laying tables; bringing up wine and beer from the cellar; the pay is nine euros an hour

(e) (i)–(ii) In any order: it's very lively; can go sailing with Uncle Udo

(f) (i)–(ii) In any order: Holland; Poland

Reading task 4

(a) C; **(b)** B; **(c)** A; **(d)** D; **(e)** A; **(f)** D; **(g)** B; **(h)** C

CHAPTER 5

Listening task 1

(a) B; **(b)** A; **(c)** A; **(d)** B; **(e)** A; **(f)** C

Listening task 2

Tina: B and D; Wolf: E and G; Chrissi: C and F; Reinhardt: H and I

Listening task 3

Reading task 1

(a) 4; **(b)** 1; **(c)** 2; **(d)** 3; **(e)** 5; **(f)** 6

Reading task 2

(a) gelernt; **(b)** sprechen; **(c)** Umwelt; **(d)** Tier-;

(e) Meere; **(f)** Treibhauseffekt; **(g)** Schock; **(h)** verrückt

Reading task 3

(a) People at home

(b) (i)–(ii) In any order: turn off the lights; don't use the TV stand-by function

(c) Sort it properly

(d) Do not use it in town

(e) Wear warmer clothing at home

(f) Do not fill it too full

(g) (i)–(iii) In any order: install a water barrel; plant a vegetable garden; build a compost heap

Reading task 4

(a) Until they left Belgium (got to Germany)

(b) Max left it at a petrol station/they had to go back /it was no longer there.

(c) Max got a fine/for no red triangle/the others had to pay.

(d) They got to the campsite too late/their place had been taken.

(e) (i)–(iii) In any order: very old; dirty; no fire alarm

(f) He smoked in bed/set the hotel on fire/got arrested.

CHAPTER 6

Listening task 1

(a) She finds him great **(i)–(iv) In any order:** she learns more with him than the previous teacher; he is funny; he speaks clearly; he laughs at their mistakes

(b) He does not think so **(i)–(iv) In any order:** he is much nicer to the girls; he is sarcastic to boys; he doesn't give them much time; the girls get better marks

(c) He was very nice.

(d) So friendly/he couldn't control the class

(e) The smallest boy was being bullied.

Listening task 2

(a) To earn money

(b) He has a little job in a sports centre

(c) Help his mother

(d) They are only a name on a list.

Listening task 3

(a) It was the worst ever

(b) All the time

(c) Problems with public transport

(d) Falling asleep

(e) Boredom

(f) (i)–(ii) In any order: they didn't like their work; they were looking for other jobs

(g) Breaking the photocopier

(h) She liked to cause him problems.

(i) He always blames someone else.

(j) She sees Sam fall asleep in front of her.

Reading task 1

(a) She has to finish her work experience/during the first week of Sam's visit.

(b) (i) She asked the office boss if Sam could come to work with her. **(ii)** Enthusiastic

(c) The firm has British customers/who always write in English/and who talk on the phone in English.

(d) (i)–(iii) Any three from: work in the office; answer letters; answer e-mails; answer faxes

(e) Sam will be well paid/while Susi is unpaid.

(f) Let Susi know straight away

CHAPTER 1
Speaking 1

Student: Last year I found myself on a school exchange visit at my exchange partner's home on the edge of the Black Forest/Schwarzwald. On the Wednesday evening, all the members of the exchange had tickets for the Rolling Bones concert in Freiburg, the capital of the Black Forest. The Rolling Bones are a hard rock group, on which I'm extremely keen. I had been looking forward to this concert for a long time. And finally at the end of April, the great day came. It was quite a warm spring evening, the sun was shining and we believed we would have a happy evening.

Teacher: Where did the concert take place and how did you travel there?

Student: We were to go to the Freiburg Stadium from my exchange partner's home on our school bus and the bus came (round) at 6pm. So far, so good. I had said to the others, we'll have an extremely good time this evening.

Teacher: And what was it like on the bus?

Student: Just great! We saw a film about the Rolling Bones and naturally we sang along (with it) and danced a bit, but the teachers didn't like the dancing! The journey lasted three quarters of an hour and we had a lot of fun on the bus without being too naughty for the teachers. As always!

Teacher: Interesting, and did you go straight to the stadium?

Student: Don't make me laugh! We had to queue for an hour and a half. And that was at the stadium entrance. It was like an audition for *X-Factor* in Manchester or Liverpool! But once in the stadium itself, we were in a better mood, because we were happy to be together and to be able to see the preparations on stage. It was highly exciting! We had a fried sausage two or three times and washed them down with coke.

Teacher: So far, so good, you said earlier. When did it begin to go wrong?

Student: It was like in England! Suddenly, the weather changed, like it often does with us! For two whole hours it poured down and we were all wet through, from head to toe. But, we all sang our hearts out during the performance. The Rolling Bones were not as wet through as us and they did their best to cheer us up.

Teacher: And later, what happened later?

Student: Two days later, I didn't feel at all good and I went to the doctor's. I had an unbelievable headache, pains in my nose, throat and stomach, and a high temperature with it. The male doctor, no, the lady doctor insisted on me going to bed and staying there for two or three days, because I had flu. That, I did – I was so sorry for myself! But, not the teachers, they can be so cruel!

Teacher: That I cannot imagine. I think you're exaggerating there!

Student: Perhaps a bit. But, I'll tell you something. In spite of the illness, I'll willingly go back with the school to the Schwarzwald next year. Hopefully, this time we'll have no disasters.

Teacher: I hope so, too, this time I'm coming with you!

Writing 1

Frauenpopmagazin: Dear readers, you will already have heard of Kris Ledermann as much for his manly beauty, as for his astounding music. A very hearty welcome to Frauenpopmagazin, Kris Ledermann.

Kris Ledermann: I thank you and I'm very happy to be here. But, I must clear something up. In no way am I handsome and superficial beauty does not interest me. But, inner beauty is something quite different.

Frauenpopmagazin: Thanks for the correction. Well, then, Kris, our readership will recognise you from your triumph at the Nixdorf pop festival last year, where you won the prizes for best singer, best lyricist, and best new talent. It was the first time that one personality has stood on the podium three times.

Kris Ledermann: True. But, I had a lot of luck. For me, it had been an awkward encounter with fame. I'm a politically involved person and it will be a better world if we can share things like prizes. No person has a right to more than one prize at such festivals. That's my opinion. The good things of this Earth, we should share as far as possible.

Frauenpopmagazin: Let's perhaps talk about your family and your circle of friends.

Kris Ledermann: Ah, now you're calling me 'du', we're making progress. We're all equal, aren't we?

Frauenpopmagazin: I'd say so, too. Your family and your circle of friends?

Kris Ledermann: Well, then, my parents, Gabi and Horst have had a considerable influence on me. Mum is a music teacher and dad is a refuse collector. He is the most civilised man/human being I've ever come across. Both of them are totally generous and very into human rights. I've also become like that and that's thanks to them. I've a brother, Fred, with whom I regularly play tennis and squash to keep fit. My friends from Harsewinkel, my home town, I see a lot.

Frauenpopmagazin: And what else do you do during your free moments/time off?

Kris Ledermann: I play the guitar and sing for the patients in the local hospitals as often as I can.

Frauenpopmagazin: That's really kind!

Kris Ledermann: It's more what I have to do. We give people what we have to give. I have a guitar and a voice and will carry on working for my fellow-beings. I will never see my career as more important than other people.

Frauenpopmagazin: Kris, you're a lesson to us all.

Writing 2

Hi Hansi!

Greetings from the Schöndorf Hospital, where I'm now a patient. Don't panic, as I'm already better and I'm only here for a short period/stay. It was right after school and I was on the way home to sort my sports kit out, before my tennis match for the county. Wishful thinking/little did I know!

Suddenly, I smelled smoke and I knew there was a fire somewhere. You know my home is tucked away on the edge of town and almost in the country. For this reason, you see no one around during the working day. I walked round the corner and to my great astonishment I saw how our only neighbour's house was already on fire.

I had my mobile phone with me and was just about to call for the fire brigade, when, at the bedroom window, I caught sight of Schnappi, our neighbour's dog that bites, as he was barking and scratching away at the panes of glass. And so, I didn't just phone for the fire brigade, but for an ambulance as well. What was I to do now? My parents would be at work for another three hours and my elder brother, who is useless in such situations, was presumably asleep next to his school books in the garden. There was only one thing to do. I shook myself, went into the smoke-filled house as quickly as possible, rushed up the stairs and got to the dog with some difficulty. He clearly knew that I was there to help him and he did not try to bite me.

While I was clambering down the stairs with Schnappi under my arm, the flames burned me a little, but I hadn't noticed it until, later, I found myself in the ambulance. The dog that bites was unharmed and licked my face! It didn't have to do that! Tomorrow, a team from the local paper is coming. A (lady) reporter will interview me and a photographer will take pictures of me. There's no way I will buy this newspaper, as you know, I can't stand seeing photos of me! See you soon, Gisela.

CHAPTER 2
Speaking 1

Teacher: I believe you smoke?

Student: Yes, I did smoke in the past. But I would never smoke again and there are three reasons for that. Firstly, smoking began to affect my health. I'm a sportswoman and represent the school and the county at tennis and basketball. I noticed that I was coughing more when I ran. That wasn't good and had a bad effect on my self-esteem/confidence.

Teacher: And the second reason was?

Student: It was costing so incredibly much. I was smoking a pack(et) a day and that cost more than a thousand pounds in a year. At the time I had and I still have a part-time job. I spent a large part of my money on cigarettes, small cigars and snuff!

Teacher: And what sort of thing is snuff?

Student: It's a brown or reddy-brown powder, which is made from dried and ground tobacco leaves. I think that you can compare it with cocaine, because it seriously damages the nose and can cause cancer.

Teacher: I understand. And were you addicted to it?

Student: I think more to the cigarettes. But, what I do know is that it was high time I saved my money and health! And I did it with nicotine patches, a whole load of nicotine patches. Fortunately it worked!

Teacher: Worked?

Student: Yes, it was a success…it worked well. I had a lot of help from my friend, Jason. We weren't going out together but we were and will always be very good friends. He gave up this poison at the same time and we did our detox together. Not easy. I wouldn't want to do something like that a second time.

Teacher: Did your parents know while you were going through it?

Student: Can't say. If they did, then they were very patient and sensitive. And perhaps that was another reason why I gave up. My parents have been so good to me. I believe I owed them it, to give up/stop.

Teacher: And the third reason?

Student: That had to do with a boy and Jason helped me with this, too. He can be honest with me and he explained to me in a sensitive way, how my clothes and my hair smelt of tobacco. I promise you something, I will never stink of tobacco again. For a young woman like me that was enough!

Teacher: And enough is enough. Thank you for an extremely interesting and lively conversation.

Student: My thanks to you too.

Writing 1

Two years ago, I believed I would never marry, because my girlfriend had left me in the lurch, but now I've a different opinion/changed my mind. In the meantime, I've been out with some girls and had good relationships with them. I'm a very sociable person and need other people's company.

But, living as a husband or partner lies a long way in the future. At sixteen, I'm much too young to be thinking about a wedding or something like that. I shall study for two more years in my comprehensive and after that will hopefully spend three or four more years at university. Besides/also, I've not yet found a person who makes the Earth move for me, as they say in pop songs!

What I can make clear is that I'm no male chauvinist pig, although I'm a rugby player and we have the reputation of being hooray Henries. I would also like to state that I'm for women's rights and for equal opportunities, as well. If my partner of the future becomes better qualified than I, has better job prospects, or just has a more interesting profession than me, I will be prepared to be a house-husband and to look after the children, provided my partner earns enough money to keep us (provide for us).

What I've learnt is that my future wife or partner will not necessarily be extremely beautiful, because the most important beauty is inside and if I find myself a person who has a great heart, makes me laugh and has sympathy with the poor of this world, that will be enough for me.

CHAPTER 3

Speaking 1

Teacher: What do you like doing in your leisure time?

Student: That depends, because it all hangs/depends on the weather. I'm a great sports fan and just love being in the open air. But, I've also got other interests, other hobbies that I can do indoors.

Teacher: Well, then, let's start with your sport. What sport do you like?

Student: I play women's football for the school and the county and table tennis for our youth club. I represented the town at tennis and till last summer I also did athletics for the district, in the 100 and 200-metre sprints, but I gave up sprinting because I had too much to do. It was a good decision. What interests me most is not competitive sport, but street hockey, which is quite disorganised. When I'm playing on the street/road with my friends, I can totally relax. That is not the case with competitive sport! And I'm not interested in being famous.

Teacher: That's impressive. Apart from sport, what are your hobbies?

Student: I like the Internet and television, but I'm really keen on quiet, calm things like reading and chess. I play chess with my father and that has become a sort of connection between us both. We often play for hours (and hours) and mum can't understand why we can sit for so long in the lounge without talking!

Teacher: And could you perhaps make a career for yourself out of one of your hobbies?

Student: I would like to be a sports/PE teacher, but I will have to study until I'm twenty-two and that's too long. I shall perhaps go to university and, as I like books so much, I could also/even become a librarian. But that also needs too much time. Perhaps I'll work in the youth service in our town. I could perhaps contribute to the youth sports programme.

Teacher: Great! At least you have a lot of possibilities.

Student: I'd say so.

Writing 1

I don't know what I would do without my mobile (phone), my MP3 and my Internet. I'm allowed to/can say my Internet, because my web page and also my Facebook have personalised it for me. But, let's start with my mobile.

It is more a good friend than a piece of technology, because it brings me and my family a kind of security. Before I had my own mobile phone, my parents didn't know where I was, at what time I would come home, what I wanted to eat and so on. And, because mum and dad are anxious people, I now have the freedom to do things, which I couldn't do before. For example, I'm allowed to go out more often than a year ago, especially because I have a reliable mobile.

My Facebook and web page have opened up the world for me. Through them, I have so many new contacts and friends that my horizons are continually extending. I feel I have more understanding of individuals because I now know so many people.

But I must admit that new technology has another, negative side. For example, let's take my MP3. The parents say that I spend all my time with my earphones on my head and that it's almost impossible to have a conversation with me at home. That's not altogether true but they are a bit right!

But, as far as pornography and paedophilia are concerned, my parents are 100% right! Facebook and chat rooms will offer mentally sick outsiders/strangers the opportunity to access our personal lives and our circle of friends. For that reason, my friends and I will be extremely careful.

Another disadvantage for me are the bills! Technology is never going to be very cheap and one day my friends and I must learn to reduce our use of the Internet and our mobile phones. Perhaps a scientist and/or a computer specialist will find a way in which we can use our new technology at almost no cost. We can all dream!

CHAPTER 4

Speaking 1

Student: Last summer my family and I had a bad experience during our holiday in Turkey. So, this August we are going to go to the South of France. With a bit of luck, we won't have to put up with last holiday's disasters all over again.

Teacher: It would be very interesting to hear your story.

Student: Where shall I start? Well, then, let's start with the airport in Turkey. We got out of the plane and went by bus to the main hall. So far, so good. No problems, either with the police or the customs. Then, we found that my sister, Anita, had got the wrong case. When we went back to the carousel, we discovered that Anita's had disappeared. The airline delivered the right bag to us at the hotel, three days later.

Teacher: And what were the other disasters?

Student: Oh, yes! The bus trip to the hotel was great, no question. The sun was shining, it was very warm and the land and seascapes gleamed so beautifully that the passengers were in a very good mood. When we arrived at the Hotel Hercules the situation soon changed.

Teacher: Tell me exactly what happened.

Student: The Hercules was not really a hotel, more a building site. We had no running water in the bathroom, a window pane was missing in the sitting room and we had insects in the beds! Dad made a complaint. We then got another apartment/flat, but it was worse than the first!

Teacher: Well, what did you do then?

Student: You don't know my father. He has daft ideas from time to time and this was one of those times! He bought a tent and we camped throughout the whole holiday. Flexitours paid us our money back but our holiday was ruined. For this reason, I'm looking forward to our next holiday in France. It'll be so much better!

Teacher: I hope so, too!

Writing 1

I should like to tell you about my summer holidays in Cornwall. They took place in the town of St Ives and we had really great fun day in day out. This part of Cornwall has the nickname of the "English Riviera" and thanks to the especially fine weather I can understand that. Mum had booked two rooms in advance in a tiny pub with bed and breakfast, which appeared to be a very good choice from the start on account of the friendliness and professionalism of the landlady. It is true that she gave us extremely large portions to eat, but that was only one side of her hospitality. She was never too busy to help the guests. When, for example, one of the guests had a flat tyre, she left the pub and changed the tyre for him!

We had so much good luck during these holidays, mostly thanks to the fantastic weather! The sun shone so often and the sea was so blue that I understood why there are so many painters, male and female, in this part of Cornwall. During the day, we spent all our time on the beach, where we went bathing and lying in the sun. In the evening it was quite different, as we found a disco at the end of the pier, where we danced for hours and hours and made (ourselves) new friends, in particular Maxi and Maria, whom I phone regularly and correspond with by Internet.

Next year all three of us will be going to Spain without the parents and we will enjoy ourselves, no question, because we get on so well. For this opportunity, I'm so grateful to mum and dad, because they have been so understanding. I can't tell you how much I'm already looking forward to this holiday. For it, I'm already learning a little Spanish and hopefully I'll be able to speak enough, to make myself understood. I'm not interested in shouting in English abroad, so that I can get something.

CHAPTER 5
Speaking 1

Teacher: What sort of environmental problems get you worried?

Student: I believe we are ill-treating the Earth and that makes me anxious. Perhaps it's already too late, but I don't know since some scientists say yes and others no. Yet I know we are doing certain things to protect the environment but it is not enough by a long way.

Teacher: And what do you actually do for your own personal environment and for the wider one?

Student: I do what I can, to protect the globe. Perhaps I don't do enough, but, yesterday, for example, I went to school on foot. My mother would always take me with her but that is twice two miles more for her. She is obliged to travel to her place of work by car, but I have my legs! When we have bad weather, I take the opportunity of travelling with mum. Storms and snow apart, the last time I got driven to school was two years ago!

Teacher: Impressive! And what else do you do for your personal and the wider environment?

Student: I obviously use public transport to travel to town. I always take my litter with me and I go to the recycling centre with the empty bottles and cans. And I don't wash the bottles in advance, because they're also washed in the centre. I don't waste any valuable water! And I do exactly the same with the power, the electricity. I switch off! Lights, television, computer. I also put only (just) enough water in the kettle. I never fill it, except when there are four or five of us!

Teacher: I'm impressed! Now we come back to what disturbs you. What would you like to say to me?

Student: To start with, I have to say that perhaps I was too pessimistic when we started this conversation. The situation is bad, but not so bad that we can't do anything about it. For example, I'm sure we'll one day be compelled to use public transport instead of our cars. To push this policy the government is going to have to improve public transport. That way, we'll cause fewer emissions, which pollute the air. That will help people like asthmatics and bring down the asthma rate. There are also particular problems, which are global, like the extinction of threatened species, dying seas, over-fishing thanks to factory ships and so on, the use of plastic bags, which kill flora and fauna and threaten the ozone layer. But, it's not really too late. We must all work together on a global level. Then, the next generation will have a beautiful world!

Teacher: Thank you for an inspiring conversation!

Writing 1

My family and I do what we can to protect the environment. Even if it is not enough, we won't need to have it on our conscience. Some scientists are of the opinion that our world is lost. I'm not totally in agreement with that. I will explain why, but first I'd like to list the things we do collectively in my small home for the local and wider environment. My parents use the car as rarely as possible and we all normally travel by public transport or bike. My sister and I are never driven to school, except in bad weather.

One of my tasks is to walk with the empty bottles and cans to the recycling centre, and I mean walk, even if the centre is quite far away. I also mow the lawn and have to put the grass on the compost heap. We have a vegetable garden and we use the compost to keep the soil in top condition! We grow enough vegetables and fruit to support us/keep us going the whole year.

Of course, we give vegetables to the neighbours and recently two or three have started their own vegetable gardens and allotments. Soon, we shall grow enough to give parcels of vegetables to the old people in the neighbourhood. I have already been working for three years in our garden and I can tell you how much enjoyment it gives me! On a global level things are, of course, rather different. Last week, I read in a German newspaper how the tiger, the whale and other species are threatened with extinction. I already know that certain seas are dying from pollution and that one or two smaller seas have already died. From this, we can see how the greenhouse effect

threatens the whole world. 'Collective action!' is the battle-cry! Otherwise, we will be in a really bad situation.

I am a positive person and will end on a positive note. The environmental movement has already begun to make real progress. Thanks to their campaigns the new plastic bags and fast-food packaging are biodegradable. Inside the European Union, they have started to build fewer roads, motorways and airports and the American president has approved the Kyoto agreement. We still have time!

CHAPTER 6
Speaking 1

Teacher: What sort of plans do you have for the future?

Student: It all began with my work experience (placement). I learnt good and bad lessons from it, as well as my strengths and weaknesses. It was an extremely interesting experience, exciting and also boring from time to time.

Teacher: And where did your work experience take place?

Student: Last June, I did unpaid work experience in a machine engineering factory in Glasgow. I had to get myself really organised for it. Firstly, I had to get up very early, as the working day began at 8.15. Perhaps that doesn't seem to be so important, but, if you can't learn to be disciplined, it can be really hard to hold down a good job. The first lesson was, no television after 10 o'clock and early to bed like my parents.

Teacher: Very good! And the second lesson was?

Student: I took the bus, train and tram to get to work. As far as public transport is concerned, before, I had no idea how much you depend on these forms of transport when you work in the city! Now, I know. But, the most important lesson was, although I was the office Girl Friday, I had to learn that we are all part of a team, male and female, almost exactly like in sport. I helped the manager, photocopied documents, took (the) phone calls, etc. I even carried the tools for the workmen once or twice. And what I have learnt is that you have to get on well with your fellow workers and be as helpful as possible. You have to work hard if you want to succeed. And so, I work very hard here and at home. I want to go into the Lower Sixth/First Year Sixth, if I get good results in my GCSEs. I will wait for the results before I make a decision.

Teacher: And what will you study in the First and Second Year Sixth?

Student: Next year, I would really like to carry on with Maths, Physics, Biology and German. German, because I hope to work in Germany one day.

Teacher: And before that, what will you do?

Student: It's my dream to be an engineer. With a bit of luck, I'll study at Imperial College. Imperial is very well-known for science, just like Massachussetts' Institute of Technology. Perhaps, one day, I could study there as well.

Teacher: I hope that for you, too! I wish you a lot of luck with it!

Writing 1

'Stress in the schools' is a hot potato and I understand only too well why. For me, this stress is a mixture of three things. Firstly, we are under pressure to maximise our results, even when we are not that intelligent. Secondly, we have the old-fashioned rules of our school routine and, thirdly, we have bullying. Bullying and brutal young people can ruin school life.

Let us start with the pressure to get the best results. Last year, my results were disastrous and I felt a total failure! I was convinced that I was making no progress, even when I was working very hard. The problem was made worse by some teachers, who can't give praise, yet have always liked criticising, a bit like my parents. They are sure that I shall be a doctor, while I know that I shall only find something mediocre.

Then comes the school routine, which creates all sorts of unnecessary pressures. Why aren't we allowed to choose what we wear? I can't understand, either, why we are not allowed to express our opinions/say what we think. I understand that we are to respect our teachers, but such rules as those I've mentioned take things too far, in my opinion. Oh, I'm sorry, I've expressed an opinion!

In our school, as everywhere (else), the worst stress is bullying, which perhaps stems from the fact that the school rules are so old-fashioned and unfair. There is so much bullying going on, especially in the schoolyard and the toilets, since, when you're not part/a member of a particular gang, you can have problems. It mostly starts with name calling, but this can hurt. Quite often, you get ignored and sometimes we get beaten up. The worst thing about it is that we can't talk about it with our teachers or parents. I would change my school, if only that were/was possible!

Listening transcripts

CHAPTER 1

Speaking 1 (track 2)

Listening 1 (track 3)

(a) Alice: Was nimmst du denn Benno?

Benno: Das ist einfach. Ich möchte gerne einen Fruchtsaft und eine Portion Pommes. Und du, Alice?

Alice: Für mich ist das auch einfach. Eine Tasse Kaffee und ein Brötchen mit Schinken.

(b) David: Was soll es denn für dich sein, Crystal?

Crystal: Eine Bratwurst und ein Glas Rotwein. Nein, ich trinke lieber ein Bier. Nimmst du das auch, David?

David: Mmmh. Ja, ich esse wie du auch eine Bratwurst aber ich trinke lieber ein Glas Rotwein.

(c) Ernst: Frankie, ich trinke eine Tasse Kaffee, du auch?

Frankie: Ja, ja. Und ich esse damit wahrscheinlich ein Brötchen mit Schinken.

Ernst: Ich nehme Pommes damit.

Listening 2 (track 4)

– Guten Abend, liebe Hörer und Hörerinnen! Willkommen bei *Jung-Gesund*, unserem Jugendmagazin, das sich für die Gesundheit der kommenden Generation spezialisiert. Fangen wir mit Angela an.

– In meinem Fall war es so, dass ich bei meiner Ärztin war und die hat mir gesagt, dass ich sehr übergewichtig bin! Die Ärztin war nett aber sie hat mir sehr direkt gesagt, dass ich 15 Kilo abnehmen muß.

– Das ist ziemlich viel, wie haben Sie reagiert?

– Ich wollte es machen, auch wenn es sehr, sehr schwierig werden würde.

– Während dieser Periode haben Sie zu rauchen begonnen. Warum?

– Um mir zu helfen das Gewicht schneller zu verlieren. Ach, nach drei Tagen rauchte ich ein Päckchen pro Tag.

– Wie haben Sie denn das Gewicht verloren?

– Ich habe fast kein Fett gegessen und ich wurde Mitglied eines Fitnessklubs.

– Was war Ihre Reaktion, als Ihr Freund meinte, Sie wären jetzt zu schlank?

– Ich habe ihm gesagt, er könnte eine andere Freundin finden!

– Und wie ist es jetzt bei der Arbeit?

– Weil ich jetzt eine so positive Person bin, hat mein Boss mir einen besseren Job gegeben.

– Darf ich Ihnen und Ihrem Freund Klaus gratulieren!

– Sprechen wir nicht von Klaus. Ich will ihn nicht mehr sehen und ich habe es ihm auch gesagt!

Listening 3 (track 5)

Karl: Aua, Fritz, das schmerzt!

Fritz: Tut mir leid, Karl. Das war ein Unfall. Ich wollte dir nicht weh tun.

Karl: Ich weiß, du bist nur ungeschickt! Aber zu Fuss kann ich nicht mehr gehen! Ich glaube, du hast mir das Bein gebrochen.

Fritz: Es tut mir so Leid! Wir müssen dich zum Krankenhaus bringen.

CHAPTER 2

Speaking 1 (track 6)

Listening 1 (track 7)

1: Günther: Es sind fünf Personen in meiner Familie. Meine Eltern sind geschieden. Wir drei Kinder wohnen mit meiner Mutter und unserem neuen Stiefvater, Konrad. Die zwei anderen Kinder sind mein Stiefbruder Alex und meine Stiefschwester Maria. Wir alle kommen miteinander sehr gut aus und wir streiten uns nicht sehr oft.

2: Günther: Letzten Sonntag hatte Alex Geburtstag. Wir sind zur Feier des Tages alle in einem Restaurant zum Essen gegangen. Er wurde fünfzehn Jahre alt. Alex hat viele Geschenke erhalten aber sein Lieblingsgeschenk war *Alienkrieg*, das neueste Computerspiel. Ich habe meinen sechzehnten Geburtstag in einem Monat und will zu einem Freizeitpark gehen und die gefährlichsten Fahrten ausprobieren!

Listening 2 (track 8)

Millie: Es war meistens in Berlin und war eine sehr unglückliche Zeit für mich. Meine Eltern hatten sich getrennt und meine Mutter fehlte mir. Ich konnte nie mit Sylvia, meiner neuen Stiefmutter, auskommen. Obwohl ich ein gutes Verhältniss zu den Kindern der Familie hatte. Um ehrlich zu sein, habe ich meine Stiefmutter gehasst. Sie hat mich geschlagen. Nur ein einziges Mal aber ich habe es nie vergessen. Aber es war dank Sylvia, dass ich meine Chance in der Filmindustrie bekommen habe. Nach einem Streit bin ich von zu Hause weg gelaufen. Ich war in einer Bar in Ostberlin, als die Filmregisseurin, Heike Linz, mich gesehen hat. Sie hat mir dort eine Rolle in Ihrem neuen Film, *Berliner Symphonie* angeboten. Jetzt ist Heike wie eine neue Mutter für mich geworden. Angelika, meine eigene Mutter ist vor drei Jahren gestorben. Sie fehlt mir ständig und ich werde sie nie vergessen. Das Leben kann hart sein. Vielleicht ist das der Grund warum ich tragische Rollen ziemlich gut interpretieren kann.

Listening 3 (track 9)

– Wir haben mit uns im Studio vier Personen, die wir heute zum ersten Mal auf der Straße getroffen haben. Sie werden uns Ihre Meinungen über die neuen Rollen in der Fernsehserie *Paradiesstrasse*, geben. Also kann es los gehen?

– (Ja! Ja! Freilich! Prima! Ohne weiteres!)

– Wie finden Sie Willi Herder, den neuen Briefträger?

– Er ist gesprächig, sehr laut und etwas snobisch.

– Ja, gut. Und Carla Heinrich, die Kassiererin im Supermarkt?

– Carla ist auch zu laut. Aber sie ist geduldig und sehr praktisch. Eine gute Person im Falle eines Straßenunfalls.

– Das ist positiv! Ist Ulrike Diederich, die Polizistin, auch eine positive Person?

– Absolut nicht. Ulrike ist eine Katastrophe. Ich finde sie gemein, aggressiv und grausam.

– Sehr interessant. Und jetzt kommen wir zur letzten Rolle, Siegfried Siedler, der Pfarrer in der evangelischen Kirche.

– Der scheint mir, ein wunderbarer Pfarrer zu sein. Er ist geduldig, gelassen und hilfsbereit.

CHAPTER 3

Speaking 1 (track 10)

Listening 1 (track 11)

Heute abend können wir nicht zum Konzert gehen. Die Eintrittskarten sind ausverkauft. Aber für morgen gibt es Karten und ich habe welche gekauft. Ruf mich an, wenn du nicht kommen kannst. Ich schlage vor, wir treffen uns vor dem Theater eine halbe Stunde vor der Aufführung, das heißt, um Schlag sieben Uhr.

Listening 2 (track 12)

Willkommen bei *Handy Dandy*. Wenn Sie einen neuen Apparat installieren möchten, drücken Sie Taste 1. Wenn Sie Kredit herunterladen möchten, drücken Sie Taste 2. Wenn Sie einen neuen Vertrag abschliessen möchten, drücken Sie Taste 3. Wenn Sie eine Beschwerde haben, drücken Sie Taste 4. Für alle andere Fragen, warten Sie bitte.

Listening 3 (track 13)

(a) Deutschlands Lieblingsrockband geht auf Tournee.

(b) Drei Personen werden nach dem starken Regen in den Alpen vermisst.

(c) In Flushing Meadow, in den USA, hat Ulrich Biedermann das Endspiel im Tennis Einzel gewonnen.

(d) Um 22.00 Uhr ein Interview mit dem russischen Präsidenten.

(e) Die Autobahn A1 ist zu vermeiden. Es gibt 20 Kilometer Stau in Richtung Süden.

(f) Bundesministerpräsidentin Merkl fliegt nach Jordan ab.

Listening 4 (track 14)

Manni: Doro, willst du zum Fußballspiel kommen? Es wird fantastisch werden.

Doro: Du weißt, dass ich Sport nicht leiden kann.

Manni: Aber ich gehe auch mit dir ins Kino um Liebesfilme zu sehen!

Doro: Ich tue auch Dinge für dich. Ich spiele Schach mit dir, obwohl ich es langweilig finde.

Manni: Aber du weißt, wie gern ich Schach spiele.

Doro: Und Karten! Du bist ein Fanatiker!

Manni: Das ist richtig aber ich verliere zu viel Geld beim Karten spielen. Ich gebe das auf!

Doro: Wie wäre es wenn wir Tanzen gehen? Du weißt, wie gerne ich tanze.

Manni: OK, wenn du nächsten Mittwoch mit mir zum Jugendklub kommst, um die Theatergruppe zu sehen.

Doro: Das ist mir recht. Ich mag Theater auch gern aber nicht so sehr wie du.

Manni: Ja, richtig und es ist genau das Gegenteil fürs Kino. Du bist Fanatikerin und ich weniger. Ja, ich ging mal ziemlich gerne ins Kino aber jetzt nicht mehr.

Listening 5 (track 15)

Heute abend präsentiert der Filmkanal Max Müllers Film vom letzten Jahr, ´Ich mache gern´. Müller, der berühmte österreichische Regisseur, hat den Oscar für den besten Film in einer Fremdsprache gewonnen. Es kostet nur zehn Euro pro Monat um den Filmkanal zu abonnieren. Die Nummer für neue Abonnenten ist 060424957.

Listening 6 (track 16)

(a) Würden Sie gern in einer Apotheke arbeiten? Sie können kranken Menschen helfen, indem Sie Medikamente empfehlen und in Kooperation mit dem Apotheker und dem Arzt arbeiten. Kontaktieren Sie *Apotheke Neugesund*, Schloßgasse 32.

(b) Ist Mode Ihr Ding? Sind Sie zwischen achtzehn und dreißig Jahre alt? Sind Sie modisch? Dann rufen Sie für Ihren Traumjob bei *Modelmode*, Steinstraße 17 an!

(c) Freundlich? Hilfsbereit? Dann könnte eine Karriere bei *Chez Martine* für Sie sein. Martines Spezialität ist das französische Essen. Sie beginnen als Kellnerin und können sich zum Chef hocharbeiten. Büdingen, Altstadtstraße, 51. Telefon: 071522896.

Listening 7 (track 17)

Um 6Uhr30 dusche ich zum ersten mal und danach kommt um 7Uhr das Frühstück. Danach habe ich eine kleine Pause und gehe um 8Uhr auf einen langen Spaziergang. Zwischen 10Uhr und 11Uhr sprinte ich. Direkt danach boxe ich eine Stunde was mich zur Mittagspause um 12Uhr bringt. Eine Stunde später um 13Uhr laufe ich für 30 Minuten. Um 13Uhr30 dusche ich dann zum zweiten Mal. Danach verbringe ich zwei Stunden im Fitnessraum, wo ich um 16Uhr30 meinen Trainingstag mit ein wenig Physiotherapie beende.

CHAPTER 4

Speaking 1 (track 18)

Listening 1 (track 19)

Der Flug 0479 nach London Heathrow fliegt vom Flugsteig 14 um 12h30 ab. Gegen einen Zuschlag wird den Flugästen in Economyclass ein Abendessen serviert werden. Passagiere der Ersten Klasse bekommen dies gratis inklusive einem Glas Champagner.

Listening 2 (track 20)

Liebe Musikfreunde! Es tut uns Leid, daß Sie Schlange stehen müssen aber wir haben immerhin eine gute Nachricht für Sie. Leider sind Freitag und Samstag Die Prinzen Konzerte ausverkauft. Es gibt aber noch Plätze zu 30 und 50 Euro für Die Prinzen Konzerte am Mittwoch und Donnerstag. Wenn Sie Karten für den Mittwoch oder Donnerstag kaufen, können Sie diese Eintrittskarten auch für die Chatshow mit den Prinzen morgen Nachmittag benutzen. Dann werden Sie die Gelegenheit haben, den Sänger persönliche Fragen zu stellen.

Listening 3 (track 21)

– Wie war es denn in Österreich?

– Bis auf das Essen ganz gut. Es war zu fett für mich.

– Und wie hast du die Österreicher gefunden?

– Sie waren ganz nett und sehr hilfsbereit.

– Und was war deine beste Erinnerung?

– Vielleicht die Ausflüge. Nein, es waren die Kinos. Viele gute Filme in schönen Kinos.

– Und die Häuser, Wohnungen und so weiter?

– Nicht so imponierend. Die Preise waren so unheimlich teuer!

– Jetzt kommen wir zum Wetter.

– Dass ich nicht lache! Schlimmer als zu Hause. Wolken, Regen, Kälte. Ich habe die schlechteste Jahreszeit gewählt.

– Okay und meine letzte Frage, wie waren die öffentlichen Verkehrsmittel?

– Die waren ganz gut. Das Problem waren die Bauarbeiten! Ich hatte schon gehört, dass es sehr viele Bauarbeiten in den Städten gibt aber das hat die Qualität der öffentlichen Verkehrsmittel nicht beeinflusst.

– Sehr interessant, ich danke dir.

– Ich danke Ihnen auch.

Listening 4 (track 22)

(a) Ihr Schnellzug kommt in Berlin um 14Uhr50 an.

(b) Ein Doppelzimmer wird 42 Euro kosten.

(c) Es ist ein Doppelzimmer mit zwei Betten plus Bad.

(d) Es ist ziemlich weit bis zum Stadtzentrum. Es ist besser mit der U-bahn zu fahren.

(e) Sie können nicht sagen, dass Sie Berlin gesehen haben, ohne die Gedächtniskirche besucht zu haben.

Listening 5 (track 23)

Christan: Wo hast du deinen Urlaub gemacht, Pia?

Pia: Am Karlschlosser Campingplatz am Strand.

Christan: Und warum hast du diesen Campingplatz gewählt?

Pia: Weil ich mich den ganzen Tag am Strand sonnen konnte.

Christan: Und was hast du abends am liebsten gemacht?

Pia: Das ist leicht. Ich habe jeden Abend in der Disko am Campingrestaurant getanzt!

Christan: Ich habe vergessen zu fragen, wie bist du nach Karlschloss gekommen?

Pia: Mit dem Fahrrad. Ich war bei Freunden circa 150 Kilometer entfernt. Ich bin von dort mit dem Rad gefahren.

Christan: Imponierend. Und meine letzte Frage, vielleicht die bedeutendste: Wie war das Wetter?

Pia: Nicht wie bei uns im Norden. Während der zwei Wochen hat die Sonne nie vergessen zu scheinen!

Listening 6 (track 24)

– Weißt du, die Zwillinge machen mir Sorgen. Der Udi hat Schwiereigkeiten sich zu organisieren und die Frankie ist meistens nicht viel besser, auch wenn sie anders denkt!

– So schlimm sind sie doch gar nicht. Ich habe Bedenken wegen der 400 Kilometer am Steuer. Das ist zu viel für unsere Tochter!

– Nein, da bin ich anderer Meinung. Ich glaube eher, dass Sie das schaffen wird.

– Aber was Landkarten betrifft ist Udi hoffnungslos!

– Unterbrich mich bitte nicht. Ich würde sagen das es mit dem Flugzeug oder auch mit dem Zug sicherer wäre. Sie würden so viel mehr sehen. Vielleicht könnten Sie wandern gehen und in Jugendherbergen übernachten, wie wir es gemacht haben.

– Aber das war vor 25 Jahren! Heute sind die Herbergen nicht so sicher wie damals. Ich bin total dagegen! Ein Hotel wäre wesentlich sicherer.

– Wie du willst! Eigentlich machen wir immer das was du sagst. Warum denn nicht Übernachtung mit Frühstück in einer Pension. Das wäre viel billiger!

– Ja, vielleicht, vielleicht! Ich habe dieses Gespräch satt. Die Zwillinge sind immerhin 18 Jahre alt. Sie können selbst entscheiden.

– Warum haben wir denn dann dieses Gespräch geführt!

– Das weiß ich auch nicht.

Listening 7 (track 25)

Liebe Zuhörerinnen, wenn Sie diesen Sommer Urlaub in Europa

machen, denken Sie an den Europapaß! Dieser Pass ermöglicht Ihnen eine 50% Ermässigung auf Ihre Fahrkarten. Er kostet nur 20 Euro und Sie können alle Städte, die sich auf dem Bahnnetz befinden, in Deutschland besuchen. Für einen Zuschlag von 25 Euro pro Strecke können Sie im Speisewagen essen und Plätze im Schlafwagen sind für 60% des normalen Preises erhältlich. Die einzigen Bedingungen: Sie dürfen keinen Zug vor 9Uhr morgens und zwischen 16h30 und 19h30 nehmen. Sie sollten zwischen 18 und 59 Jahre alt sein, um den Pass zu bekommen. Besuchen Sie den nächsten Hauptbahnhof in Ihrer Umgebung mit Ihrem Reisepaß oder Personalausweis.

Listening 8 (track 26)
Jutta: Ich weiß nicht, ob die Rolle für mich geeignet ist, da ich London langweilig finde.
Karl: London ist wie Berlin. Ich glaube, ich verstehe die Londoner. Ich möchte gerne in dem Film mitspielen.
Farida: Das könnte eine große Gelegenheit für mich sein, aber mein Asthma ist schlimmer wegen der Luftverschmutzung. Ich muss nach Hause.
Michael: Ich bin total begeistert. Es gibt so viele Sehenswürdigkeiten zu sehen. Ich möchte unbedingt eine Rolle bekommen.
Thea: Ich finde die Leute ganz toll und freundlich. Ich würde gerne eine Rolle spielen aber ob ich genug Talent habe?

Listening 9 (track 27)
1: Heine: Wo machst du diesen Sommer Urlaub?
Sophie: Ich bin zu Hause aber Urlaub mache ich nicht. Ich habe kein Geld. Ich muss für die Uni sparen. Und du, Heine, fliegst du auf die Bahamas?
Heine: Nein, leider nicht, dafür habe ich nicht genug Geld. Ich werde im Schwarzwald zelten.
2: Helga: Willi, wann fahren wir in den Urlaub?
Willi: Tut mir Leid aber wir können nicht fahren. Ich habe eine Panne gehabt.
Helga: Wir könnten mit meinem Wagen nach Berlin fahren.
Willi: Okay, wir benutzen deinen Wagen. Aber nicht nach Berlin. Ich habe diese Stadt satt.
3: Hanna: Also Leute, wir haben die Broschüren studiert und lange diskutiert. Wohin wollen wir fahren und mit welchem Transportmittel? Fangen wir mit Thea an. Thea?
Thea: Ich möchte gerne mit der Fähre nach Schottland.
Hanna: Und du, Wolf?
Wolf: Ihr wisst, ich bin ein echter Zugfreund. Für mich ist es Spanien mit der Bahn.
Hanna: Peter?
Peter: Das ist eine gute Frage. Vielleicht nach Edinburg wie Thea, aber ich möchte lieber fliegen. Und du, Hanna?
Hanna: Ich möchte auch fliegen aber nicht nach Schottland. Lieber in die USA.

CHAPTER 5
Speaking 1 (track 28)
Listening 1 (track 29)
1: – Entschuldigung, ich suche mein Kind. Wie komme ich am besten zum Spielplatz?
– Er ist nur 200 Meter entfernt. Sie fahren die erste Strasse links und dann sind Sie da.
2: – Entschuldigen Sie bitte, ich kenne die Stadt nicht. Ich muss zum Krankenhaus.
– Ich glaube, Sie gehen links. Nein, nein. Sie gehen geradeaus.
3: – Entschuldigen Sie bitte, wie komme ich zur U-Bahn?
– Keine Angst, Sie sind fast da. Links haben Sie den Ausgang des Bahnhofes, aber zur U-Bahn, müssen Sie rechts gehen.

Listening 2 (track 30)
– Tina, was machst du zu Hause, um zu helfen?
Tina: Bügeln kann ich nicht und die Gartenarbeit ist zu hart. Also spüle ich und erledige die Einkäufe so oft ich kann.
– Und du, Wolf, was machst du?
Wolf: So wenig wie möglich! Nein, das ist nicht richtig. Ich interessiere mich für Autos und deshalb wasche ich Vatis Volkswagen. Ich helfe auch von Zeit zu Zeit im Garten.

– Und, du, Chrissi, hilfst du deinen Eltern auch?
Chrissi: Natürlich. Ich bin fantastisch mit dem Staubsauger, laut meiner Mutti! Und ich koche gern. Also helfe ich in der Küche.
– Und du, Reinhardt, überläßt du alles deinen Eltern?
Reinhardt: Dass ich nicht lache! Ich bin der Sklave der Familie, da ich die Betten für die ganze Familie mache! Ich spiele auch die Putzfrau!

Listening 3 (track 31)
Hier der Wetterbericht für ganz Deutschland. Im Norden bekommen wir demnächst den Wind aus Russland. Erwarten Sie einen windigen Tag. Wenn Sie nichts als Sonne wollen, müssen wir in den Süden fahren. Dort scheint den ganzen Tag die Sonne. In Mitteldeutschland kann man Regen erwarten. Gehen Sie nicht ohne Regenschirm oder Regenmantel raus! Im Westen wird es nur kalt sein. Kein Regen aber auch keine Sonne und, wie gesagt, kalt, sehr kalt für die Jahreszeit. Was haben wir vergessen? Nur den Osten und hier wird es nebelig sein und, wie Sie wissen, Nebel kann Unfälle auf der Strasse verursachen. In einer Stunde bin ich wieder bei Ihnen!

CHAPTER 6
Speaking 1 (track 32)
Listening 1 (track 33)
Stephan: Sag mal, Ulrike, wie findest du den neuen Englischlehrer?
Ulrike: In einem Wort: toll! In drei Stunden mit ihm habe ich mehr gelernt als in einem Semester mit dem alten Lehrer. Er ist lustig, spricht klar und er lacht über unsere Fehler.
Stephan: Hmmm. Für mich ist es nicht so. Er ist viel netter zu Mädchen als Jungen. Für uns ist er ein bisschen sarkastisch. Er gibt uns wenig Zeit und die Mädchen kriegen bessere Noten.
Ulrike: Unglaublich, ich sehe einen ganz anderen Menschen! Heute morgen zum Beispiel war er äußerst freundlich.
Stephan: Ja, so freundlich, dass er die Klasse nicht kontrollieren konnte. Ganz hinten schikanierte einer den Kleinsten in der Klasse.

Listening 2 (track 34)
Dieter: Danke, dass Sie mir Zeit geben über die Probleme in meiner Schule zu sprechen. Ich gehe nicht mehr in die Schule weil meine Mutter alleinstehend ist. Ich habe einen kleinen Job im Sportzentrum gefunden. Da verdiene ich genug, um meine Mutter zu unterstützen. Es gibt eine ganze Menge anderer Schüler und Schülerinnen, die ständig abwesend sind, weil sie nur ein Name auf einer Liste sind. Was kann man dagegen tun? Ich würde gerne die Antworten von Ihren Zuhörern hören.

Listening 3 (track 35)
Teacher: Sam, das ist das schlechteste Zeugnis für ein Arbeitspraktikum, das ich je gesehen habe.
Sam: Es war nicht meine Schuld. Der Leiter konnte mich nicht leiden. Ich verstehe nicht warum.
Teacher: Laut dem Zeugnis kamst du immer zu spät zur Arbeit.
Sam: Das ist nicht wahr. Es ist richtig, dass ich einige Probleme mit den öffentlichen Verkehrsmitteln hatte, aber es war nur die Hälfte der Zeit.
Teacher: Ach, so! Der Leiter der Textilfirma hat geschrieben, "Mindestens sechs Mal ist Sam eingeschlafen und das kann in einer Fabrik sehr gefährlich sein."
Sam: Das stimmt auch nicht. Es war nur fünfmal und die Arbeit war so langweilig! Niemand da mochte seine Arbeit. Alle haben gesagt, sie würden eine andere Stelle finden, aber es gibt keine Jobs in der Gegend.
Teacher: Ich habe das eindeutige Gefühl, dass du dich nicht gut organisieren kannst.
Sam: Das ist so aber nicht richtig. Es war nur ein unbezahltes Praktikum und ich habe mein Bestes getan.
Teacher: Kannst du mir sagen, wie du den Fotokopierer kaputt gemacht hast?
Sam: Das war nicht ich! Es war die Informatikerin, die immer über mich gelacht hat und versucht hat Probleme für mich zu machen!
Teacher: Ich habe den Eindruck, dass du nie für die Dinge verantwortlich bist. Es sind immer die Anderen. Sam! Sam! Unglaublich! Er ist vor meinen Augen eingeschlafen!

Index